The List

The Uses and Pleasures of Cataloguing

ROBERT E. BELKNAP

Yale University Press New Haven & London

Designed by James J. Johnson and set in Minion Roman types by The Composing Room of Michigan, Inc.

Printed in the United States of America.

Library of Congress Cataloging-in-Publication Data

Belknap, Robert E., 1966–
    The list : the uses and pleasures of cataloguing / Robert E. Belknap.
        p. cm.
    Includes bibliographical references and index.
    ISBN 0-300-10383-2 (alk. paper)

    1. American literature—19th century—History and criticism.   2. Lists in litera-
ture.   3. Emerson, Ralph Waldo, 1803–1882—Technique.   4. Thoreau, Henry David,
1817–1862—Technique.   5. Melville, Herman, 1819–1891—Technique.   6. Whitman,
Walt, 1819–1892—Technique.   7. Catalogs in literature.   I. Title.
    PS217.L57B45 2004
    810.9'2—dc22

                                      2004016113

A catalogue record for this book is available from the British Library.

The paper in this book meets the guidelines for permanence and durability of the Committee on Production Guidelines for Book Longevity of the Council on Library Resources.

10   9   8   7   6   5   4   3   2   1

For B.H.B.

A Motto from Emerson

He will perceive that there are far more excellent qualities in the student than preciseness and infallibility; that a guess is often more fruitful than an indisputable affirmation, and that a dream may let us deeper into the secret of nature than a hundred concerted experiments.

Contents

✳ ✺ ✳

Preface

✳ ✣ ✳

January is a terrible time to be considering lists. Readers have just been inundated by end-of-year retrospectives from newspapers and magazines, and the predictable rankings sprout like so many spreading weeds: "Top Stories of the Year," "Top People of the Year," "Biggest Grossing Films of the Year," "Craziest Fads of the Year." Mention lists and these are what spring to mind, in part because they are everywhere. Perhaps we do not recall specific examples, but the general idea of a top-down ordering of things (or sometimes the reverse—to heighten suspense, I suppose) comes to predominate at the expense, unfortunately, of all other permutations. These rankings have a certain power: they either succeed in flattering us by inviting our approval and agreement or overmaster us by implicitly remarking, "This is the way things are; we know!" We can accept the editors' decisions, or we can just go make our own lists. The whole process seems to me an exercise in comparative discrimination, a way to prove that the compiler alone possesses the judgment and sensitivity to distinguish what ranks as a 3, for example, from what earns only a 6.

I admit that these appraisals can be informative, even fun, but I dislike the way their evaluative view of things comes to dominate, as though the aim of everything—every experience, every work of art, every personality, every event—were to find its place in a single hierarchical plan. I don't know where the impulse to evaluate and rate may have come from (could David Letterman's "Top Ten" lists have had that much influence on us?); I can only lament the fact that like an invading species these rankings edge out other, more fragile varieties of listing with their popular appeal and opportunistic simplicity. I confess that I have a low estimation of rankings. It may be because of my contrarian nature—I want to do my own ordering—but mostly it is because I think that giving predominance to rankings impoverishes the imagination.

I first started paying attention to lists one summer after reading James Agee's wonderful document *Let Us Now Praise Famous Men*. I was drawn particularly to the spare itemizations of possessions Agee recorded for the families he studied. There, in strikingly short lists, Agee had taken account of all the belongings of each family. The idea that everything an entire family owned, socks and all, could be counted out and still sum to so little, virtually nothing, left a deep impression me. I thought of my own possessions and of how embarrassingly long their reckoning would be in comparison with this powerful, graphic representation of poverty. Agee's lists were so cold, so objective, so compelling. Their precision and detail, their arrangement, drew me. Of all the extraordinary things in that book, including the sober faces captured by Walker Evans's photographs, it was the lists that fixed me.

That September I worked as a tutor for Daily Themes, Yale's oldest creative writing course. In Daily Themes, students are introduced to a variety of aspects of literature—tone, voice, point of view—and then given nightly assignments to practice what they have learned, accumulating a portfolio of writings by the end of the semester. One week the primary theme was lists, and passages from

Dickens and Joyce, Shakespeare and children's rhymes were passed around the lecture hall. I recall nothing of the lecture; my mind was adrift in speculation, musing on the notion that lists themselves might be something one could study.

My conviction was sealed soon afterward. While studying for my orals, I had been reading and rereading the literature of the American Renaissance. I worked through Emerson, set out with *Moby-Dick,* and took refuge in Thoreau. With the idea of lists fresh in my mind, I seemed to find them everywhere. My roommate was likewise preparing for his impending orals, and when I tried to engage him on Whitman's chants or Ishmael's digressions, he simply dismissed them, stating, "I just skip over all that stuff." I was surprised that he could dispense with them so easily. Did he not savor the catalogue of trees in Thoreau's Concord woods? Was he not invigorated by Emerson's relentless gathering of examples? Delighted by Ishmael's garrulous amplifications? Swept away by Whitman's dizzying collections?

No one asked me any list questions on my exam, but I still dwelt on them. There were mysteries about lists that I wanted to investigate, but I didn't know where to begin. In search of a guide, I practiced formulating my ideas. I knew that if there were anyone who might find merit in the undertaking, it would be John Hollander, and to my delight, Professor Hollander readily engaged the topic, suggesting numerous approaches with enthusiasm. He wisely advised me to begin by taking a survey of the list as it had been used throughout literature. Once I had established some history and defined some terms useful for discussing lists, I could begin to engage the questions I had for the four authors—Emerson, Whitman, Melville, and Thoreau—who most interested me.

During this preparatory stage I became aware of a shared delight in lists among many readers; friends and even strangers would stop me and ask whether I had considered the lists in *Alice in Wonderland* or *Gravity's Rainbow,* Cole Porter's lyrics, or the odd list by

Harry Crosby. In lists, I had found something that had a wide appeal, a construct that took many forms and patterns and invited many uses and interpretations. Accumulating samples was easy—I had such a big collection that I feared my dissertation would become "The Book of Lists" and I might be forever known as "the List Man." But over time I was able to prune my own listings into a form that eventually became the book you have here.

Our fascination with lists is old and continuing. Perhaps competitive social pressures influence us to deal in rankings, but we can unroll lists for other reasons as well—inventorying our possessions and taking the measure of ourselves, lumping and splitting, grouping and dividing the world about us, finding similarities and differences between things and creating patterns of possibility with them, making assessments of things that are important to us, memorializing the fallen, the lost, the loved. Perhaps listing is simply play, mixing and matching for sheer pleasure like fancy-led children. Maybe the creation of lists echoes some distant poetic impulse, the chanting of the names of objects: sun moon stars me you. Perhaps, as in that earliest time, such a calling of things empowers us by momentarily allowing us to order our surrounding world, verbally or symbolically putting everything into a sequence and an arrangement we desire, if only for that instant. With the multitude of things and signs from which to choose, it can be exceedingly gratifying to get our list exactly right—and then to remake it all over again.

Reading lists, as opposed to creating them, offers its own pleasures. Many of the lists we use in everyday life are utilitarian: they tell us what courses are offered, what is on television, what ingredients we need for a recipe, or which gate our plane leaves from. But they can be captivating as well as serviceable. How inviting to the imagination they can be, and how personal as well. How often have we found ourselves reading someone else's grocery list, left behind in a shopping cart? Menus always trouble me, teasing me with the burden of making a choice. (I usually stick to the same thing.)

The Internet, with its handy listing machines, the ever-necessary search engines, has lately made available a stupendously large quantity of lists, a vast volume that can inform, distract, tempt, or swallow us, leaving no trace. The apotheosis of the list, the point-and-click world now enables us to scroll and link at will through an expanding network of possibility. Online booksellers catalogue everything ever written, it seems, and they cheerfully grab our attention and our wallets by simplifying our access while leading us on to further items. Ingeniously, Amazon.com has tapped into the human penchant for lists and listing by inviting its clientele to create and post their own rosters in its exercise-in-democracy marketing ploy, "Listmania." Like reggae?—click here for The Essentials (A Desert-Island Disc-List by Joe). A Jane Austen fan?—click here (A List of Austenalia by J-D). Interested in crime fiction?—Here's some you might not have heard of (A List by SmOk).

We can end the virtual world's siren call by turning off the computer. Withdrawing from that vast ocean, we can savor the many lists that appear in the world's literatures, those that I call in this book literary lists. They are the ones that are set apart from pragmatic lists, preserved by marked artistic endeavor, even if they may not appear to be. Literary lists afford us particular attractions and pleasures. The rhythm of the repetition interrupts the forward drive of the text, and for a moment we are invited to dance.

Sometimes we delight in the pattern unwinding before our eyes as its creator sequences the items with a regularity we can keep in step with: we follow its progression, priding ourselves on seeing and predicting connections and inclusions. Sometimes the pace or the tune alters, but we follow willingly, challenged yet undeterred by the transitions, winding around and through the possibilities.

Sometimes all hell breaks loose, and in some psychedelic jam of language an ecstasy overwhelms us, sustainable for only a moment.

My family has owned a small parcel of land in northern Michigan for nearly a hundred years. For many summers, Belknaps of all ages have enjoyed its woods and open spaces. I recently spent a great deal of a vacation removing by hand as much of the garlic mustard that invades it as I possibly could. Garlic mustard is a hardy but charmless weed that disperses its numerous seeds with great success, edging out the occasional wildflower that blooms around our cottage. The more delicate flowers whose company I enjoy are seriously endangered; harebell, starflower, sweet william, bloodroot, jack-in-the-pulpit, northern lily, and many others whose names I do not know all lose ground against the invader. At least, this is what I fear will happen if I am not out there pulling at all hours. My battle with garlic mustard has become something of an obsession, much to the consternation of my wife. But I love to stroll in the garden and savor the variety of color, shape, scent, and attitude that a mixture of wildflowers can provide, and to do so I need to create a space for these flowers, a space that is completely free of garlic mustard.

It is with a similar motivation that I decided at the outset to speak against certain kinds of lists. Lists as rankings—I won't call them "popular" because I think they are purely media-generated—threaten to crowd out the other, fragile, more intriguing, and unique lists. I want to clear a space in which those lists can thrive, and then spend some time pondering and appreciating them, especially the oddities, the rarities—lists that are beautifully flawed, or at least less "efficient."

I am interested in structure, and lists are structures that, like wildflowers, invite us to reflect, to wonder. Why? Why this form? Why here? A list gathers together a collection of items, and, as in many personal collections, it is the special items we most enjoy. Of the many possible candidates in the literary firmament, I have chosen to linger over one particular galaxy, not because the lists of the American Renaissance are the brightest or the most brilliant, the ones with the most fascinating arrangements or the oldest histories, but because they are the ones that have captured my imagination. They have intrigued and puzzled me, and in this book I try to pin down what they mean to me.

Lists are personal constructions that invite different interpretations from different readers. I don't wish to be authoritative, and I don't believe that it is possible to be comprehensive with this protean form. From the outset I wished to explore aspects of selected lists and try to answer some questions I had about them. I hope that my offerings will in turn encourage others to take their own flights with these obsessive elements. The value of lists is that they ask us to make them meaningful. Writing in his introduction to *Nature* about the vast surrounding Creation, rather than our pen and paper orderings, Emerson put it best: "We must trust the perfection of the creation so far as to believe that whatever curiosity the order of things has awakened in our minds, the order of things can satisfy."

Acknowledgments

✳ ✴ ✳

I am grateful to a great number of people who in various ways made this book possible. Some helped with guidance and instruction, some with encouragement, and some with love. In roles both minor and major, these individuals nurtured this book from its first vague dream through to its final draft. Foremost, I wish to thank John Hollander for his gracious guidance and support of this undertaking. Professor Hollander generously encouraged me in many ways, including helping me to see clearly and then present in a coherent fashion what began as a simple and somewhat unconventional interest in literary lists. Without him this project simply would not have been possible. I am grateful to him for his resourcefulness, for his ability to help me view various situations in unforeseen ways, and for the remarkable skill he demonstrated in clarifying the complex. I also wish to thank the other individuals who read various sections of my manuscript and helped me give it its final shape. These include my fellow students at Yale, Charles Baraw and Isaac Cates, deep into their own thesis work, and Yale faculty members

Nigel Alderman, Annabel Patterson, and Alan Trachtenberg. I especially wish to thank Wai Chee Dimock and Harold Bloom for their encouragement and support.

My thanks are also owed to Lawrence Rosenwald, who provided many helpful suggestions; to Sally Spence, who published the first chapter as "The Literary List: A Survey of Its Uses and Deployments" in *Literary Imagination;* and to John Kulka and Susan Laity of Yale University Press, who turned a dream into a real, honest-to-goodness book. Finally, I wish to thank the technology and library staff of Saint Mary's School for their help, and my colleagues there for their enthusiasm as this book came to fruition.

This project could not have been undertaken without the love and understanding of my family. This book is dedicated to the memory of my father, Benjamin H. Belknap, who provided necessary encouragement and confidence. It is also for my dear daughters, Rim and Lys, who have so greatly enriched my life. A la famille Metina, merci pour tout. To the two people who encouraged me daily, my wife, Nadia, and my mother, Kathleen, I thank you for your patience, your support, and your ability to boost flagging spirits. You both are in these pages more than you may know.

List of Abbreviations

✳ ✳ ✳

E   Ralph Waldo Emerson, *Essays and Lectures*
MA   Herman Melville, *Mardi*
MD   Herman Melville, *Moby-Dick*
T   Henry David Thoreau, "*A Week on the Concord and Merrimack Rivers,*" "*Walden,*" "*The Maine Woods,*" and "*Cape Cod*"
W   Walt Whitman, *Leaves of Grass*

1

The Literary List

＊ ❈ ＊

When Randall Jarrell considered the pages of ecstatic list-ing in *Leaves of Grass,* he described them as "little systems as beautifully and astonishingly ordered as the rings and satellites of Saturn."[1] This analogy is fitting not only because it evokes the stratification implicit in Whitman's lines—and the sometimes barely perceptible orbits the poems fulfill—but also because it suggests the sense of wonder the lists can arouse in readers. Most of us are curious about why a disorderly array of interplanetary debris orders itself so gracefully in the heavens; even when we have heard the accounts and theories of experts, we still marvel. Whitman's lines, whether we understand their organization or not, similarly fill us with wonder. In their motions, their inclusions, and their exclusions, they seem to be continuously in play, tumbling but controlled.

Whitman was a great lister, a writer who experimented with the list and exploited its capacity to accumulate elements and yoke together phenomena. Because of its generative qualities—because it can be considered shapeless it has the capacity to spark endless connections and inclusions in a multiplicity of forms—the list is a device that writers have frequently employed to display the pleasurable infinitude of language. Faced with the great variety of its uses in literature, how can we best define what the list is?

At their most simple, lists are frameworks that hold separate and disparate items together. Lists are plastic, flexible structures in which an array of constituent units coheres through specific relations generated by specific forces of attraction. Writers can build these structures so that they appear random or create them so they seem to be organized by some overt principle. The versatility of these structures has without doubt led to their use throughout history by both literary and nonliterary, utilitarian compilers. Indeed, one would need the prodigious talent of Callimachus, who organized and catalogued the vast holdings (some 700,000 volumes) of the great library of Alexandria, to completely categorize the uses writers and compilers have found for the list form. Although an exhaustive listing is beyond this discussion, I would like here to survey the use of the list in literature in order to illustrate its advantages as a literary construct, present terminology useful for discussing it, and examine the literary heritage of compilation that the four main authors of this study—Emerson, Whitman, Melville, and Thoreau—inherited and on which they left their lasting marks.

A complete discussion of the list must cover all its aspects. These include the sorts of elements that make up its constituent parts, how the compiler arranges these parts, and what circumstances occasion a particular arrangement. We need to explore the nature and function of both literary and nonliterary compilations, as well as listing devices that have been used both pragmatically and artistically. A list of listings would include the catalogue, the inventory, the itinerary, and the lexicon. Lists differ from catalogues in presenting a simple series of units, without the descriptive enhancement a catalogue usually provides. The catalogue is more comprehensive, conveys more information, and is more amenable to digression than the list. In the inventory, words representing names or things are collected by a conceptual principle. In the itinerary, actions are ordered through time: the continuum of a single motion may be subdivided into discrete elements, or narrative in general may be conceived of as an elaborate listing of a series of events. In the lexicon, words are inventoried with their definitions, ordered and arranged for ease of accessibility.

Other pragmatic listing forms that find rhetorical use include the invoice and the last will and testament. Many writers exploit or elaborate upon listing techniques to achieve a particular effect: the suggestion of plenitude, of rapid motion, or of the joyful concatenation of a number of possible mixtures of language.

Both pragmatic and literary lists are organized to display information. As repositories of information, they are meaningful to those who read or access them. Connections between elements in a list may be readily apparent or vague and indistinct, depending on what role the list is intended to serve. On the one hand, a list may fulfill a reference function, acting as a resource in which information is ordered so it can be swiftly and easily located. On the other, a list may convey a specific impression; its role is the creation of meaning, rather than merely the storage of it. In such a way a writer might present numerous entities to a reader, setting them side by side in display, or might particularize an individual object, indicating its components or qualities. A list like Edmund Spenser's celebrated catalogue of trees from the first canto of *The Faerie Queene*, for example, serves multiple purposes. Taking shelter from a storm, Una and the Red Crosse Knight survey the wood:

> Much can they prayse the trees so straight and hy,
> The sayling Pine, the Cedar proud and tall,
> The vine-prop Elme, the Poplar neuer dry,
> The builder Oake, sole king of forrests all,
> The Aspen good for staues, the Cypresse funerall.

The Laurell, meed of mightie Conquerors
    And Poets sage, the Firre that weepeth still,
    The Willow worne of forlorne Paramours,
    The Eugh obedient to the benders will,
    The Birch for shaftes, the Sallow for the mill,
    The Mirrhe sweet bleeding in the bitter wound,
    The warlike Beech, the Ash for nothing ill,
    The fruitfull Oliue, and the Plantane round,
The Carver Holme, the Maple seeldom inward sound. [1.1.8–9]

Here the list structure is relevant to the theme of its occasion: the list is an economical way to get the couple lost, and its effect is to simultaneously suspend and advance the narrative of the poem. As the list develops, we, like the two characters "led with delight," penetrate deeper into the forest, distracted by the game of arboreal identification.[2] The close packing of the species reflects the density of the wood, but the lack of sensory description reveals the Knight's failure to attend to his surroundings, and Spenser's application of epithets to each species reveals the hero's complacent preoccupation with humanity's supposed mastery over the natural world.

The lines conclude with our hollow realization of his mistake, ironically juxtaposing the anticlimax of the Maple's inutility with the climax of the unretraceable path. The unsound center of the tree forewarns of the monster lurking within the "shady grove," the allegory of human hubris. In addition its deliberate construction (A. C. Hamilton notes that Spenser arranges the trees in stanza 8 by their height),[3] the list serves to associate the poet with other poets who have assembled well-known catalogues of trees: Ovid, Virgil, and Chaucer. Placed near the beginning of the poem, the compilation proclaims Spenser's position in poetic tradition; the setpiece announces, as Anne Ferry writes, the poet's place within a "subliminal catalogue of immortal names."[4] When Whitman and Thoreau continue the tradition by constructing their own lists of trees, as we shall see in the "Song of the Broad-Axe" and the opening of the

"Baker Farm" chapter of *Walden*, respectively, they do so in new and original ways.

When we search for information in a utilitarian list, we are satisfied when it is organized by a sensible principle. The literary list, however, is complex in precisely the way a pragmatic list must not be. In a literary work, lists and compilations appeal for different reasons. Here we do not hunt for a specific piece of information but rather receive the information the writer wishes to communicate to us. There can be great satisfaction in the search for order in a list, whether that feeling be due to an appreciation of explicitly patterned artistry, a delight in unforeseen and unexpected combinations, or the writer's invitation to the reader to generate his or her own sense of meaning, to piece matters together in whatever way seems right. Emerson, inspired by the Transcendental "convertibility of every thing into every other thing," acknowledges this invitation, writing in "The Poet," "Bare lists of words are found suggestive to an imaginative and excited mind" (*E*, 455). In a sense, we all take up the invitation: a modern neurological view finds that the human brain "looks for ways to lower the entropy of a collection of items by reducing the number of ways in which they can be arranged. . . . If the items display no obvious relationships, no discernible pattern, the brain will invent relationships, imposing some arbitrary order on the disorderliness of the material."[5]

Nonliterary lists must have a practical composition in order to be useful, but literary compilations, though they generally have some inner logic of form, have no such obligation. For the critic there is thus the ever-present danger of interpretive overdetermination. Eager to decipher the disorder that is evident in the open, suggestive nature of the list, the critic who strives to find meaning by making coherent messages from these loose formations can err badly. As Dr. Johnson noted of one commentator's praise of a connective order found in Pope's *Essay on Criticism*—an order the author himself had not intended—the result may be "a concatenation of intermediate ideas such as, when it is once shewn, shall appear natural; but if this order be reversed, another mode of connection equally specious may be found or made."[6] Conscious of the danger Dr. Johnson warns of, the critic nevertheless may find it rewarding to apply the same investigative rigor given other elements of a literary work to a writer's use of lists and listing strategies.

Lists consist of arrangements of entries and have been used for varied purposes throughout history. Lists enumerate, account, remind, memorialize, order. Lists take a number of sizes, shapes, and functions, ranging from directories and historical records to edicts and instructions. Francis Spufford, who has put together a beautiful (but incomplete) collection of literary lists, asks whether lists are simply too various to have a character. He writes, "The separateness of the extraordinary variety of ways of using lists inevitably raises an uncomfortable question—whether 'lists' are at all a unified category of literary endeavor or whether 'a list' is only a name for something completely determined by what is put in it, like a paragraph."[7]

In an effort to manage this great variety William Gass suggests a good general taxonomy of three basic families into which lists can be categorized.[8] He defines these families according to their different degrees of organization. First are lists built without a formal organizing principle that take shape as elements emerge "out of thin air" or as objects are come upon, either from pressed memory ("what did I need today?") or, as at a police station, items are removed from a suspect and inventoried. Gass's second category of list includes everything arranged by a particular principle: alphabetically, numerically, hierarchically, geographically, chronologically, and so on. In the final category are lists that are built through an externally imposed system, as the structure of a table of contents of a book, for example, is dictated by the sequence of the book's parts.

In contrast to the pragmatic list, however, the literary list must be allowed an additional category that is neither truly random nor strictly principled. Writers present these textual lists to their readers much as they do other aspects of literature, such as rhyme or plot—to mark off the literary from the nonliterary. By design, these un-rolled lists may begin according to a specific principle, but they may show build, movement, or deviation as they progress. Alternately, they might spiral into their own constellations of form for which there is no identifying label. Some literary lists have their own traditions from which to abide by or depart—the roll call of leaders in epic poetry is a cardinal example—and their appearance has an aspect of tradition. Others represent deliberately the informal, makeshift, or random aspects of experience. The literary listing is thus a quite different entity from the pragmatic list since its craft of composition pushes it, as Stephen Barney writes, "beyond the minimum requirements of listing into ornament."[9]

Patterns of listing have been identified and conceptually categorized, however. In the sixteenth century, Henry Peacham recorded many of these strategies in his catalogue of rhetoric *The Garden of Eloquence.*

Congeries—A multiplication or heaping together of many words signifying diverse things of like nature.

Conglobatio—When we bring in many definitions of one thing, yet no such definitions as do declare the pith of the matter, but others of another kind all heaped together, which do amplify most pleasantly.

Dinumeratio—When we number up many things for the love of amplifying. This differeth from Congeries, for Congeries heapeth up words, and this sentences.

Distributio—When we dilate and spread abroad the general kind by numbering and reckoning the special kinds; the whole by dividing it into parts . . . the General into the Special (which distributeth to every person his due business).

Enumeratio—When we gather together those things into a certain number, which straightaway we do briefly declare.

Expolitio—When we abide still in one place yet seem to speak many things, many times repeating one sentence, but with other words and figures.

Incrementum—When by degrees we ascend to the top of something, or rather above the top; that is, when we make our saying grow and increase by an orderly placing of our words, making the latter word always exceed the former. . . . In this figure, order must be diligently observed, that the stronger may follow the weaker, and the worthier the less worthy; otherwise you shall not increase the Oration, but make a mingle mangle, as doth the ignorant, or else make a great heap, as doth Congeries.

Ordinatio—A figure which doth not only number the facts before they be said, but also doth order those facts, and maketh them plain by a kind of definition.

Partitio—When the whole is divided into parts.

Synonimia—When by a variation and change of words that be of like signification we iterate one thing diverse times.

The list form is the predominant mode of organizing data relevant to human functioning in the world, from financial transactions to knowledge of tides. Lists consisting of sequential signs appear as early as 3200 B.C. and mark the distant origin of a means of communication that will develop into written language. Listing itself developed in numerous ways worldwide, though most systems were initiated to establish a reliable means to store information necessary to record commercial exchanges or property ownership. Schemes of accountancy and record keeping provided for the mechanical collection and retrieval of data with the "reasonable" amount of unambiguous exactness necessary for trade and administration. Codification of quickly learned and easily performed systems facilitated transactions, becoming increasingly organized as economic, civic, and religious life became more complex.[10]

Signifying artifacts that predate writing, such as tallies and tokens, suggest the earliest occurrences of the concept of a pragmatic listing device. Notches cut in wood documented debts or receipt of payments. They were also useful in circumstances where a more permanent record was preferable to individual or collective memory, such as registering the duration of a journey, the number of animals hunted, the number of enemies slain, and so on. Ancient peoples also used tokens to represent commodities, employing counters of fixed shapes that corresponded to specific articles. Carried loosely in thick clay envelopes, these tokens were arranged in patterns so that participants in commercial transactions could visualize quantities. Eventually clerks marked the outer surface of the envelopes with impressions of the tokens inside them, thereby rendering the contents—both number and shape—visible at all times. Merchants later replaced the containers with tablets bearing the serial impressions, and early tabulation began.[11] (When Emerson in *Nature* describes the use of nature as a vehicle for human thought, he writes, "We are thus assisted by natural objects in the expression of particular meanings." He continues, however, to lament the underutilization of this rich resource: "But how great a language to convey such pepper-corn informations. Did it need such noble races of creatures, this profusion of forms, this host of orbs in Heaven, to furnish man with the dictionary and grammar of his municipal speech?" [*E*, 23].)

Accountancy and record keeping similarly drove the invention and progressive refinement of cuneiform writing. Although most of the Sumerian tablets that have been recovered are clerical records, some are lists of standardized terminology from exercises for scribal training in cuneiform. Such lists represent a mode of compilation different from that of commodity, debt, or occurrence enumeration, one that demonstrates a conscious awareness of the development of written language. Documenting the standardization of terms used in clerical transactions, these exercises represent the earliest lexicons and the approximate point from which advanced reference works (syllabaries, bilingual dictionaries, phrase books, grammars) originate. As civilization progressed and commercial and bureaucratic workings became more and more complex, cuneiform developed further in precision and refinement. Finally, as writing evolved to approximate spoken language, it no longer served a purely functional use but began to be employed for rhetorical purposes as well, branching, as M. W. Green writes, "out from the documentary into the narrative and creative literary spheres."[12]

The written list, itself born as a purely serviceable budgetary and mnemonic device, thus helped to bring further modes of writing into existence. It should be noted, however, as does Alastair Fowler in *Kinds of Literature*, that though "lists of a practical character" are among our earliest writings, it is probable that forms of oral listing developed even earlier.[13] The oral passing of family histories and genealogies, as well as the instruction of skills, could have possessed a listlike structure. Songs driven by anaphora—in which a word or phrase repeats at the beginning of subsequent clauses— or those with repeated phrases in refrain or reprise could certainly predate written lists and command listing strategies of their own.

Indeed, cataloguing is a major component of elaborate monumental works like the *Iliad,* even though the great list of ships may have been omitted in some oral reproductions in periods when historical and geographical enumeration held no interest.[14] Such versions of the poem may have left off just after the series of similes that are used to evoke the massive number of soldiers (the flames, the flocks, and the flies) and resumed after the conclusion of the register, sadly overlooking one of the poem's important features. Homer's documentation of everyone involved in the assault of Troy serves the greater song in significant ways, through both instruction and art. The great sweep of this list conjures up the magnitude of the impending war, but it also provides a historical and geographic lesson in an era when there were virtually no other means by which to hand on information. The list enumerates participants, using anecdote and epithet to pass along a remembered history. The past evoked is both collective, because of the unified undertaking of the war, and individual, appealing to listeners to recognize the membership of their homelands in the effort. As Cedric Whitman observes, "In Antiquity, a hymn to a god recounted his deeds; the hymn to an army recounts its constituents."[15]

There is, however, a didactic caveat in that this list, though generally correct in its broad outline of history, does contain factual errors and liberties, as well as stylistic peculiarities; as Nicholas Howe observes, "the use of traditional material does not preclude poetic invention."[16] Geography is an important factor here, in that it forces the poet, who must meet specific metrical requirements, to accommodate a diversity of different-sounding place names and manipulate traditional and improvised epithets. Without variation the enumeration would quickly become monotonous. The poet employs this variation not only with regard to the epithets—doing so would just be mixing around labels—but also by providing inset illustrations of either individuals or the legacy of a particular locale.

Although it appears ordered, the prebattle procession is presented not merely as a passing parade: the catalogue moves in and out, alternating grand sweep with intimate portrait. With narrative dynamism it also moves backward and forward in time relative to the assault, flashing back to a death early in the invasion, and, in the congruent catalogue of Trojans, forward to a fated death at the hands of Achilles. Portraits of Agamemnon and Achilles also frame the catalogue in a significant way, bracketing the enumeration and further suggesting a mixture of motivations and states of mind before the battle proper. A glimpse of Agamemnon, presented in the midst of the mass, precedes the list. When recounting the troops, the list locates the hero in his own position in the middle. In contrast, Achilles, raging apart, is shown only after the catalogue of Achaeans concludes.

Finally, it should be noted that the list could also have served as an acknowledgment of patrons for whom the poem was sung. Though a stylistically isolated incident in the *Iliad,* the device was copied by subsequent authors who sought to imitate or surpass Homer, and it became a hallmark of epic literature. *Paradise Lost* draws on this epic tradition and further illustrates how the significance of the catalogue can change with the passing of time. As William Hunter observes, several passages of this epic poem are

made up of lists and catalogues (except for the compilation of dev-
ils) which are all but incomprehensible to modern readers but
which contain information easily understood and appreciated by
an educated reader of Milton's era.[17]

As a structure, the list remains with us in both pragmatic and
literary forms. Through the millennia, the pragmatic list has been
used and continues to be used for commercial, reference, and
mnemonic purposes. But representations of such functional lists
are frequently incorporated into literary works in the same way
other aspects of daily human life are. Just as writers simulate
speech, conversation, and other verbal communications within a
text, so too may they generate pragmatic lists that fulfill a literary
service while ostensibly fulfilling a functional one. Thus in "The
Decanter" chapter of *Moby-Dick*, Melville offers this inventory,
which Ishmael transcribes from "an ancient and learned Low
Dutch book":

400,000	lbs. of beef.
60,000	lbs. of Friesland pork.
150,000	lbs. of stock fish.
550,000	lbs. of biscuit.
72,000	lbs. of soft bread.
2,800	firkins of butter.
20,000	lbs. Texel & Leyden cheese.
144,000	lbs. cheese (probably an inferior article).
550	ankers of Geneva.
10,800	barrels of beer. [*MD*, 499]

As a pragmatic inventory, this list presents a straightforward record
of the supplies necessary to outfit a fleet of whalers, providing details important to the narrator's agenda of presenting the entire
compass of whaling life. As a literary device, Melville's list triggers
Ishmael's own analysis and his further digressions down unforeseen avenues of thought. Although Ishmael amasses such details
throughout the novel, his manner of collecting brings confusion
rather than clarity. The search for truth, signified by the hunt for the

whale, is carried out, ultimately, not through scientific investigation but through the creative literary power of the imagination.[18] On the other hand, facts and the reckoning of facts have enormous significance for a writer like Thoreau. Thoreau commits himself to making *Walden* a complete accounting, though the work includes both actual and fictive occurrences and is a report in which events have been selected, ordered, altered, and mythologized.

Prose, in its less hindered duplication of the external world in writing, has a great advantage over poetry in the incorporation of the pragmatic list, especially in its capacity to assimilate all written forms. Nevertheless, in poetry, the near-approximations of the pragmatic list, or at least principles of pragmatic listing made to accommodate verse form, predate those of prose. A convenient example is Ben Jonson's Epigram 73, "To Fine Grand":

> What is't, fine Grand, makes thee my friendship flye,
>   Or take an Epigramme so fearefully:
> As't were a challenge, or a borrower's letter?
>   The world must know your greatnesse is my debter.
> In-primis, Grand, you owe me for a jest;
>   I lent you, on meere acquaintance, at a feast.
> Item, a tale or two, some fortnight after;
>   That yet maintaynes you, and your house in laughter.
> Item, the babylonian song you sing;
>   Item, a faire greeke poesie for a ring:
> With which a learned Madame you belye.
>   Item, a charme surrounding fearefully,
> Your partie-per-pale picture, one halfe drawne
>   In solemne cypres, the other cob-web-lawne.
> Item, a gulling imprese for you, at tilt.
>   Item, your mistris anagram, i'your hilt.
> Item, your owne, sew'd in your mistris smock.
>   Item, an epitaph on my lord's cock,
> In most vile verses, and cost me more paine,
>   Then had I made 'hem good, to fit your vaine.
> Fortie things more, deare Grand, which you know true,
>   For which, or pay me quickly, or Ile pay you.

An imitation of a bill, Jonson's poem appropriates the actuarial nature of the list in a complex manner. In counting out its items one by one, Jonson's poem is an "enumeration," a specific kind of particularization and collection. In its itemization and transformation of witty constructs into goods and services rendered—commodities—the poem shows how one can assign a measure of value to and exchange things even as immaterial as jokes and sayings. Jonson performs some budgetary alchemy here, provocatively suggesting that if something can be encompassed in words it can then be registered as a unit inside a list frame, and if that structure is a bill, it implies purchase or payment. Through his enumeration, the poet translates a general sense of bonhomie into a series of uncredited gestures. This reflects the capacity of interconvertability (economic or otherwise) suggested by the list.

In the satiric distributions of "The Legacy," François Villon offers another illustration of how the list form can function as a frame within which he can combine, add and subtract, and tabulate things according to a fantastic, weirdly mathematical principle. Among his bequeathed imagined objects—things made substantial by their creative articulation—Villon gives to one recipient

> every day a greasy goose
> And a nice plump capon,
> And ten vats of wine white as chalk,

to which are added, prophylactically, "two lawsuits, so he won't get too fat."[19]

Jonson's Epigram 73 also serves as a good reference for exploring other list features. The poem begins its reckoning (though the reckoning does not begin the poem) with the quasi-assimilated Latin *Inprimis*, meaning "in the first place" and originally used to introduce the first member of a series. I say quasi-assimilated because the term has disappeared from common use and been replaced by *item*, originally meaning "likewise" and used to introduce subsequent facts or statements but now used for all elements in a series including the first. The *Oxford English Dictionary* gives two definitions of the noun form of *item* relevant to this study. The first calls it "an article or unit of any kind in an enumeration, computation or sum total; an entry or thing entered into an account or register." The second defines it as "any member of a set of linguistic units." When discussing components of a list here, I use *item* in both these senses.

Finally, it is important to observe the singular advantage poetry has over prose in the creation of lists. As the Jonson epigram makes clear, poems usually take forms that provide a natural environment for lists. The stacked lines of a verse provide virtual ledger entries in which the poet can itemize, registering and elaborating a certain number of items per line (in this case one). This loose framework lets the poet enumerate or accumulate, amplify or distribute, mount or diminish, suggest completion or unending plenitude, according to a custom-made formula.

How do we define what a list is? A list is a formally organized block of information that is composed of a set of members. Nicholas Howe notes that medieval encyclopedias were at once accretive and discontinuous, a definition that aptly describes the list as well.[20] This is to say that the list is simultaneously the sum of its parts and the individual parts themselves. By accretion, the separate units cohere to fulfill some function as a combined whole, and by discontinuity the individuality of each unit is maintained as a particular instance, a particular attribute, a particular object or person. Like the conjunction *and,* the list joins and separates at the same time.[21] Each unit in a list possesses an individual significance but also a specific meaning by virtue of its membership with the other units in the compilation (though this is not to say that the units are always equally significant). Writers find a wide range of application for lists because of this capability, and subsequently critics offer a variety of readings.

The list is the site where "completeness in separation" balances "the identity of the Union," as Kenneth Burke notes in a discussion of Whitman.[22] Thomas Rosenmeyer sees the list form as "the single most effective and congenial literary device of the pastoral lyric" because of this quality of simultaneous inclusion and partition. The list is both distributive and associative, an apt form in which to represent the "harmonious grove" through its "formal combination of a delight in separateness with its insistence on kinship."[23]

Because of their dual nature, lists must therefore be looked at from two opposing viewpoints: the individual units that make up a list (what does it hold?) and the function or purpose of the list as a whole (how does it hold together?). The study of literary lists will often reveal such patterned relations among the contiguous components as equality, contrast, gradation, progression, and further networks that expand out from the lists into the works in which they are embedded. Pragmatic lists also can be made to indicate inequality (a coaches' poll of the nation's best ball teams hierarchically arranged according to perceived ability) or equality (a team roster—though this will probably also have an internal organization, which could be numerical, alphabetical, or even hierarchical [captain, varsity, junior varsity]).

Because speech and writing are sequential, units heard or read in a list are comprehended first as having individual, discrete meaning, and then as having significance determined by relations to the preceding units. Furthermore, the dynamics and balance of lists adjust and shift as subsequent units are added, when relations realign and metrical patterns emerge. Relations among constituents give the list coherence. Interior elements can demonstrate new relations that may never have been considered except by their juxtaposition; unanticipated dynamics develop when such "strangers" are held together. The writer may force equality or contrast between elements, or both, when making the constituents copresent in the list structure.

Extrasystemically, as Stephen Barney notes, these crafted com-

pilations "potentially react with the narrative that encloses [them],"
operating as "intruders" that interrupt but represent some relation
to the greater work.[24] Mark Twain's miscellany of the contents of
Tom Sawyer's pockets is a delightful example: "a lump of chalk, an
indiarubber ball, three fish-hooks, and one of that kind of marbles
known as a 'sure 'nough crystal'" (*The Adventures of Tom Sawyer*,
chap. 14). This short list, much like the longer one recording Tom's
whitewash takings, reveals both the character's and the author's
love of collecting. For Tom such things are worth retaining because
of their inherent power to actually do something (chalk can mark
walls; fishhooks can hook fish) or a firm belief that they will potentially do something (a sure 'nough crystal will get you out of a jam
in a game of marbles—and it sure enough is crystal, really). It is
hard to resist indulging in the longer list, just to reinforce the splendid variety:

> There was no lack of material; boys happened along every little
> while; they came to jeer, but remained to whitewash. By the
> time Ben was fagged out, Tom had traded the next chance to
> Billy Fisher for a kite in good repair; and when he played out,
> Johnny Miller bought in for a dead rat and a string to swing it
> with; and so on, and so on, hour after hour. And when the mid-
> dle of the afternoon came, from being a poor poverty-stricken
> boy in the morning, Tom was literally rolling in wealth. He
> had, besides the things I have mentioned, twelve marbles, part
> of a jew's harp, a piece of blue bottle-glass to look through, a
> spoon-cannon, a key that wouldn't unlock anything, a frag-
> ment of chalk, a glass stopper of a decanter, a tin soldier, a cou-
> ple of tadpoles, six fire-crackers, a kitten with only one eye, a
> brass door-knob, a dog-collar—but no dog—the handle of a
> knife, four pieces of orange-peel, and a dilapidated old win-
> dow-sash. . . . If he hadn't run out of whitewash he would have
> bankrupted every boy in the village.
>
> [chap. 2]

One might observe, here, that the very miscellaneousness of this
kind of collection is itself a kind of unity. The dictum of Wallace

Stevens's Connoisseur of Chaos is fitting here as well: "A great disorder is an order." Still, excess like this is always funny: all the author needs is what Spufford calls "a willingness to halt a horizontal march across the plains of narrative to build a sudden tower of words of no obvious usefulness."[25]

But this list isn't useless. Here the collections of "certain schoolboy treasures of inestimable value" serve the work at large by making explicit the value system under which the novel will operate, one that endows ordinary objects with childhood fascination and wonder. The worth of these objects is determined by a sort of secret underground economy that thrives beneath the awareness and certainly the understanding of the adult world. As a "history of a boy," *The Adventures of Tom Sawyer* reflects Twain's fascination with boyhood play, and as such, these lists substantiate the intersection of this world of children's imagination with the world of grown-up reality, a juncture that is one theme of the novel.

On the author's part, the list presents an understanding of how the frame can be filled with stylistically different structural formulations reflecting an array of possibilities that is as surprising and heterogeneous as the objects collected. Twain's list could have been composed of equivalent units such as "a chalk, a ball, a hook, a marble," but to build it in that way would have been to disregard the richness of language and its capacity to express the richness of the world we live in, a wealth the imagination renders even richer. Twain modifies each object in a different way, using language to describe each by a different quality—shape, composition, quantity, appearance—and each through syntactically different approaches. Twain's narrative virtuosity and his ear for language are revealed in the arrangement of this list: the chalk rests inert as a lump until used for marking; the india-rubber ball practically bounces; the three fishhooks are carefully, precisely accounted for (you wouldn't want to get poked); and the marble, the special, valuable treasure, is granted an elaborate, almost mythical, description ("one of those known as") and the privileged, anchoring, final spot.

Lists are adaptable containers that hold information selected from the mind-deep pool of possibility. As the Twain list shows, they grow by the will of the compiler, by whose discretion the number and order of elements are decided. The ability to select gives the writer enormous power in determining which things to enumerate, what will appear in the procession, exactly how and in what relations an object will be perceived. When a writer creates a list, he or she makes choices of inclusion or exclusion based on some desired criteria. As Patti White observes, compilers must observe distinctions and make decisions, otherwise everything would be eligible for inclusion (and imagine poor Tom's pockets then!).[26] Decisions to accept or reject elements involve multiple comparisons based on how one element adapts to the growing structure so that, to adapt Claude Lévi-Strauss, "the decision as to what to put in each place depends on the possibility of putting a different element there instead, so that each choice which is made [involves] a complete reorganization of the structure, which [is never] the same as one vaguely imagined or as some other which might have been preferred to it."[27] Indeed, because the list structure may absorb any kind of component, readers can imagine their own conceptual alternatives adjacent to it and wonder, "Why was such-an-such an item included? Why not substitute this one?" We can consider what it was about one series that led to its being chosen compared to others that were not chosen.

I have suggested that a list is constructed of elemental units. Before looking further at how writers may arrange these parts, it is worth investigating what sort of things actually constitute parts. Generally, a list is nominal. This is to say that usually nouns are compiled, whether persons, found objects, store inventories, features of an individual, or the days of the year. This is particularly true of non-literary compilations—for example, where a record is kept of units of currency or particular events. But in the literary sphere, to list nouns is to do more than record; it is to display, to lay out, to arrange—to create reality—whether that be to represent a moment of complete awareness of the world or just to experiment, to conjure by naming. As Walt Whitman writes in *An American Primer*, "A perfect user of words uses things. . . . They exude in power and beauty from him . . . poured copiously."[28]

Though nouns—individuals, objects, dates—may dominate the list, other parts of speech (words being particulate in nature) are also readily compiled. Descriptive listing allows a writer to combine appropriate adjectives to present an object as accurately as possible using a language system which, though vast, does not have a vocabulary large enough to represent every shade, gradation, and possible combination of attributes. By compiling, a writer can evoke for the reader an object or an action in all its definite and peculiar aspects. The components, as Gass notes, "assert the joint dependency of every element in the pursuit of the truth."[29] (In contrast, Emerson writes in *Nature*, "Words are finite organs of the infinite mind. They cannot cover the dimensions of what is in truth. They break, chop and impoverish it" [*E*, 30].)

A pure delight in words themselves may also drive listing, where meaning is less important than sound. Joyce masterfully heaps up such accumulations, exploiting listing to reveal and celebrate the infinitude of language:

> Thither the extremely large wains bring foison of the fields, flaskets of cauliflowers, floats of spinach, pineapple chunks, Rangoon beans, strikes of tomatoes, drums of figs, drills of Swedes, spherical potatoes and tallies of iridescent kale, York and Savoy, and trays of onions, pearls of the earth, and punnets of mushrooms and custard marrows and fat vetches and bere and rape and red yellow brown russet sweet big bitter ripe pomellated apples and chips of strawberries and sieves of gooseberries, pulpy and pelurious, and strawberries fit for princes and raspberries from their canes.

(Indeed, this description of the Dublin market from the "Cyclops" chapter is a rather tame excerpt from *Ulysses;* in some passages, Joyce compiles such word-heaps that meaning is entirely obscured.)

Written lists, both utilitarian and literary, may develop along two different axes, horizontal or vertical. We can borrow an illustration from elementary physics to demonstrate the difference between the horizontal and vertical arrangements. In electronics, one can arrange circuits, discrete units analogous to items in a list, in two manners: in series and in parallel. Circuits in series are arranged end to end so that the entire current passes through each element without branching, much as one would read a horizontal list:

A parallel arrangement of circuits is a less exact analogy since the passing current is divided among the circuits in inverse proportion to their resistances in a way that our reading attention is not, but it nevertheless can serve as a visual illustration of how the vertical list is exhibited:

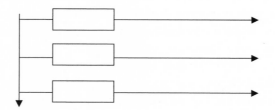

In literary listings, prose compilations, except in imitation of nonliterary itemizations such as bills, guest lists, or inventories, generally progress horizontally, moving along the page through the sentence. Verse lists can both stack vertically and develop sequentially along a line. An example is Pope's recapitulation of the survey of Belinda's dressing table in *The Rape of the Lock*. Here, a deliberate presentation, in which each item receives satirical amplification, concludes as a rather untidy, crowded miscellaneous collection:

> This Casket India's glowing Gems unlocks
> And all Arabia breathes from yonder Box.
> The Tortoise and the Elephant unite,
> Transform'd to Combs, the speckled and the white.
> Here Files of Pins extend their shining Rows,
> Puffs, Powders, Patches, Bibles, Billet-doux. [1.133–138]

In addition to the alliterative organization of the concluding line—one that foregrounds an aural mode of association while its very contents seem to fluctuate—there is further evidence of deliberate arrangement in the structure of this excerpt. As Pope lays out the cosmetics, the casket seems to be placed on one side of the table, while "yonder Box" is at a distance. This is also reflected in the relative positions of the two at the beginning and end of their respective lines. Furthermore, the chiasmus of Casket:India—Arabia:Box reinforces linguistically the sense of a sweeping examination across the entire surface of the dressing table.

In devising the congeries that bedecks this table, Pope accomplishes an extraordinary feat—his lines convey a sense of clutter that a contemporary reader may find hard to believe. The incongruous presence of "Bibles" in the boudoir is striking, though in keeping with the tenor of a work that exposes hypocrisy. But what is truly remarkable here is that scholarship has only added to the confusion, in this case to the benefit of the poem, by making the tabletop seem even more disarranged. While one scholar verifies the existence of decorative Bibles as fashionable eighteenth-century accessories, another deduces that *Bibles* is a variation or contraction of *bibelots*—trinkets—and these alternatives, each one with its merits, jostle for prominence in the mind of the reader. Even if the collected mass is in part philologically artificial, the effect of overabundant particularity it generates is akin to the residual washings of Swift's "City Shower," a list that one sensitive reader tellingly described as "a harmony of garbage":[30]

> Sweepings from Butchers Stalls, Dung, Guts, and Blood,
> Drown'd Puppies, stinking Sprats, all drench'd in Mud,
> Dead Cats and Turnip-Tops come tumbling down the Flood.
> [61–63]

The format of a list, its vertical or horizontal orientation, is simply another feature of its versatility. Whereas a vertical list stacks items, a horizontal list places one item directly after another. Here the demands of lineation impinge to a lesser degree, and a horizontal listing may have more grammatical continuity. One example is line 9 of Shakespeare's sonnet 106, where one item directly follows another: "Of hand, of foot, of lip, of eye, of brow." This innocent-appearing line is really quite devious in its subversion of the *blason*, a poetic genre dedicated to the praise of the female by the particularization of her attributes. This technique conventionally allowed the poet to describe or metaphorically elaborate one feature per line, creating a vertical compilation whose constituents are thematically continuous but linearly independent. Stephen Booth, in his commentary on Shakespeare's sonnets, presents as an example of the blason at its most conventional this poem by Bartholomew Griffin:

> My Lady's hair is threads of beaten gold,
> > Her front the purest Chrystal eye hath seen:
> Her eyes the brightest stars the heavens hold,
> > Her cheeks red roses such as seld have been:
> Her pretty lips of red vermillion dye,
> > Her hands of ivory the purest white:
> Her blush Aurora, or the morning sky,
> > Her breast displays two silver mountains bright,
> The spheres her voice, her grace the Graces three,
> > Her body is the Saint that I adore,
> Her smiles and favors sweet as honey be,
> > Her feet fair Thetis praiseth evermore.
> But ah the worst and last is yet behind,
> > For of a Gryphon she doth bear the mind.[31]

In sonnet 106, Shakespeare dispenses with the comparisons and collapses the blason topos (signaled by name in a previous line) from a sonnet-length poem to a single line, displaying a further flourish by disrupting the standard head-to-toe descent. Beyond merely elaborating on the convention in original ways, the poet here captures the entire genre by reference, not simple imitation.

As a convention the blason typically presented the mistress's features in a fixed sequence, and as a convention it typically invited talented writers to challenge its principles, to dazzle, and to create lasting art. Shakespeare does this by compression in sonnet 106 and by feigned disassociation from the genre in sonnet 130, "My mistress' eyes are nothing like the sun," in which he invalidates a series of comparisons yet still employs its enumerative practice:

> My mistress' eyes are nothing like the sun;
> Coral is far more red than her lips' red;
> If snow be white, why then her breasts are dun;
> If hairs be wires, black wires grow on her head.
> I have seen roses damask'd, red and white,
> But no such roses see I in her cheeks,
> And in some perfumes is there more delight
> Than in the breath that from my mistress reeks.
> I love to hear her speak, yet well I know
> That music hath a far more pleasing sound;
> I grant I never saw a goddess go,
> My mistress when she walks treads on the ground.
>> And yet, by heaven, I think my love as rare
>> As any she belied with false compare.

In its listing of attributes, the blason provides a sequence that is voyeuristically followed by the reader. Poets arranged the individual features so as to guide the reader through a particular way of seeing the beloved. By convention, it usually followed a head-to-toe sequence, but often it is not so much the contents of the sequence but the arrangement and manipulation (where does it start, where does it end) that reveal its underlying purpose. In a head-to-toe description, it is nearly impossible to develop an emotional climax peaking at the beloved's feet. Recognizing this, poets have manipulated the form by arranging its components for more satisfactory results. Some poems may linger on specific elements, shifting the emphasis or abandoning the convention. Some may abbreviate the enumeration by leaving off at strategically suggestive locations. Still others may use the sequence of comparisons to progress not in a direction of physical observation but into a different dimension altogether: away from corporeal loveliness toward a transcending spiritual beauty.

In contrast to the blason's account of the presence of features, the *ubi sunt* poem uses the list structure to reckon absence. By convention, the ubi sunt lists the names of individuals who have died, pressing the notion that despite the heterogeneity of individuals and fortunes, death ends all lives. In this roll call, the dead are simultaneously revived and reburied, brought to life momentarily through the poet's naming, and re-entombed by the occasion of that action. The genre provides momentary repossession of the departed but reminds the reader of the ultimate dispossession. In the face of its authoritarian last word, this convention also invites challenge. Into the substitutional array of the list of names, for example, Byron inserts "Where is Lord This? And where my Lady That?" and Villon adds, "And the good king of Spain / Whose name I can't recall?"[32] The ciphers of each of these accurately reflect the human condition as well as the naming of any person.

The ubi sunt poem may have one of any number of intentions, and like other literary lists it is unrolled in a deliberate manner. Dante Gabriel Rossetti's "Ballad of Dead Ladies," translated from Villon's "Dictes moi ou, n'en quel pays," provides a further illustration of the variety of form within the verse listing:

> Tell me now in what hidden way is
> > Lady Flora, the lovely Roman?
> Where's Hipparchia, and where is Thais
> > Neither of them the fairer woman?
> Where is Echo, beheld of no man,
> > Only heard on river and mere,—
> She whose beauty was more than human?
> > But where are the snows of yesteryear?

Where's Héloise, the learned nun,
    For whose sake, Abaillard, I ween,
Lost manhood and put priesthood on
    (From Love he won such dule and teen!)
And where, I pray you, is the Queen
    Who willed that Buridan should steer
Sewed in a sack's mouth down the Seine?
    But where are the snows of yesteryear?

White Queen Blanche, like a queen of lilies,
    With a voice like any mermaiden,—
Bertha Broadfoot, Beatrice, Alice,
    And Ermengarde the lady of Maine,—
And that good Joan whom Englishmen
    At Rouen doomed and burned her there,—
Mother of God, where are they then?
    But where are the snows of yesteryear?

Nay, never ask this week, fair lord,
    Where they are gone, nor yet this year,
Save with thus much for an overword,—
    But where are the snows of yesteryear?

The poem emphasizes the transitoriness of life through the trope of past winters, in which snowfalls leave no lasting marks but register a trace of their existence only in our memories. The persistent contemporaneity of the poem with each recital, reinforced by the *now* of the first line, augments the gulf between the impermanence of life and its endurance as art or record. Suggesting the brevity of beauty in the first stanza, the poet departs from the one line–one item format in significant stylistic ways: the first personage, Lady Flora, is deferred to the second line, "hidden" away through a complex syntax that separates her existence from the present moment; Hipparchia and Thais, neither one the fairer and therefore neither one privileged or elevated over the other, share their line; Echo, whose beauty is beyond comparison, receives an augmented three-line entry.

The second stanza refers to only two women, but here the poem moves beyond the fading and inevitable death of beauty. The speaker does not even mention beauty in this stanza. Instead he provides examples of lives that inspired stories or reputation, where again the record remains but the person does not. The third stanza rolls out further names but concludes abruptly with Joan of Arc. In Joan's case the vanished snowfall is an inexact metaphor for the dead woman except perhaps in some grotesque way, yet the variety of human experiences and fates also includes burnings, so these too must be reckoned in a poem about mortality.

Nicholas Howe describes the list as "catenulate," a term the *Oxford English Dictionary* defines as "formed of parts united end to end like links in a chain."[33] Such a definition accurately reflects the joined but flexible nature of list components, operating somewhere between the extremes of detached isolation and rigid unification. Nonliterary lists form their linkages by externally imposed methods: additional units of information are plugged into a database such as a phone book, a dictionary, or an itinerary after they have been shaped for assimilation; heterogeneous lists such as "to do" or grocery lists link items together under a general mnemonic rubric. Textual, literary lists become chainlike by forming thematic or rhetorical links. The blason with its itemization of features and the ubi sunt poem with its recollection of departed personages are examples of thematic listing. Rhetorical listing is grammatically additive and can be elaborated in one of a number of ways, each of which carries a particular nuance.

The shortest chain must have two links. (Louis Milic asserts that a list, however, must have a minimum of four units—fewer than four are conventionally defined by the rhetorical terms *doublet* and *tricolon*).[34] One kind of list uses the word *and* to pair objects in various ways. It can hold, one in each hand as it were, items that are complementary and belong together, like "ham and eggs," or opposites, like "fire and ice" or "good and evil." *And* may also yoke words that are different but similar enough in meaning to be redundant: "That, sir, is a false and untrue statement!" (a pleonasm). The comma silently fuses together components, as it would do in Whitman's line were we quietly to add a comma: "A noiseless[,] patient spider."

Chains grow longer with the addition of links, and lists expand with the addition of items. In polysyndeton all the constituents are joined by a conjunction, often the word *and*. The repetition of the conjunction serves to call equal attention to each item in the list, as well as to generate momentum: "Lions and tigers and bears (O my!)." In combinations of more than two constituents, *and* usually joins the penultimate and ultimate items; the other connections are made through punctuation. In this standard, sedate format, *and* signals the arrival of the concluding element and thus the end of the list. In lists formed by polysyndeton, however, the common expectation of termination is suspended. As readers or listeners, we don't know when the compilation will conclude. The effect on us can be peculiar. A prose writer like Dickens uses the technique to heap up such an exhaustive accumulation of things, that, as Gass observes, "it implies that he is not telling us the half of it."[35]

> There were frowzy fields, and cow-houses, and dunghills and dustheaps, and ditches, and gardens, and summerhouses, and carpet-beating grounds, at the very door of the railway. Little tumuli of oyster shells in the oyster season, and of lobster shells in the lobster season, and of broken crockery and faded cabbage leaves in all seasons, encroached upon its high places. Posts, and rails, and old cautions to trespassers, and backs of mean houses, and patches of wretched vegetation, stared it out of countenance. [*Dombey and Son*, chap. 6, "Paul's Second Derivation"]

Dos Passos can also use conjunctions to excess, as in this passage mimicking anecdotal garrulity (and she hasn't told us the half of it!):

Then she talked about her best friend when she'd been a girl who'd been an Irish girl with red hair and a clear warm white skin like Crown Darby, my dear, and how she'd gone to India and died of the fever, and how Miss Oliphant had never thought to survive her grief and how Crown Darby had been invented and the inventor had spent his last penny working on the formula for this wonderful china and had needed some gold as the last ingredient, and they had been starving to death and there had been nothing left but his wife's wedding ring and how they kept the fire in the furnace going with chairs and tables and at least he had produced this wonderful china that the royal family used exclusively. [*The 42nd Parallel*, "Eleanor Stoddard"]

"The continuator," as Milic terms it, in these passages is used to suggest two different modes of copiousness.[36] In the first, the accumulation of objects, though exhaustive, seems incomplete, implying that the scene is so chaotic that it is beyond language to accurately enumerate and present; it can be evoked only by a kind of resigned approximation. In the second, by connecting whole clauses, not merely objects and their descriptors, the writer conveys an unbroken chain of empty talk propelled by an unchecked mind skipping from thought to thought.

Purely a connector—the device that creates the philological linkage between the links—*and* joins what comes before it to what comes after it, without regard to syntactic size or configuration, or to the relation of the two components so joined. In this way it differs from the use of more specialized connective words, for example *begat,* which also joins two components, although the connection is the progenerative capacity of one generation to the next: "Abraham begat Isaac, Isaac begat Jacob, Jacob begat Judah," and so on. *Begat* is a verb that reproduces, whereas *and* is a straightforward conjunction. (Dupriez defines this use of a repeated word to connect one clause to another as "concatenation.")[37] Polysyndeton can be used to create grammatical manipulations not only with regard to degree of compilation but in subtle, slippery ways as well. Faulkner provides a good example in "A Note on Sherwood Anderson": "purity and integrity and hard and unremitting work and accomplishment." The arc of such a line appears to follow the formula $A+B+C+D+E+F$, but the trajectory is more accurately represented by $(A+B)+([C+D][E+F])$.[38]

When conjunctions are omitted entirely the effect is quite different. Asyndeton suggests that the list will continue beyond its last member. Milic notes that this tactic seems to imply that the list is longer than is revealed and that something further remains unsaid. Alternately, Curtius describes a "verse-filling asyndeton" used by Horace to dismiss a class of things such as superstitions or objects of value, in which the entire line is filled, leaving no room for the superfluous *and*.[39]

Another way of creating chains is through seriation, in which a series of statements is presented in succession. Melville is particularly skilled at this reiteration and restatement in *Moby-Dick*, where wave after wave of illustrations, "facts," and comparisons accumulate. The heaping up of example derives from an irrepressible urge to amplify—to generate and churn out example after example, regardless of authenticity. Though they retard the narrative, these facts, some genuine, some fantastic, persuade. As Barney writes of the justifications of listing in oratory, "If one dart in the list fails to hit the opponent, another may." In the words of George Puttenham, this tactic of amplification can "enforce persuasion mightily."[40]

A grocery list scrawled on the back of an envelope compiles in one location items the writer wants to buy at a store. This list serves as a receptacle to hold a set of items. It may have a scheme of organization that gives it form—alphabetical, by location in store, the sequence in which the writer thought of the items—but it also demonstrates another feature of lists: it has no requisite force of closure. Although there may be a hierarchy apparent in the list (some items may be substituted for others or specific items might be purchased only if the shopper has enough money or an item is on sale), additional items can always be added to the written list itself. This expandability holds true as well for such obvious compilations as a telephone directory, which retains numbers of individual entries and orders them according to a straightforward principle for ease of use. In this instance, elements are added alphabetically, rather than tacked on at the end, but fundamentally both the grocery list and the telephone book readily assimilate additional members.

The principle of expandability may apply in theory to literary lists, but in practice these lists are regulated by aesthetic requirements as well. The list form may suggest the idea of inclusivity and expansive accretion, but literary compilations have a limit to the number of items they can hold, beyond which the addition of further units becomes detrimental. One of the things that can go awry with a list is that it can go on for too long: though without bounds in principle, the list has a load limit of what it can skillfully hold. In verse, metrical patterns and boundaries impose absolute restrictions—a sonnet must conclude after fourteen lines, a line of iambic pentameter must contain at least five stresses. With such impositions, it is impossible to attain telephone-directory exhaustiveness.

Nonetheless, poets of great ability are able to fill the fixed size and shape of their forms to the greatest possible capacity, as Milton does in the inspired line "Rocks, caves, lakes, fens, bogs, dens and shades of death." Here within the parameters of his required ten beats, the poet evokes all the conceivable barren or empty spaces of Hell, using the list to create a sonically inhospitable landscape. The harsh, splintering consonants and the incremental progression, one propulsive monosyllable after another, blast life itself from the line, the life that poetry normally conveys through rhythm. Nevertheless, the rhyme *fens/dens*, straddling the boggy middle, and the repetition of the "s" sound throughout hold the line together just as suspension wires support a bridge.

Similarly, though the list of George Herbert's "Prayer (I)" is restricted by the fourteen-line obligation of a sonnet, the poem achieves a sublime effect of seeming to expand with the opening against restriction in the spiritual relief that comes with the contemplation of God.

> Prayer the Church's banquet, Angels' age,
> > God's breath in man returning to his birth,
> > The soul in paraphrase, heart in pilgrimage,
> The Christian plummet sounding heaven and earth;
> Engine against the Almighty, sinners' tower,
> > Reversed thunder, Christ-side-piercing spear,
> > The six-day's world transposing in an hour,
> A kind of tune, which all things hear and fear;
> Softness, and peace, and joy, and love, and bliss,
> > Exalted manna, gladness of the best
> > Heaven in ordinary, man well dressed,
> The milky way, the bird of paradise,
> Church-bells beyond the stars heard, the soul's blood,
> > The land of spices; something understood.

The sonnet consists of a series of items that present the nature of prayer, held together without a verb. The poem defines prayer as each of these paraphrases, and the progression from one to the next blends them all together, despite marked differences between them. Prayer thus encompasses all modes of thinking of God, whether rapt wonder, worship, comfort, desperate pleading, or unsure questioning. As Arnold Stein notes, "prayer is neither definable nor wholly expressible," but through the list the poet is able to array its potential approximations.[41] This concentrated accumulation gives the poem an incantatory effect.

In only fourteen lines, Herbert packs the poem with twenty-eight items. Nevertheless, the series reads as no mere listing, an effect the poet achieves by its deliberate construction. By omitting the verb, he suspends the resolution of the sentence. (This assumes, of course, that poetry is supposed to progress grammatically, although

Herbert's intent may be to evoke a sensation of concentration or meditation in which grammatical movement is irrelevant.) Though it may be understood by ellipsis after *Prayer,* the omission is significant. As we move down the list of examples, we abandon the expectation of a grammatical conclusion, and the poem resolves itself as "something understood." Without being explicit, the poet has suggested something between the lines, as it were, communicating the nature of prayer to us as though it were something we did not need to be told about, in the same manner in which we come to understand the latency of the verb.

Herbert's list is remarkable as well because it is such a heterogeneous assortment, and this diversity requires special note. The items differ with regard to both their attitude toward prayer and their syntactic construction, illustrating how flexible a container the list can be. Examination of this list reveals that it includes examples of prayer as solace, thanks, anger, and querying, among others. "Engine against the Almighty" is active; "God's breath in man returning" seems passive. Some of the items require an entire line to describe, while others ("Softness") stand alone. Herbert mixes generalities with particularly precise or elaborate metaphors: we have "peace" and "love," but also a spear—a specific, "Christ-side piercing spear" to be exact. Others ("A kind of tune") are remarkably vague. E. B. Greenwood describes this list as "an asyndetic series of parallel statements,"[42] and Herbert does indeed withhold the conjunctions to augment the concentration, except for the ninth line. Here, at the turn between octave and sestet, the poem becomes meditative, the polysyndetonic line held together and broken up by commas and conjunctions. The effect is incantatory. How different the line would be without the commas, its headlong momentum then unbroken. That the line is free of intellectually challenging imagery adds to the sense of refuge.

We can point to Twain's collection or Herbert's sonnet to show how dissimilar units can join, chainlike, to make up a list. Both examples illustrate the variations of internal contrast achieved by het-

erogeneity of form as well as meaning. In both, the chain incorporates links of diverse size and shape, and we might say, of color or
texture too. Ultimately, it is not individual links by themselves that
make up a chain but rather the linkages made between them that
give coherence: a handful of loose loops is very different from the
same loops coupled into a series. It is by bringing this varied collection together and then creating linkages between them—as Herbert does through suggesting paraphrases for prayer or Twain does
by imagining his protagonist's possessions—that a list conveys
meaning.

A repeated single item makes for a very boring list but may have
important nonliterary functions:[43] markings on a cell wall record
the number of years imprisoned; carvings on a coconut tree on a
deserted island record days since the shipwreck; jottings in a log-
book by a birdwatcher at a sanctuary record the number of tufted
marsh grebes seen on a particular visit. In these examples, the element tallied does not vary, but the length of the tallying presents
very different stories and significances: what is the magnitude of
the crime committed? how much of the sentence has been served?
how does that service correlate with the private thoughts of the
prisoner? (Is there regret or remorse? or even guilt?—the tallying
has a very different effect if the prisoner is innocent.) How many
days' supply of food is there? Has construction of the airport af-
fected migration patterns? In the spectrum of lists, from pragmatic
to literary, meaning is determined not only by variation but by duration.

To build lists, the compiler connects one link to another. These
chains can have all kinds of compositions, an endless variety of
lengths, and any number of purposes. As Barney notes of this elusive, protean construct, "the numberlessness of a list makes it an apt
vehicle for enumeration, and its random sequence makes it apt for
a display of formal order."[44] To catalogue the list is an enormous
undertaking, for the structure has an infinitely interchangeable potential. Lists have been unrolled with exuberance and tedium, with

surprise and as expected. To explore the list in Joyce or Rabelais calls
for a book in itself. I have argued that lists are deliberate structures,
built with care and craft, perfectly suited to rigorous analysis. The
list offers a marvelous venue for literary and linguistic spectacle. Let
us now look at how four great, very different American compilers
have occupied this arena.

2

Emerson

"Each and All"

※ ⚙ ※

L ists appear with great frequency throughout American literature. Sometimes they are incidental or minor, sometimes
they carry considerable artistic and intellectual weight. Most
of the lists of the early literature of North America are practical in
character: in 1519 Hernán Cortés inventoried the rich trove of gifts
given him by the Aztecs; in 1607 George Percy matter-of-factly catalogued the deaths of members of the Jamestown colony; in 1620
William Bradford registered the terms of a peace treaty; in 1624
John Smith documented the possessions of various Indian groups
and their trades with the early colonists; in 1643 Roger Williams
recorded a guide for native languages; in 1710 Cotton Mather completed his "Parental Resolutions" for "doing good," assembled in his
Bonifacius; and in his 1821 autobiography, Thomas Jefferson reiterated the injuries and crimes committed by the tyranny of George III
listed in the Declaration of Independence.

It was Benjamin Franklin who turned to more extensive and
elaborate systems of listing, especially when he chronicled his at-

tempts at self-improvement in his *Autobiography*. Franklin frequently compiled lists of aphorisms, but he also developed more ornate catalogues as well. As he recorded in the *Autobiography*, he began by compiling a select array of virtues culled from similar compendiums. He combined and consolidated his categories and worked to rank them in a meaningful, progressive way, whereby succeeding virtues built on and extended specific qualities of those that had previously been mastered:

> I proposed to myself, for the sake of clearness, to use rather more names, with fewer ideas annexed to each, than a few names with more ideas; and I included under thirteen names of virtues all that at that time occurred to me as necessary or desirable, and annexed to each a short precept, which fully expressed the extent I gave to its meaning.
>
> These names of virtues, with their precepts, were:
>
> 1. TEMPERANCE. Eat not to dullness; drink not to elevation.
>
> 2. SILENCE. Speak not but what may benefit others or yourself; avoid trifling conversation.
>
> 3. ORDER. Let all your things have their places; let each part of your business have its time.
>
> 4. RESOLUTION. Resolve to perform what you ought; perform without fail what you resolve.
>
> 5. FRUGALITY. Make no expense but to do good to others or yourself; *i.e.,* waste nothing.
>
> 6. INDUSTRY. Lose no time; be always employed in something useful; cut off all unnecessary actions.
>
> 7. SINCERITY. Use no hurtful deceit; think innocently and justly, and, if you speak, speak accordingly.
>
> 8. JUSTICE. Wrong none by means of doing injuries, or omitting the benefits that are your duty.
>
> 9. MODERATION. Avoid extremes; forebear resenting injuries so much as you think they deserve.
>
> 10. CLEANLINESS. Tolerate no uncleanliness in body, clothes, or habitation.
>
> 11. TRANQUILITY. Be not disturbed at trifles, or at accidents common or unavoidable.

12. CHASTITY. Rarely use venery but for health or off-spring, never to dullness, weakness, or the injury of your own or another's peace or reputation.

13. HUMILITY. Imitate Jesus and Socrates.

It was Franklin's intention to acquire these habitudes incrementally rather than all at once, and his arrangement reflected the fashion in which he proposed to do so: when mastered, the virtues at the top of the list, he believed, would aid him in attaining those that followed. Temperance would aid him in achieving silence, which would in turn lead to order, resolution, frugality, industry, and so forth. Franklin developed a tabulated system designed to record and lead to the betterment of his character.

In a less orderly and systematic fashion, Franklin also used a variation of listing to create his famous prefaces to his popular publication *Poor Richard's Almanac*. The preface to one particular edition, "The Way to Wealth" (1758), contained a medley of pragmatic maxims attributed to Poor Richard. Here a substantial volume's worth of well-known sayings have been thrown together and presented through the speeches of Franklin's prudent mouthpiece, Father Abraham. A portion of Father Abraham's declamation gives an idea of the overwhelming compilation of detail:

> How much more than is necessary do we spend in Sleep! Forgetting that *The sleeping Fox catches no poultry,* and that *There will be sleeping enough in the Grave,* as *Poor Richard says.* If Time be of all things the most precious, *wasting Time* must be, as *Poor Richard* says, *the greatest Prodigality,* since, as he elsewhere tells us, *Lost Time is never found again;* and what we call *Time-enough, always proves little enough:* Let us then up and be doing, and doing to the Purpose; so by Diligence shall we do more with less Perplexity. *Sloth makes all Things difficult, but industry all easy,* as *Poor Richard* says; and *He that riseth late, must trot all Day, and shall scarce overtake his Business at Night.* While *Laziness travels so slowly, that Poverty soon overtakes him,* as we read in *Poor Richard,* who adds, *Drive thy Business, let not*

that drive thee; and *Early to Bed, and early to rise, makes a Man
healthy, wealthy and wise.*

If Franklin found new ways to use listing and compilation effectively, nonetheless the practice did not become widespread until
some eighty years later. Lists do make appearances in sermons and
diaries as a conventional form employed to help organize the lecture and documentation, but only with the publication of a radical
new book did the practice of listing begin a new and dramatic
resurgence. This pioneering text, innovative and challenging on
many levels, possessed, in addition to its other stylistic peculiarities,
an energetic propensity toward listing. The book was Emerson's
Nature, appearing in 1836. The statement of its author's "First Philosophy," the work had a significant impact on American letters and
thought for years to come.

Never uncomplicated or unadorned, or even practical, Emerson's unorthodox essay contained exceptional lists, some of which
were almost rhapsodic. One passage confidently unrolls a vast, varied itemization in a swiftly widening sprawl to achieve a grand
sweep over all things animal, mineral, and vegetable: "All things are
moral; and in their boundless changes have an unceasing reference
to spiritual nature. Therefore is nature glorious with form, color,
and motion; that every globe in the remotest heaven, every chemical change from the rudest crystal up to the laws of life, every
change of vegetation from the first principle of growth in the eye of
a leaf, to the tropical forest and antediluvian coal-mine, every animal function from the sponge up to Hercules, shall hint or thunder
to man the laws of right and wrong, and echo the Ten Command-
ments" (*E*, 28).

Emerson's lists often draw us with their fascinating, sometimes
bewildering progression of examples. Indeed, while catalogues are
employed on many occasions for many purposes, they are most often used to name specimens with some shared characteristic, even
if finding that commonality forces the reader along a circuitous and

unpredictable path. Emerson's sequences are intended as illustrations, even if they seem to deviate from the anticipated formula. The passage just quoted follows no easy calculus of connection other than a whirling, exponential acceleration from the point as near as possible to zero to some ne plus ultra at the other end. What does this sampling from "Discipline" teach? Not only that all things are moral, as begins the passage, but that when Emerson says "all things" he means all things; this collection is meant to be comprehensive, "boundless."

This sweep of synonyms spans the universe, specifying changes, processes, functions. In its roughly three sets of pairings (Emerson characteristically complicates its symmetry) the movement seems to be from the lowest end of the register—the least significant, most minute, infinitesimal change that can still be recorded as change—to the the highest state, the most intense degree, the acme. The first pairing (the crystal/the laws of life) moves from the pinpoint of a single particle to the grandest natural principles. The second pairing similarly accelerates from the one to the many (the leaf/the rainforest), from the single smallest instance to its culmination when multiplied trillions of times over. However, this exponential progression of foliage also irregularly connects to something that is not easily correlative, unless we think of the outward sense of growth and expansion in juxtaposition with a feeling of descent and penetration, a plunge both into the earth and back in time as the leaf pairs with the antediluvian coal mine. The leaf connects to the rain forest in an obvious synechdochic way, but its connection to the second partner, the coal mine, is less evident, though both potential pairs share a rushing arc of motion. The final pair (the sponge/Hercules) ascends from seemingly inert existence to passionate, heroic, mythological life that is larger than the bounds of the human.

In another passage, the text encompasses a great range of human accomplishments, coloring advances in mechanization and subsequent impacts on the individual and society through its unique viewpoint:

The useful arts are reproductions or new combinations by the wit of man, of the same natural benefactors. He no longer waits for favoring gales, but by means of steam, he realizes the fable of Aeolus's bag, and carries the two and thirty winds in the boiler of his boat. To diminish friction, he paves the road with iron bars, and, mounting a coach with a ship-load of men, animals, and merchandise behind him, he darts through the country, from town to town, like an eagle or a swallow through the air. By the aggregate of these aids, how is the face of the world changed, from the era of Noah to that of Napoleon! The private poor man hath cities, ships, canals, bridges, built for him. He goes to the post-office, and the human race run on his errands; to the book-shop, and the human race read and write of all that happens, for him; to the court-house, and nations repair his wrongs. He sets his house upon the road, and the human race go forth every morning, and shovel out the snow, and cut a path for him. [*E*, 12–13]

Here, in the chapter "Commodity," Emerson presents man's mastery over nature. Man is no longer at the mercy of favorable conditions; he now can make those conditions. They are at his convenience; he is not helpless but industrious and enterprising. Directing nature, man dominates even myth and legend and attains a kind of enviable liberty (though this freedom is still chained to commerce). In the second half of the passage, however, things change. The hapless fellow—not so much poor in the financial sense as in his nameless, faceless existence—finds that many worthy services are provided for him, performed for him virtually without his stirring. He is the beneficiary of all the enterprising endeavors of his fellows. Insistently anthropocentric, the closing repetitions enforce the fact that the activities of society operate around man; he is the hub of the complex commercial, intellectual, and political machinery.

In its relative brevity—nine chapters, approximately fifteen thousand words—Emerson's *Nature* contains some fifteen or sixteen (depending on how one counts) passages of extended itemization or listing. Often the passages lay out distinguishable examples and illustrations to give Emerson's ideas their widest possible currency. In other places and by more gradual means, the lists create the impression of a greater totality, as in this passage, where Emerson methodically compartmentalizes each moment of the perpetually changing, variegated tapestry of our surroundings:

> To the attentive eye, each moment of the year has its own beauty, and in the same field, it beholds, every hour, a picture which was never seen before, and which shall never be seen again. The heavens change every moment, and reflect their glory or their gloom on the plains beneath. The state of the crop in the surrounding farms alters the expression of the earth from week to week. The succession of native plants in the pastures and roadsides, which makes the silent clock by which time tells the summer hours, will make even the divisions of the day sensible to a keen observer. The tribes of birds and insects, like the plants punctual to their time, follow each other, and the year has room for all. By watercourses, the variety is greater. In July, the blue pontrederia or pickerel-weed blooms in large beds in the shallow parts of our pleasant river, and swarms with yellow butterflies in continual motion. Art cannot rival this pomp of purple and gold. Indeed the river is a perpetual gala, and boasts each month a new ornament. [*E*, 15–16]

A modern analogy for Emerson's presentation of this obvious truth—that the world is a place of perpetual change—is time-lapse photography, whereby the experience is condensed and sped up to allow us to better grasp the nature of the changes taking place. Emerson's nearly parallel series of examples—the heavens, the crops, the plants, the birds and insects—similarly attest to the pervasiveness of change. Because the individual elements are commonly apprehended and local, the changes Emerson describes are uncontestable. He interrupts the categorical patterning, with its broad references to earth and sky, with one specific instance, however, a curiously arresting, vibrant July moment (evocative of similar instances in the writings of Emerson's sometime friend Thoreau). Backing away, however, Emerson states that this evident beauty of nature is its "least part" and cautions that it will become nothing more than a show "if too eagerly hunted." The beauty that nature radiates disappears when pursued.

Emerson's complex treatise on nature resonated with many authors, some of whom rallied behind the ideas suggested in it while others worked in opposition to it. The complexities of the reaction are too extensive to detail here, but it is clear that *Nature* was a work that changed everything, and the effects it came to have on Thoreau, Melville, and Whitman have been detected by numerous scholars and readers.

First, there are the obvious echoes. When, for example, Emerson discusses the restoration of the facts of natural history through marriage to human history, Thoreau comes to mind. Thoreau conceived of natural facts as holding meanings that were rich in significance and assiduously collected them. "Let us not underrate the value of a fact," he wrote in his essay "The Natural History of Massachusetts," "it will one day flower in a truth." Melville retained fundamental reservations about Emerson, but he nonetheless became a great practitioner of the "perpetual allegories" that Emerson described. We see this most clearly in Ishmael, a character whose creative and intellectual motions throughout *Moby-Dick* repeatedly caused "a material object more or less luminous [to arise] in his mind, contemporaneous with every thought" (*E*, 44). The debt is evident even in the novel's individual chapter headings, in which a vast array of material objects undergo extensive metaphorical transformations, and the author, in his true capacity of poet, perceives the affinities between things. From "The Carpet-bag" to "The Cassock" to "The Great Heidelburgh Tun," Melville is able "to make free with the most imposing forms and phenomena of the world" (*E*, 36).

In a similar manner, Whitman used material things as symbols of his "heroic passion." He "conform[ed] things to his thoughts," and, conscious of the fluidity of the material world, "impress[ed] his being thereon" (*E*, 34). Later, when Emerson composed "The Poet," he seemed to be directly foreseeing and summoning the encyclopedic verse of Whitman's *Leaves of Grass:* "We have yet had no genius in America, with tyrannous eye, which knew the value of our incomparable materials. . . . Our log-rolling, our stumps and their politics, our fisheries, our Negroes and Indians, our boats and our repudiations, the wrath of rogues and the pusillanimity of honest men, the northern trade, the southern planting, the western clearing, Oregon and Texas, are yet unsung. Yet America is a poem in our eyes; its ample geography dazzles the imagination, and it will not wait long for meters" (*E*, 465). The many complexities of the interrelationships among these authors have been elucidated elsewhere, but by examining the practice of listing in Emerson we can begin to assess how its multifarious uses aid in enlivening the writing of the American Renaissance.

Emerson may have chosen the list for many reasons. As an extremely adaptable construct it could be used in numerous ways for a variety of purposes. This would of course be true for any writer, so why should it occur so frequently with this one? What purpose did listing fulfill, what features did it have, that made it so well suited for Emerson's aims in *Nature* and a great many of his other writings?

Stylistically, the list is a structure with which Emerson would have been familiar. He could have found the technique of reiteration and the practice of cataloguing in the Psalms and elsewhere in the Bible. In addition to these and the models of numerous sermons, Emerson seems to have found the list conducive to the development of his own writing style. He himself recognized his own compositions as "incompressible . . . with each sentence an infinitely repellent particle." This particulate characterization suggests that Emerson sensed that his writing failed to cohere smoothly;

rather, it accumulated as a series of discrete statements. An unspecified force of repulsion enveloped and separated each unit and seemed to prevent absorption of sentences into paragraphs, paragraphs into essays. Certainly written sentences cohere through connection, but Emerson's seem to chain together (or chain apart?) to a high degree. Indeed, this quality accounts for some of the attractiveness of his prose. In one of his exchanges with Emerson, Carlyle famously validated this aspect of Emerson's writing: the sentences, he observed, "do not rightly stick to their foregoers and followers; the paragraph [is] not as a beaten *ingot,* but as a beautiful square bag of duck-shot held together by canvas!"[1]

Carlyle's language is telling. To begin with, an *ingot,* emphasized by Carlyle, is a mass of a substance, usually metal, slagged together to be used for some secondary purpose. Ingots are molded or beaten to be reformed into another shape. The "duck-shot" designation, taken by itself, seems to slight the quality of Emerson's prose as partial, scrappy, perhaps insufficient or unfinished. Carlyle is careful to qualify this, however, and we should be reminded that the container holding all these bits together is notably "beautiful." The assembled contents give the bag an appeal which would be lost by their dispersal.

It would be too totalizing to attribute Emerson's penchant for listing solely to style. While lists do function as containers, they would also have been suitable for Emerson for other reasons as well. The convention of listing was tremendously useful for demonstrating in a diagrammatic way one of Emersonian Transcendentalism's central concepts, the idea of the microcosm, that the world exists in miniature in each of nature's objects. Emerson wrote repeatedly of this correlative aspect of things. The unity of diversity was first affirmed in the "Discipline" section of *Nature:* "Herein is especially apprehended the unity of Nature,—the unity in variety,—which meets us everywhere. All the endless variety of things make an identical impression. . . . A leaf, a drop, a crystal, a moment in time, is related to the whole, and partakes of the perfection of the whole. Each particle is a microcosm, and faithfully renders the likeness of the world" (*E*, 30).

This is further elaborated in the later essay "Compensation":

> These appearances indicate the fact that the universe is repre-
> sented in every one of its particles. Every thing in nature con-
> tains all the powers of nature. Every thing is made of one hid-
> den stuff; as the naturalist sees one type running under every
> metamorphosis, and regards a horse as a running man, a fish as
> a swimming man, a bird as a flying man, a tree as a rooted man.
> Each new form repeats not only the main character of the type,
> but part for part all the details, all the aims, furtherances, hin-
> drances, energies, and whole system of every other. Every oc-
> cupation, trade, art, transaction, is a compend of the world,
> and a correlative of every other. Each one is an entire emblem
> of human life; of its good and ill, its trials, its enemies, its
> course and its end. And each one must somehow accommo-
> date the whole man, and recite all his destiny.
>
> The world globes itself in a drop of dew. The microscope
> cannot find the animalcule which is less perfect for being little.
> Eyes, ears, taste, smell, motion, resistance, appetite, and organs
> of reproduction that take hold on eternity,—all find room to
> consist in the small creature. So do we put our life into every
> act. The true doctrine of omnipresence, is that God reappears
> with all his parts in every moss and cobweb. The value of the
> universe contrives to throw itself into every point. If the good
> is there, so is the evil; if the affinity, so the repulsion; if the
> force, so the limitation. [*E*, 289]

This shared commonality, this identity of all things beneath or within their outward differences, equated them. Such equality al-lowed any one thing to substitute for any other. Because of its in-herent structural qualities, the list was the perfect vehicle to illus-trate the act of changing or exchanging one thing for another, for in the practice of passing from one thing to another, a residual trail would be left, and that trail would be a list.

Lawrence Buell has commented on a remarkable affinity among

list-making Transcendentalist authors that is noticeable in the parat-actic, reiterative nature of their writings. It is an affinity so strong, he notes, that in some places the prose of Emerson or Thoreau is "indis-tinguishable" from Whitman's verse. There are no doubt other stylis-tic reasons for this, but Buell further observes that it is the essence of the catalogue itself that gives shape to "a particular way of looking at the world," an outlook that was shared to varying degrees by this group of writers. He writes that Transcendentalist literature was in general rather formless, and he attributes this to the fact that Emer-son, Thoreau, and Whitman "all regarded art pragmatically . . . as properly the expression of something beyond itself." For them, he continues, "the secret of design in art rested rather in the ability to perceive the natural order than in imposing an aesthetic order upon their perception."[2]

For Buell, this meant that the catalogue or list offered a purely practical format since it enabled an adequate representation of the interlinkage and connectivity of *all* things by the collection of a few. The shape of the list, the actual sequence of items in the list (or what those items were), was less important than the fact that it illustrated the indispensable principle that informed the philosophy: all things blended together and each could equally represent spirit. Transcen-dentalism effectively implied that if individually each particular of nature could be a symbol of the total spirit, then all particulars of nature, no matter how divergent, were consequently analogous. Therefore any item chosen was as good as any other in a sequence of this sort, for "each creature is only a modification of the other" (*E*, 30). All the items in a list were fundamentally the same.

Despite their deliberate construction, the seemingly random structuring of Emerson's catalogues is difficult to discount. His lists seem to have less crisp distinction than those of other writers, un-less they egregiously violate our expectations. Emerson's lists are not as conspicuous as those of boisterous Melville or iterative Whit-man—except when they are outrageous in their sweep. Christo-pher Cranch, the fellow Transcendalist who showed himself per-

haps excessively conscious of the absurd in Emerson in his carica-
ture of the all-seeing eyeball, was especially drawn to one purgative
list at the conclusion of *Nature*, often considered one of the essay's
weak points: "As fast as you conform your life to the pure idea in
your mind, that will unfold its great proportions. A correspondent
revolution in things will attend the influx of spirit. So fast will disagreeable appearances, swine, spiders, snakes, pests, mad-houses,
prisons, enemies, vanish: they are temporary and shall be no more
seen. The sordor and filths of nature, the sun shall dry up and the
wind exhale" (*E*, 48–49). (In a cartoon, Cranch depicts a seated
Emerson serenely watching as crude figures flee—a pig, a snake, a
monstrous spider, and two four-legged buildings!)

This list reads like a categorical casting out of a collection of
phobias. It has been considered wishful thinking by some and flatly
ridiculous by others, and it stands out as memorable even without
Cranch's sketch of Emerson watching the various offenders fleeing.
What is remarkable here is the absence of a sense of magnitude regarding each of these "disagreeable" things, for surely one must re-
spond differently to enemies than to swine, and certainly a world in
which no enemies existed would be different from a world without
pigs. But that is not what we have here—instead, a variety of offensive things are said to be melted, dried, and removed by "the influx
of spirit," and because they each receive identical treatment they are
all normalized, all equalized.

In this particular idealization, such offensive things can become
desiccated and be swept away, but for Emerson all the things of nature were similar in an important aspect despite their superficial
differences. Emerson acknowledged the disparity of forms that the
objects of nature could take, but he affirmed their greater shared,
singular property of beauty when he noted that each creature was
only a modification of the other; "the likeness in them is more than
the difference, and their radical law is one and the same" (*E*, 30). He
wrote of nature as "a sea of forms" that was paradoxically "radically
alike and even unique." This formulation captures the essential

contradiction that the works of nature are fundamentally similar and single while also being innumerable and different. Consequently, when in one seemingly casual sequence Emerson writes that "a leaf, a sunbeam, a landscape, the ocean, make an analogous impression on the mind" (*E*, 18), his expression of the nullification of differences between the chosen items operates on two levels, splitting signifier from signified. It is clear that the various constituents of this listed sequence are diverse, but it is the deeply felt end effect, the impression on the mind rather than a sensory sensation, that unites them. Furthermore, while the quiddities of the things signified are refined to a higher, uniform beauty, the signifiers of these things undergo a transformation as well: in the sequence, what sets them apart as different *words* is made to recede behind a higher syntactical imperative, the grammatical fulfillment of a sentence, the communication of an assertion. What is common to both signified and signifier is a transformation that standardizes them, one at a Transcendental and the other at a semantic level. Put another way, as any natural form engenders the idea of beauty in the mind, any word representing such a form can be substituted in Emerson's declaration to complete his thought—a pebble, a rivulet, a field, a feather.

It is this underlying sense of divine immanence, concurrence, and unity in endless variety, coupled with the vast store of words available to language, that ultimately sets the Transcendentalist catalogue apart from other literary catalogues. This difference comes with some consequence. If any one thing in a list is as good as anything else, then the acts of selecting and ordering are themselves discounted, and the rapid metamorphosis of one thing into another eclipses any design or plan that may have brought this specific group of items together to begin with. As Julie Ellison explains, "The metaphoric chain reaction is an ongoing act of mastering the object world. . . . Since any word or image can 'represent the world,' and since transition can occur between any two words or images, the chain reaction can go on forever, fueled by the infinite number of possible substitutions." In the natural consummation of the chain reaction of pure Transcendentalism, compilations that are genuinely without an order would consequently be random— though it should be kept in mind that these would be different from compilations having an agenda of apparent randomness. True randomness, as Richard Wilbur asserts, may affirm that there exists "a vast reservoir" of things that might just as well be used, but it might also sustain interest for only so long, as he warns, "in the absence of deliberate human meaning."[3]

What saves a literary list from this terminal monotony of sequential randomness is the deliberate working over of items, as imperceptible as it might appear to be. For Emerson, this means that the selection and order of listed items follow a deliberate process. The items in a particular list might derive from random locations or sources, but they are still worked over by the mind. For a given instance, the mind collects and assembles fragments, as Emerson suggested in one journal entry: "By a multitude of trials and a thousand rejections and the using and perusing of what was already written . . . a poem made that shall thrill the world by the mere juxtaposition and interaction of lines and sentences that singly would have been of little worth and short date. . . . Every link in this living chain he found separate; one, ten years ago; one last week; some of them he found in his father's house or at school when a boy; some of them by his losses; some of them by his sickness; some by his sins."[4]

The elements are drawn from various experiences, but they are not indiscriminately gathered. Furthermore, in his critique of Lord Bacon, Emerson defined a higher order of organization that could be distinguished from a lower, more mercantile collocation. Assemblages of items—in this case, facts—could be made in the manner of Bacon, but they would express the methodical yet sterile organization of the discount retailer instead of the miraculous, systematic harmony of a living thing. Accordingly, Bacon's collections lacked quickening power: "All his work lies along the ground a vast unfinished city. He did not arrange but unceasingly collect[ed] facts. His own Intellect often acts little on what he collects. Very much stands as he found it—mere lists of facts. . . . The fire has hardly passed over it and given it fusion and a new order from his mind. It is sand without lime. . . . It is a vast collection of proverbs, all wise but the order is much of it quite mechanical, things on one subject being thrown together; the order of a shop and not that of a tree or an animal where perfect assimilation has taken place and all the parts have a perfect unity." The conclusion Ellison draws is that "in the absence of energy, solid objects become oppressive," adding that "the writer cannot muster sufficient force to overcome the inertia of his raw material."[5]

Perhaps it is unfair to extrapolate from Emerson's censure of Bacon that his own collections possess this intrinsic vitalizing capacity, but his words do suggest that the ideal—and in a document as studied and perfected as *Nature,* what would be constructed as less than ideal?—informs Emerson's collections and their lesser siblings, his lists. There is some kind of order behind what appears to be without order, some working of the mind that has achieved a fusion evident as form rather than formlessness.

A simple illustration from *Nature* in which order seems to play a negligible role will demonstrate this point. In the section "Beauty," Emerson characteristically brings together an unremarkable collection of items: "But besides this general grace diffused over nature, almost all the individual forms are agreeable to the eye, as is proved by our endless imitations of some of them, as the acorn, the grape, the pine-cone, the wheat-ear, the egg, the wings and forms of most birds, the lion's claw, the serpent, the butterfly, seashells, flames, clouds, buds, leaves, and the forms of many trees, as the palm" (*E,* 14). To read through this list is to walk through an antique shop with a master-carver, a person who can point out all the accomplishments of woodworkers in re-creating the forms of nature in the decorative arts.

As Emerson explicitly notes when introducing this list, these are not all the forms of nature—that would be a quantity too large to enumerate—but rather "some of them," a portion of the subsection of forms that have been imitated and that adorn humanmade objects, such as jewelry or furniture: the lion's claw on the foot of the table leg, the buds and leaves carved over the archway, the acorn blazoned on the family crest, the seashells on the face of the grandfather clock. It is probably impossible to determine the narrative thread that orders this sequence of items, but this is not to deny the movement and changing rhythm of this passage. It develops stepwise, type by type, and the reader serially approves each specimen:

1. Yes, it is unique (the shape of the pinecone is different from that of the serpent).
2. Yes, it is agreeable to the eye (though it would be interesting to know what forms Emerson would exclude: he begins the roll by stating "almost all" are agreeable, implying that there must be some that are not, although earlier he writes that "even the corpse has its own beauty").
3. Yes, it has been imitated by craftsmen as major or minor decoration or adornment.

By the tenth entry there is a change in the rhythm of the sequence. Dropping the articles, Emerson brings forward additional examples at a faster rate, as though more and more possibilities are springing to mind, and the list must adapt to keep up. At risk of appearing to overanalyze what is really only a minor passage in an extremely complex work, I point out that this list only appears to be formless. It seems to be an unbidden pronouncement of interchangeable items that happen to come to mind. But even if one thing is as good as another, the list is still regulated, even if only at a grammatical level. Dropping the article also acknowledges that some generic categories of form are themselves heterogeneous. These categories constitute a variety of shapes: an egg is an egg, but a scallop shell differs from a conch; an oak leaf differs from a maple leaf; a stratus differs from a cumulus; and a flame—well, a flame is never the same twice, as it flickers through a range of characteristic outlines.

Although the things of nature may each engender a similar impression of beauty on the mind, it would be a misrepresentation to say that Emerson reduced the panoply of the world by taking the perceivable variety out of it. Nature's abundance of forms serves to educate humans because nature in total is "a discipline of the understanding in intellectual truths." Nature brings before us an array of sensible objects; it is "a constant exercise in the necessary lessons of difference, of likeness, of order, of being and seeming, of progressive arrangement, of ascent from particular to general, of combination to one end of manifold forces" (*E*, 26).

How strikingly like a list of the properties of a list this is! Lists themselves bring together a hodgepodge of items, or a collection of identical items, or some "progressive arrangement" whereby near neighbors are comparable but widely separated individuals are not. Accordingly, Emerson claims that nature is constituted by these disparate forms in order that "man may know that things are not huddled and lumped, but sundered and individual." With regard to beauty, the objects of the world are interchangeable and equivalent, and a leaf is as worthy an example as a sunset. In other circumstances, however, the sensible differentiation between things has a more important meaning. The ability to perceive difference and distinction, the capacity for discretion, are attributes of the wise, while in contrast, "the foolish have no range in their scale, but suppose every man is as every other man. What is not good they call the worst, and what is not hateful they call the best" (*E*, 27).

This introduces the opposite quality of list making as Emerson uses it: items can be arranged to separate and distinguish, rather than join and unite. In just this way Emerson celebrates the range and difference that the natural world affords us, the "prodigal provision that has been made for [our] support and delight on this green ball that floats [us] through the heavens." Marveling at his surroundings, Emerson turns to a list to convey his sense of wonder: "What angels invented these splendid ornaments, these rich conveniences, this ocean of air above, this ocean of water beneath, this firmament of earth between? this zodiac of lights, this tent of dropping clouds, this splendid coat of climates, this four-fold year?" (*E*, 12). Appearing in the section "Commodity," what is remarkable about this sequence is how quickly and easily Emerson dispenses with the manifold tangible, practical furnishings of nature that we can exploit ("ornaments" and "conveniences") before moving upward and outward to things more sublime.

Where one might expect a Whitmanesque inventory of the bounty of nature, this quick dispatch reminds us that the use of nature as commodity is "low," the only use that "all men apprehend." The "rich conveniences" provide "a benefit which is temporary and mediate, not ultimate," and as such they are relegated to positions of inferior stature as the progression swells from ornaments to more ethereal stations. The splendid ornaments and rich conveniences provided by the conjectural angels initially sound resplendent, but they are soon outclassed by the grandeur of the following entries. Indeed, they seem dime-store and domestic compared to the more lofty expression of the other items.

This effect is owing in part to Emerson's use of the demonstrative adjectives *these* and *this* for each unit in the series. The diffuseness of the plural form, comprising various entities, contrasts with the declarative, gestural force of the singular with which Emerson indicates, with noteworthy exactness, several overarching layers whose circumjacent immensities dwarf and shrink to inconsequence the mundane concerns of day-to-day existence. Furthermore, the patterned repetition of "the ocean of air above" and the correspondent "ocean of water beneath" reinforces the magnitude of the great circle of the horizon, and the alliteration of "coat of climates" and "four-fold year" augments the majesty of environmental forces (from *environ*, "encircle") indifferent to humans.

The character of this list stems from Emerson's desire to move from the more to the less evident uses of nature. The employment of *ornaments* and *conveniences* handily packs together an impracticable assemblage that would grievously ground matters in a roll call of

minor "mercenary" (Emerson's term) benefits. Speaking of the several attributes of Laertes, an impatient Hamlet tells Osric, "to divide
him inventorially would dozy th'arithmetic of memory." Likewise
Emerson, in a preemptive curtailment, cuts short potentially diver-
sionary listing by drawing "Commodity," the shortest section of *Nature,* to an abrupt close: "But there is no need of specific particulars
in this class of uses. The catalogue is endless, and the examples so obvious that I shall leave them to the reader's reflection" (*E*, 13).

As short as it is, "Commodity" houses a concentration of listlike
passages. Another section, while providing sufficient evidence of
our adaptation of nature to suit modest but not ultimate goals, reminds us of a still greater interconnection among things, this time
from the perspective of interrelated processes rather than shared
transcendental commonality. Here all nature is again at the service
of humans, with the complexity of its machinery tightly integrated
in a vast system of productivity. "All the parts incessantly work into
each other's hands for the profit of man," Emerson asserts before
tracking through one possible network of reciprocal relation: "The
wind sows the seed; the sun evaporates the sea; the wind blows the
vapor to the field; the ice, on the other side of the planet, condenses
rain on this; the rain feeds the plant; the plant feeds the animal; and
thus the endless circulations of the divine charity nourish man" (*E*,
12). Reminiscent of Abraham Cowley's Anacreontic poem "Drinking," with which Emerson was certainly familiar, this passage suggests a similar enclosed system of circulation in which "an eternal
health goes round." The progressive interconnection of things is evident in both:

> The thirsty earth soaks up the rain,
> And drinks, and gapes for drink again.
> The plants suck in the earth, and are
> With constant drinking fresh and fair.
> The sea itself, which one would think
> Should have but little need of drink,
> Drinks ten thousand rivers up,

So fill'd that they o'erflow the cup.
The busy sun (and one would guess
By's drunken fiery face no less)
Drinks up the sea, and when h'as done,
The moon and stars drink up the sun.
They drink and dance by their own light,
They drink and revel all the night.
Nothing in Nature's sober found,
But an eternal health goes round.
Fill up the bowl then, fill it high,
Fill all the glasses there, for why
Should every creature drink but I,
Why, man of morals, tell me why?

According with the "steady and prodigal provision" mentioned by Emerson, the terminal goal, from the commissarial point of view of nature—in which the world is a stocked storehouse—is to nourish and sustain human beings. To this purpose this great web of inter-relation works, spanning the globe and incorporating a series of distinct transducing operations that all lead to one desirable end. In this determinedly anthropocentric view, the processes of nature conspire to funnel resources toward our subsistence: but in Emerson the provision is made that "a man is fed, not that he may be fed, but that he may work" (*E*, 13).

So ends the "Commodity" chapter. But Emerson continues to use lists to describe how nature fulfills still greater purposes, especially as the treasury through which spiritual truths are made available to humans. Postulating the distant origins of language in the "Language" chapter, Emerson begins by observing that nature had provided the necessary standard by which meaning could be agreed upon. Made conventional by reference to apparent truths of nature, meanings could be fixed to words and then used and understood by a considerable community. As he explains how nature provides the book of forms on which humans draw to develop language, Emerson gives the brief lexicon that constitutes perhaps his best-known list: "Every word which is used to express a moral or intellectual fact, if traced to its root, is found to be borrowed from some material appearance. *Right* means *straight; wrong* means *twisted; spirit* means *wind; transgression,* the *crossing of a line; supercilious,* the *raising of the eyebrow"* (*E,* 20).

Laid etymologically bare (*right* derives from *rectus,* "straight," *wrong* from *rangr,* "awry," and so on), this group of five examples makes evident the concept without stopping to explain. Beginning with a pair of opposites and moving toward unexpected though no less suitable illustrations, the sequence is eyecatching, providing a fitting representation of the varied range of adaptable meanings nature makes available. Emerson further justifies the validity of his linguistic theory with the observation that time-honored moral truths are delivered in the language of natural truths. Briefly *Nature* becomes a miscellany of aphorisms: "The memorable words of history and the proverbs of nations consist usually of a natural fact, selected as a picture or a parable of a moral truth. Thus: A rolling stone gathers no moss; A bird in the hand is worth two in the bush; A cripple in the right way will beat a racer in the wrong; Make hay while the sun shines; 'Tis hard to carry a full cup even; Vinegar is the son of wine; The last ounce broke the camel's back; Long-lived trees make roots first;—and the like" (*E,* 35).

Emerson continues to elaborate the expressive utility of nature in "The Poet." There he announces that "Nature offers all her creatures to him as a picture-language. . . . Things admit of being used as symbols because nature is a symbol, in the whole, and in every part" (*E,* 227). This doctrine of universal correspondence is further elaborated:

> Beyond this universality of the symbolic language, we are apprised of the divineness of this superior use of things, whereby the world is a temple whose walls are covered with emblems, pictures and commandments of the Deity,—in this sense, that there is no fact in nature which does not carry the whole sense of nature; and the distinctions which we make in events and in affairs, of low and high, honest and base, disappear when na-

ture is used as a symbol. Thought makes everything fit for use.
The vocabulary of an omniscient man would embrace words
and images excluded from polite conversation. What would be
base, or even obscene, to the obscene, becomes illustrious, spoken in connection to thought. [*E*, 229]

Barbara Packer notes that Emerson took great pleasure in believing that some unknown meaning concealed itself in the common things of the world. She importantly indicates that "what
something signifies matters less than the fact of significance itself."
This relation of correspondence between natural and spiritual facts
implied that nature's text, transcribed from spirit, was "mysteri-
ously encoded but potentially decipherable."[6] *Nature* itself serves as
one such elementary text. In it Emerson describes the relation and
provides a sampling of examples from a hypothetical reference
work illustrating the doctrine of correspondence with the uniform
clarity of a children's picture book:

> It is not words only that are emblematic; it is things which are
> emblematic. Every natural fact is a symbol of some spiritual
> fact. Every appearance in nature corresponds to some state of
> mind, and that state of mind can only be described by present-
> ing that natural appearance as its picture. An enraged man is a
> lion, a cunning man is a fox, a firm man is a rock, a learned
> man is a torch. A lamb is innocence, a snake is subtle spite;
> flowers express to us the delicate affections. Light and darkness
> are our familiar expression for knowledge and ignorance; and
> heat for love. Visible distance behind and before us, is respec-
> tively our image of memory and hope. [*E*, 20–21]

The basis for this conceptual congruence is Emerson's assertion
that the elements of nature are the final emanations of spirit: "A fact
is the end or last issue of spirit. The visible creation is the terminus
or the circumference of the invisible world" (*E*, 25). All the facts of
nature "preexist in the necessary Ideas in the mind of God," and the
better aligned we become with nature and truth the more the world
becomes "an open book" (*E*, 25).

Simplicity is necessary for Emerson's purposes here, and the select lists are presented to solidify our belief in the symbolic role of nature's components. Under this commission they are repetitive, pedantic, lacking in dynamism. Their objective is to drive home the conviction that this is the way of things, not because Emerson himself has attained the proper posture and now all things are transparent to him but rather because he believes in the validity of correspondence. If the relation is true for the dozen or so items listed—true in the sense that they are commonly apprehended and understood—then the principle must hold true for the countless other possible sets that we have yet to become aware of. Taken together, the sum of Emerson's lists cannot become the one great, comprehensive book open to us all, for he himself is not and will not become capable of seeing into all things. He can, however, recognize enough of the obvious points of connection to contour for us the grand design.

Finally, the only evidence he can present must be as obvious and as straightforward as possible, otherwise the enterprise will collapse. It is the fact of universal application ventured from a handful of instances that is essential; hence there cannot be examples that could be misread or disputed. Ultimately, the list of correspondences Emerson provides is not itself the great book to which he refers; it can be only a primer, a grammar that must be mastered before the great book can be read. Because Emerson must teach us to read in an entirely different way—reading the things of the world rather than the words he has written on the page—the beginners' text he offers must pose as little difficulty as possible. Each set in the collection is an exercise designed to encourage us, not turn us away through trickery and complexity.

For his other purposes, Emerson's lists need not be as declarative and accessible; in fact, there are situations in which it is only by forcing readers to grapple with difficult transitions between items that a list becomes advantageous. Occasionally a series of items will contain a vague conceptual similarity in the manner of a collection of synonyms. In such cases the items may possess a degree of like-ness the way different words can possess an equivalence of mean-ing. Much like a thesaurus, such a set becomes a list of words that purport "to be interchangeable," as one scholar describes it, but col-lectively extend "the meaning of any one of them." When we read them we recognize that there are "connotative differences that pre-vent the words from being truly equivalent." The degree of resem-blance does not necessarily entail absolute conformity or perfect parallel replication, however. In fact, bringing together a great number of items tends to foreground their differences,[7] as we see in this sample from *Nature:*

> Not only resemblances exist in things whose analogy is obvi-ous, as when we detect the type of the human hand in the flip-per of the fossil saurus, but also in objects wherein there is great superficial unlikeness. Thus architecture is called "frozen mu-sic," by De Stael and Goethe. Vitruvius thought an architect should be a musician. "A Gothic church," said Coleridge "is a petrified religion." Michel Angelo maintained, that, to an archi-tect, a knowledge of anatomy is essential. In Haydn's oratorios, the notes present to the imagination not only motions, as of the snake, the stag, and the elephant, but colors also; as the green grass. The law of the harmonic sounds reappears in the har-monic colors. The granite is differenced in its laws only by the more or less heat from the river that wears it away. The river, as it flows, resembles the air that flows over it; the air resembles the light which traverses it with more subtle currents; the light re-sembles the heat which rides with it through Space. [*E*, 30]

When we read through this collection, what may have appeared its one essential truth is surprisingly fractured into many, slightly dif-ferentiated truths. The thread of connection twists through ana-tomy and architecture, music and nature; the concept of resem-blance is colored in a finer and finer way.

Slight differences of meaning can also reinforce what Alan Hodder identifies in Emerson as the movement of the spiral. "The spiral's distinction is that it conveys an impression of movement within stasis," he writes, adding that "it appears to move ahead while at the same time circling back upon its point of origin." Conversely, it may also seem to circle back while really guiding the progression in new directions. Certain sequences may gradually deviate from a given trajectory in an illusory fashion, seeming to repeat a concept many times over but actually advancing it minutely or with a deft sleight of hand. The spiral is really, as Hodder writes, "an interplay of centripetal and centrifugal forces," and by extension these functions can accommodate a range of variables so as to advance as well as reverse their course.[8]

The spiral is one pattern of arrangement, potentially turning from a central path at a greater or lesser rate. Another way to empower a list is by forcing the reader's mind to make great leaps between the items presented in a sequence. Different effects are attained when different methods of transition are used, as Ellison has described. For example, a series in which items are repeatedly connected with the conjunction *or* forces us to remove one element and exchange it for another, generating a sense of disjunction and even a kind of mistrust. Skepticism can arise if there are too many rapid replacements in sequence, undermining faith in the compiler's ability to make an assertion without equivocation. The joining word *and,* by contrast, vigorously builds cumulative elements in a way that elaborates, enhances, and complicates the original item in a positive way. In such moments, Ellison notes, "we feel that conviction, not doubt, has motivated its redundancies."[9]

In actuality, however, Emerson rarely uses conjunctions to lengthen his lists, except when he is pairing items and couples them with *and.*[10] He generally prefers to compress his lists by omitting conjunctions altogether, increasing the pace of the appearance of new items and testing the reader's capacity for making transitions. Shared concepts may be implicit among the items, or the collective sequence may be more difficult to understand. Similarities may allow gradual progressions, but commonalities that are not evident force the reader to make sometimes bewildering shifts between the items in a list or sequence. This exercise of leaping from one thing to the next forces the reader to undertake a kind of mental gymnastics that strengthens the mind's comprehensive power. If the sequence of items is irregular or perceptibly flawed, then the experience of moving from one to the next becomes more dramatic, even delirious. As Ellison describes the sensation, "The further apart the statements are, so to speak, the more aware the mind is of its power in moving from one to the next." In making connections, bridging possible chasms between things, the mind becomes aware of its own potency. Flitting between disparate items, the intellect engages in what Ellison accurately terms "play for its own sake."[11]

A late excerpt from "Prospects" exhibits this playfulness as Emerson matter-of-factly specifies the qualified ways we humans make use of nature, then follows this with a series of examples showing the occasional moments in which we open ourselves to nature's greater promises:

> [Man's] relation to nature, his power over it, is through the understanding, as by manure; the economic use of fire, wind, water, and the mariner's needle; steam, coal, chemical agriculture; the repairs of the human body by the dentist and the surgeon. This is such a resumption of power as if a banished king should buy his territories inch by inch, instead of vaulting at once into his throne. Meantime, in the thick darkness, there are not wanting gleams of a better light,—occasional examples of the action of man upon nature with his entire force,—with reason as well as understanding. Such examples are, the traditions of miracles in the earliest antiquity of all nations; the history of Jesus Christ; the achievements of a principle, as in religious or political revolutions, and in the abolition of the slave-trade; the miracles of enthusiasm, as those reported of Swedenborg, Hohenlohe, and the Shakers; many obscure and yet contested facts, now arranged under the name of Animal Magnetism; prayer; eloquence; self-healing; and the wisdom of children. These are examples of Reason's momentary grasp of the scepter. [E, 46–47]

Here Emerson looks forward toward greater utilizations of nature than those that we have thus far achieved. The passage opens with a listing of the ways we have harnessed and domesticated the processes of nature, and what consequences these processes provide for human benefit. Our understanding has captured the elements, though they need not exist exclusively to be used in such ways by us. This is to say that our exploitation of these benefits, which Emerson does not deny is productive and worthwhile, may not be their primary or even ultimate purpose. We can sense a greater energy in the sequence that follows than in the unscintillating list of utilitarian achievements; indeed the first list starts ominously with the word *manure!* As his analogy suggests, the common, profitable uses of nature are yet pedestrian and tentative; they are timid rather than strong, dramatic, or heroic.

But as the second list makes evident, the fullest applications of our assertions over nature do occasionally take fire. These achievements are rapturous, awakening, rebellious, and committed, but also surprising, questioned, and doubted, achieving full fruition only in the face of adversity. The particulars named in the dynamic hodgepodge attain their status only when they struggle against doubt, skepticism, and mockery, and with them Emerson encourages forward thinking, mustering the will to advance toward a fuller, more powerful instrumentality of nature.

Although Emerson clearly believed there was a design in nature and also valued design in art, Buell noted that he did not believe in making the latter an end in itself. In this Buell sided with F. O. Matthiessen's judgment that Emerson's works, including the lists and catalogues incorporated into them, privileged content over form. However, if Emerson's appeal is more intellectual than sensual, it is not for lack of effort. Maurice Gonnaud summarizes much Emerson criticism as pointing to "a radical tension" between

"the trained rhetorician . . . and the bold, stumbling artist"—that
is, Emerson struggled to articulate in both prose and verse something that ultimately eluded expression in words. Getting something of significance said, either with art or without it, was his first
concern, as Stephen Whicher has emphasized.[12]

His intellectual stature aside, Emerson was one of the few writers who compiled lists in both prose and verse formats, each with
specific designs and intentions. If an ultimate similarity of purpose
is evident in the two modes, each deserves individual attention to
delineate their variety, which is not readily reducible entirely to
principles of unity in diversity, correspondence, or transition. It is
important to heed Whicher's warning that Emerson is "a dangerous
man to pigeonhole."[13] Poetry in general depends more on the precise arrangement of words than do essays, and Emerson struggled
with such refined expression. He revealed his own candid assessment of his abilities in a letter to Lydia Jackson, who was soon to be
his wife: "I am born a poet, of a low class without doubt yet a poet.
That is my nature & vocation. My singing to be sure is very 'husky,'
& is for the most part in prose" (1 February 1835). For Emerson the
thought expressed by a poem was more critical than the art used to
shape it. The symbol a poem offered was the source of its power and
was, as he idealized it in "The Poet," the product of "a thought so
passionate and alive that like the spirit of a plant or an animal it has
an architecture of its own, and adorns nature with a new thing" (*E,*
450, emphasis added).

Given such a mandate, structure becomes secondary, derived
from within rather than imposed from without. The lists found
within Emerson's poems are less programmatic than those found in
Whitman's verse and, indeed, may be something of a red herring on
occasion. This is not to say, however, that when a list does appear it
is inessential to the poem, some inconsequential or vestigial feature
of "the instant dependence of form upon the soul" (*E,* 447). A list
can provide a fruitful clue to how to read the poem. Consider the
beginning of "Hamatreya":

Bulkeley, Hunt, Willard, Hosmer, Meriam, Flint,
Possessed the land which rendered to their toil
Hay, corn, roots, hemp, flax, apples, wool and wood.

Here a roll call of names on one side and a simple list of agricultural products on the other bracket the poem's central concern. "Hamatreya" is about humility in its most literal sense: going into the earth (*humus*). Spiritual or psychological humility, as opposed to physical humility, comes in the speaker's realization that it is an illusion for men to think that they possess the earth. Individuality, suggested by the series of personal names, gives way to anonymity, and Emerson debunks the popularly prized notion that ownership permanently validates existence. The six names that open the poem stand for the proprietary division of an entity that withstands division, one that in the end inevitably incorporates its dividers into itself.

The six men named are actual settlers of Concord; the first is in fact one of Emerson's ancestors, Peter Bulkeley.[14] The sequence is thus darkly and prophetically intimate; Emerson personalizes it in an uncomfortably particular way, singling out specific individuals instead of generic figures. However, just as the six stand for but one patch of the world, they are also metonymically representative of the whole. With deference and submission to something greater, the speaker solemnly observes the dividers' inattention to the real truth: the undeniable fact that they will be anonymously assimilated into what they have futilely expanded, divided, subdivided, and arrogantly claimed as their own. "Ah! the hot owner sees not Death, who adds / Him to his land, a lump of mold the more," the speaker observes. Witness to the fate of the "hot" landowners, the speaker's own heat humbly cools "like lust in the chill of the grave."

Although the greater purpose of "Hamatreya" may be to humble readers in a memento mori–like fashion, the poem begins with the assumption that the laws of property are what drive and maintain society. Throughout his life, Emerson noted that civil institutions chose to safeguard property, or property rights, to the detriment and deterioration of the "culture" of persons. Those who "created" their lands, establishing their homesteads, did so through honored acts of application, self-reliance. The act itself was self-improving: as Emerson declared in "Circles," "That which builds is better than that which is built" (*E*, 404). But the passing of property to those who did not create it engendered a society that had lost sight of such cultivating aims and now geared itself to the preservation of ownership at the expense of "living property." This led the human community to "measure their esteem of each other by what each has, and not by what each is," as Emerson formulated it in "Self-Reliance" (*E*, 281).

Societal pressures gave property and material goods preeminence. In a stinging critique of the times, Emerson wrote of the reliance on property in his "Ode to Channing," employing a pattern of repetition to establish this servile state of affairs:

> The horseman serves the horse,
> The neatherd serves the neat,
> The merchant serves the purse,
> The eater serves his meat,
> 'Tis the day of the chattel,
> Web to weave, and corn to grind,
> Things are in the saddle,
> And ride mankind.

Before the passage of the Fugitive Slave Law, which seems to have galvanized him to uncompromising support of the antislavery cause, Emerson held abolitionism in low esteem. He believed that unless the black population carried within itself "an indispensable element of a new and coming civilization," it would either forever serve or be extinguished; he himself had "other slaves to free," namely the "imprisoned spirits, imprisoned thoughts, far back in the brain of man." A reluctant radical, he wrote the ode in response to William Henry Channing's goadings that he be more outspoken for the abolitionist movement.

Channing, a fervent partisan and abolitionist, opposed Emerson's individualism: "You deny the Human Race," he wrote Emerson upon reading the *Divinity School Address,* "You stand, or rather seek to stand, a complete Adam. But you cannot do it." In contrast to the essays and other writings that examine the "two laws discrete . . . Law for man, and law for thing" with an optimism that aims at redressing the situation, Emerson's "Ode to Channing" seems to capitulate to the status quo. As David Bromwich describes it, the reiterative middle portion of the ode stands as a "survey of America's estate, with the admission that evil *is* abroad in the land, but an evil that has come to dominate nature itself, to the point where all action is equally useless, and equally blameless":[15]

> 'Tis fit the forest fall,
> The steep be grounded,
> The mountain tunneled,
> The sand shaded,
> The orchard planted,
> The glebe tilled,
> The prairie granted,
> The steamer built.

Acknowledging that it is the "law for thing" that drives civilization—the force that gets things done and "builds town and ship"—the poem advocates a remarkably resigned hands-off approach to counter Channing's calls for activism. "Let man serve law for man" and the state will eventually follow "as Olympus follows Jove." This is the way things are, the poem seems to say, and it calls for the patience to let events sort themselves out. "Every one to his chosen work," the speaker encourages in this precursor to Whitman's vision of America, listing its productive activity on many fronts; yet the poem continues to advise restraint, since "Foolish hands may mix and mar."

Whereas the list that opens "Hamatreya" gives an advance summary of the poem as a whole—while crops emerge from the land, rising out of it, men go down into it, in spite of their minor cos-

metic tinkerings—in "The Humble-Bee," Emerson creates a different kind of list, one that suggestively encapsulates the carefree terri-
tory of the blissful dozing voyager:

> Aught unsavory or unclean
> Hath my insect never seen;
> But violets and bilberry bells,
> Maple-sap and daffodels,
> Grass with green flag half-mast high,
> Succory to match the sky,
> Columbine with horn of honey,
> Scented fern, and agrimony,
> Clover, catchfly, adder's tongue,
> And brier-roses, dwelt among;
> All beside was unknown waste,
> All was picture as he passed.

Written approximately one year after the death of his brother
Charles, possibly while Emerson was in the midst of depression, the
poem presents the bee as a symbol that evades misery, "Seeing only
what is fair, / Sipping only what is sweet." The bee roams a delightful garden described by the list above, from which "aught unsavory
or unclean" is excluded. Regardless of whether the bee is physically
confined to the pleasing park or is simply the antithesis of Milton's
Satan, knowing only delight ("Which way I fly is paradise"), the list
is impervious to unpleasantness; all waste is pushed to the exterior
while an arrangement of wildflowers thrives within it.

The catalogue in "The Humble-Bee," fenced in as it were from
the "want and woe" that are willfully excluded from it, provides an
example of a list that constitutes most of a stanza. It reproduces
graphically an area of delight from which trouble, care, and adversity are expelled. The plastic structure of the list, enabling the collection of various entities, as though in a garden, further informs a
poem like "Each and All." (The list, approximative though it may
be, is the form resorted to most frequently by Emerson and others
to represent totality.) The title of the poem focuses on a fundamen-

tal aspect of the list as such and makes plain its subject: the relation of the part to the ensemble. The poem illustrates the lesson that "All are needed by each one; / Nothing is fair or good alone." This thesis statement is abruptly inserted after ten lines. Matthiessen compares the poem to this passage Emerson had written about the lesson he teaches here: "I remember when I was a boy going upon the beach and being charmed with the colors and forms of the shells. I gathered up many and put them in my pocket. When I got home I could find nothing that I gathered—nothing but some dry, ugly mussel and snail shells. Thence I learned that composition was more important than the beauty of individual forms to effect."[16]

The poem begins with a series of illustrations in which connections between things go unrecognized:

> Little thinks, in the field, yon red-cloaked clown
> Of thee from the hill-top looking down;
> The heifer that lows in the upland farm,
> Far-heard, lows not thine ear to charm;
> The sexton, tolling his bell at noon,
> Deems not that great Napoleon
> Stops his horse, and lists with delight,
> Whilst his files sweep round yon Alpine height;
> Nor knowest thou what argument
> Thy life to thy neighbor's creed has lent.

It then recounts three instances in which the speaker sought to hold individual things, not perceiving that their beauty depended on their integration within a whole greater than he could possibly possess:

> I thought the sparrow's note from heaven;
> Singing at dawn on the alder bough;
> I brought him home, in his nest, at even;
> He sings the song, but it cheers not now,
> For I did not bring home the river and sky;—
> He sang to my ear,—they sang to my eye.
> The delicate shells lay on the shore;

The bubbles of the latest wave
Fresh pearls to their enamel gave,
And the bellowing of the savage sea
Greeted their safe escape to me.
I wiped away the weeds and foam,
I fetched my sea-born treasures home;
But the poor, unsightly, noisome things
Had left their beauty on the shore
With the sun and sand and the wild uproar.
The lover watched his graceful maid,
As 'mid the virgin train she strayed,
Nor knew her beauty's best attire
Was woven still by the snow-white choir.
At last she came to his hermitage,
Like the bird from the woodlands to the cage;—
The gay enchantment was undone,
A gentle wife, but fairy none.

The attempts to isolate the things from their surroundings render them empty and hollow, neutralizing them by severing the unperceived or unacknowledged connections of cosmic coherence that gave them beauty to begin with.

The acquisitive speaker, who fragments the collection by trying to possess what he thinks are its most valuable parts, converts in the end to a person who is rewarded with beauty by relinquishing claims to beauty. The possession of parts fails, and the speaker gives over to the whole, with predictable results:

As I spoke, beneath my feet
The ground-pine curled its pretty wreath,
Running over club-moss burrs;
I inhaled the violet's breath;
Around me stood the oaks and firs;
Pine-cones and acorns lay on the ground;
Over me soared the eternal sky;
Full of light and deity;
Again I saw, again I heard,
The rolling river, the morning bird;—

Beauty through my senses stole;
I yielded myself to the perfect whole.

"Each and All" is meant as a demonstration of Emerson's assertion in *Nature* that "Nothing is quite beautiful alone; nothing but is
beautiful in the whole." If the poem seems without conviction, or
mechanically delivered, this is only because of its instant revelation,
the "hey, presto!" moment in which the sudden inflooding of the
"all" comes when the speaker renounces the immature desire to
possess "each." (Matthiessen noted that while Emerson could perceive beauty in delicate and poignant moments, "when he came to
set [these moments] down on paper, the rhythmical wholeness of
experience slipped away from him, and the residue seemed to turn
into a lifeless gray.")[17]

There are abundant lists to draw upon throughout Emerson's writings, lists that take a variety of shapes. As Jonathan Bishop observes,
"A series repeats an identical form of grammar several times running in the midst of an ever-varying actuality of utterance, and
Emerson delighted in them."[18] In his excellent book *Emerson on the
Soul,* Bishop asks where it is possible to find "a center of core imaginative activity" that readers can identify as "Emerson" in the mass
of essays, journals, and letters, and demonstrates that it resides in
"the literary manifestations of his genius"—the style, tone, metaphors, prose rhythms, and syntax of his sentences. We can extend
the sites in which to locate the "true" Emerson to his lists as well.

The basic structure of the list provided him with an opportunity to bring many divergent items together, either to stress an attribute common to them or to delight in their difference and disparity. A list of items could represent a broad swath of the world or
of nature. On other occasions, for rhetorical purposes, a list could
be used to illustrate a principle: a handful (or more) of representa-

tive illustrations, with a degree of diversity, could be presented to persuade where the assertion of a single specimen might fail. The list provided Emerson with the perfect format in which to display, to realize graphically, important ideas. It was the site that best represented the relation of the part to the whole: any given item clearly had an individual identity as a separate thing, but a different, latent quality emerged when it was included in a collection.

The list also served to a limited degree as the great book of correspondences in miniature, gathering a few pieces of our multifaceted world together with their conceptual correlations. And it could embody, after a fashion, the concept of composition, whereby parts are viewed together in a collective whole that is superior to their sundered, isolated individuality. Finally, the list served Emerson in his claim of Transcendental immanence, in which the divine is found not over and above but through all individual things, a mode of Romantic epiphany that Harold Bloom notes is "discontinuous in the extreme."[19]

If, as Bishop writes, "the qualities of Emerson's style are somehow close to the center of imaginative action,"[20] then I assert that in the lists and linked series of his prose and verse, we can also rediscover Emerson's messages. The skips and leaps we make in reading from one item to the next are compelling, occasionally disorienting. In their unpredictable courses, Emerson's lists force us to make unforeseen connections or even bridges of thought where we think no connection is possible. They simply and ingeniously fire and excite our minds.

3

Whitman

"Looking with side-curved head curious
what will come next"

※ ※ ※

Whitman's technique of accumulating and unfurling seemingly effortless, potentially endless lists has been considered by some critics a sign of his limitation as a poet and by others an indication of the essence of his genius. On the negative side, the detractions have been blunt. "I expected him to make the songs of the nation, but he seems content to make the inventories," Emerson once wrote, belittling Whitman's poetic accomplishments and retracting his earlier praise (for example, from his letter of July 21, 1855: "I find incomparable things said incomparably well, as they must be. I find the courage of *treatment,* which so delights us, and which large perception only can inspire.").[1]

Other critics too have failed to find merit in Whitman's original style. John Bailey, writing in 1926, commented on Whitman's "auctioneering inventories," and asserted that they derived from the "insatiable appetite of the uneducated for insignificant and disconnected occurrences."[2] Whitman's lists, he added, arose only in moments of intellectual laxity, and he further denied to their apparent formlessness any conceptual or artistic achievement. George Santayana, in his biting commentary "The Poetry of Barbarism," berated Whitman's poetry as artistic waste. He found *Leaves of Grass* to be devoid of substance and ignorant of the form and content of inherited tradition. In Whitman's poetic accumulations, Santayana detected only an "abundance of detail without organization" and a "wealth of perception without intelligence." In comments that focus his disdain for the work directly on Whitman's propensity to list, Santayana wrote: "It is a phantasmagoria of continuous visions, vivid, impressive but monotonous and hard to distinguish in memory, like the waves of the sea or decorations of some barbarous temple, sublime only by the infinite aggregation of parts."[3]

Of the pervasiveness of this poetic technique, however, Mattie Swayne notes, "If Whitman's critics object to the catalogue only in its unadorned state, their objection applies to relatively few lines of his poetry; if, on the other hand, they object to the catalogue formula, however applied, there is little left in his work for them to approve."[4] What seemed to Santayana a clear indication of ignorance is now generally considered evidence of genuine poetic innovation and a purposeful challenge to the English poetic tradition.

Indeed, on the positive side, it has been proposed that Whitman's tendency to list, to work catalogues into his poems, and to turn whole poems into catalogues is a significant feature of his artistic and thematic vision. Sometimes he used lists to accumulate factual detail, sometimes to collect impressionistic sense data. In other instances the inclusivity of the list becomes universally welcoming, open to all facets of life, according to his vision of a plural America. In just this way the extensive catalogues of "Song of Myself" allow him to represent an "ensemble" of particulars and emphasize both the total collective and the components that constitute it. It is through this device, as Edward Dowden observed, that "the individual suggests a group, and the group a multitude, each unit of which is as interesting as every other unit, and possesses equal claim to recognition."[5]

Absorbing and accruing items, the list in Whitman's verse gives an impression of multitude and variety in its imaginative reach, and of union and cohesion in its interlocking of lines. In "such join'd unended links" the poet found formal advantages he could use to suggest comprehensiveness, to reconcile opposites, to imitate patterns of motion, and to embrace motley America. Yet what he created made his readers—even his admirers—uncomfortable. Writing on the centenary of the publication of the 1855 edition of *Leaves of Grass,* Kenneth Burke explored the volume's "salient traits." In addition to its zestfulness and exhilaration, Burke (who elsewhere confessed that "one inclines to skim through [the catalogues] somewhat as when running the eye down a column of a telephone directory") celebrated its "oceanic accumulation of details," and suggested what might be found therein: "It is possible that, after long inspection, we might find some 'overarching' principle of development that 'underlies' [Whitman's] typical lists. Always, of course, they can be found to embody some principle of repetitive form, some principle of classification whereby the various items fall under the same head. . . . Some critic might discern a regular canon of development in such 'turbulent' heapings. Meanwhile, there are the many variations by internal contrast, and even where epanaphora is extreme, there are large tidal changes from stanza to stanza, or the rhetorical forms that suggest the shifting of troops in military maneuvers."[6]

Although writers have always resorted to the list for special effects, none has made the practice of listing as integral to his or her creative work as Whitman did in the poetry of *Leaves of Grass.* Indeed, no one has experimented so much with the form as Whitman; no one has even approximated his efforts to create a poetics of listing.

The generic list possesses numerous qualities, not all of which the compiler can exploit at the same time. As has been noted, of principal importance for particular occasions may be the variations of internal relations that can be perfected through the arrangement of contents. In other instances the list may function as an envelope, a receptacle inside which various things are loosely contained or sorted, filed, and stacked with managerial efficiency. Filling such an envelope may be a way of celebrating the plenitude of the world and the plenitude of language striving to match it, or it may be a means of establishing a restricted membership by incorporating only those things that meet desired criteria and excluding the rest.

In some instances in *Leaves of Grass,* the list may be no more than a bare series of words ("Blacksmithing, glass-blowing, nail-making, coopering, tin- / roofing, shingle-dressing" ["A Song for Occupations," *W,* 360]). In others, an entire line of verse may be given to a single element that is modified or elaborated by adjectives and clauses. In compilations of individual terms, the poet may select items for the qualities they possess as words or items for the qualities possessed by the things those words designate. This is to say that items can be chosen for their suitability either as signifiers or as signifieds. Certain catalogues in which each entry is composed of a line of verse may be constructed by exploiting conventions of syntax or by amplifying certain grammatical divisions and subdivisions. While there may be no "typical" Whitmanian list, the various permutations enable a poetry that develops, according to David Daiches, "length-wise, but not depth-wise."[7]

Readers may gain insight into a particular list by measuring it along various evaluative axes. Thus it may be described by its degree of inclusion or exclusion, order or disorder, movement or stasis. Furthermore, in the development of a discourse, as Roman Jakobson observed, "one topic may lead toward another either through their similarity or through their contiguity."[8] Likewise, readers may characterize the sequencing through a list of items by either metaphoric or metonymic relations, or by some pattern of modulation between the two. Finally, the assembly of particulars may either tend toward realism through the accumulation of detail or push beyond, toward surrealism, through an explosion of unrestrained collection. And, indeed, the dividing line between sufficiency and surfeit may itself be influenced by the motives of the compiler, who may strive for an adequate representation of reality or revel in language for its own sake.

Through listing, a series may amplify by gradations, progress on a roundabout journey, or unite dissimilar members through a single common feature. The various forms the list takes in *Leaves of Grass* exhibit a number of rhetorical and structural possibilities. The catalogues of professions, motions, and anatomies, the strings of native place-names, and the modulation of line-initiating prepositions reveal not only the poet's imaginative reach and fecundity of invention but also his deft capability to manipulate language, an ability that is paramount in any definition of poetry. Writing on Transcendentalist catalogue rhetoric, Lawrence Buell accurately qualifies the limitations and advantages of Whitman's lists: "Often, it is true, the structure of his catalogues consists almost wholly in their plenitude, in the parallelism of piled-up, end-stopped lines, producing, at its worst, rudimentary paeans or chants like litanies from the *Book of Common Prayer*. But often enough both tone and structure are more complex, creating tapestries of imagery and rhetoric which are fine by any standard."[9]

Although not every listing by Whitman is successful (some are, as Dowden commented, "delighted—not perhaps delightful"),[10] many achieve a unique synthesis of form with content. Far from intellectual laxity, Whitman's lists reveal intellectual rigor and a thorough understanding of listing as a vehicle for communication. One finds in these lists a facility for language as well-matched to the substance of his poetry as other poets have displayed with rhyme and rhythm. Readers frequently tend to attribute the list structure at work throughout Whitman's writing solely to impulses of inclusion and Adamic naming. But to read all of Whitman in such a way is to discount his true ability as a poet and the craft with which some of his poems are wrought.

It is certainly true that at times Whitman employs lists to be as broadly encompassing as possible. Through this method the poet can add new elements to an increasing series, provide a slightly different point of view, or suggest one further connection, spatially, temporally or linguistically. However, these are not the only goals of the practice. Although many Whitman poems seem to add ever more exempla or items, most reveal a deliberate awareness of design that extends beyond exhaustive incorporation. As Stanley Coffman observed, Whitman ordered his lists so that they would be "aesthetically expressive" and convey "meaning by their form." Coffman reminds us that Whitman took care to manipulate his itemizations, in contrast to the "incessant metamorphosis" of the Emersonian interconvertability of every thing into every other thing, a principle that could be adequately expressed through any purely random sequence.[11]

Compare, for example, the practice of listing in two superficially similar but thematically different poems, "We Two Boys Together Clinging" and "Patroling Barnegat." "We Two Boys," which first appeared in "Calamus" in the 1860 edition of *Leaves of Grass,* is a collection of present participles. Its formal regularity is enforced by the repeated ending "-ing." The effect of this grammatical choice is that each item of the list freezes the figures in a continuous action, though the list as a whole, as we progress from one item to the next, has the almost contrapuntal character of undermining stability through continual mutation:

> We two boys together clinging,
> One the other never leaving,
> Up and down the roads going, North and South excursions
>   making,
> Power enjoying, elbows stretching, fingers clutching,
> Arm'd and fearless, eating, drinking, sleeping, loving,
> No law less than ourselves owning, sailing, soldiering,
>   thieving, threatening,
> Misers, menials, priests alarming, air breathing, water
>   drinking, on the turf or sea-beach dancing,

> Cities wrenching, ease scorning, statutes mocking, feebleness
> chasing,
> Fulfilling our foray. [*W*, 282]

The list here seems broadly inclusive, generally disordered except for some alliterative relations, and static. The items vary from the trivial to the common to the boyishly hyperbolic, but the congeries of activities seems to arrest and coalesce the two figures, rendering them indistinguishable and creating a fusion that is literalized in "one the other never leaving." The relentlessness of the accumulation has the effect of intermixing and subsuming the two separate identities. There is a focus on shared activity, but the list packs items so closely, and we read through them so quickly, that no clear image of the companions endures. The result is that the piling-up of gerunds agglutinates into an abstracted, generalized intimation of confraternity.

In the sonnetlike "Patroling Barnegat," appearing some twenty years later in "Sea-Drift" in the 1881–1882 edition of *Leaves of Grass*, Whitman uses a variation of listing to layer detail, presenting the image of a single storm scene. On first glance, the poem also seems to compile numerous "-ing" endings. Again there is a repetition of present participles; but here they conclude each line in a manner that pitches the reader into the immediacy of the tempestuous situation, in a moment that is eternally suspended. The narrative of the poem goes unresolved, agonizingly arrested at the peak of its drama:

> Wild, wild the storm, and the sea high running,
> Steady the roar of the gale, with incessant undertone
> muttering,
> Shouts of demonic laughter fitfully piercing and pealing,
> Waves, air, midnight, their savagest trinity lashing,
> Out in the shadows there milk-white combs careering,
> On beachy slush and sand spirts of snow fierce slanting,
> Where through the murk the easterly death-wind breasting,
> Through cutting swirl and spray watchful and firm
> advancing,

(That in the distance! is that a wreck? is the red signal flaring?)
Slush and sand of the beach tireless till daylight wending,
Steadily, slowly, through hoarse roar never remitting,
Along the midnight edge of those milk-white combs
    careering,
A group of dim, weird forms, struggling, the night
    confronting,
That savage trinity warily watching. [*W,* 402]

Although this list may give an impression of chaos and exhilaration, because of its controlled grammatical structuring it is really quite ordered. The first six lines enumerate the different elements that make up the storm. Each component in the "sestet"—the gale, the high seas, the breaking waves, and the shore—is modified by its own present participle, but while the eight lines following continue the pattern of concluding with present participles, in each line in the "octave" the participle refers to a single deferred referent, the group of forms identified in line 13. The lines of the octave enumerate the endeavors of this group of figures to surmount the dangers listed in the sestet. If at first glance this poem seems, like "We Two Boys," to be a miscellaneous accumulation of participles,

    running
    muttering
    pealing
    lashing
    careering
    slanting
    breasting
    advancing
    flaring
    wending
    never remitting
    careering
    confronting
    watching,

on closer examination it shows a more delicate configuration. It breaks between sestet and octave to distinguish heroic humans from the environmental challenges they must encounter in the natural world. Because of its skillful syntactical manipulation, the list has a more intricate arrangement, one that might be schematically presented like this:

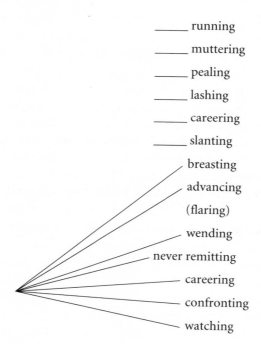

_____ running

_____ muttering

_____ pealing

_____ lashing

_____ careering

_____ slanting

breasting

advancing

(flaring)

wending

never remitting

careering

confronting

watching

Lawrence Buell comments that "the element of structure in a Whitman catalogue—indeed any Whitman poem—even where refined, is relatively unstressed."[12] This statement occurs in a paragraph warning against the dangers of overreading or too persistently stressing the architecture that gives form to Whitman's instances of cataloguing or listing. For Buell the sense of design in such an occurrence is less significant than the sensual and emotional responses it evokes, and less important than the sense of plenitude it suggests. According to this view, the primary intention of such a collection is to draw the reader's attention away from the precise arrangement of its parts through appeals to the senses, the memory, and the imagination. The poet often presents these synesthetic lists as variegated bouquets:

> Roots and leaves themselves alone are these,
> Scents brought to men and women from the wild woods and
>   pond-side,
> Breast-sorrel and pinks of love, fingers that wind around
>   tighter than vines,
> Gushes from the throats of birds hid in the foliage of trees as
>   the sun is risen,
> Breezes of land and love set from living shores to you on the
>   living sea, to you O sailors!
> Frost-mellow'd berries and Third-month twigs offer'd fresh
> to young persons wandering out in the fields when the winter
>   breaks up,
> Love-buds put before you and within you whoever you are
> Buds to be unfolded on the old terms. [*W,* 277–278]

The configuration of the list, of course, is important in creating these effects. Lists and catalogues have high degrees of organization, if only by virtue of the process of selection or omission necessary to their composition. The compiler bases standards of incorporation on the specific requirements of the individual poem. In *Leaves of Grass* these vary from an immersive tally of the environment immediately pressing itself on the senses to a broad inclusion of the whole range of American possibilities. The type of arrangement is made to seem appropriate to the textual situation. In the above passage, for example, the complex assemblage of mixed metonymic ("roots," "leaves," "scents") and metaphoric ("fingers," "breezes of love") components mirrors the poet's agenda of indicating both the palpable presence of objects and their symbolic values. This reinforces the figuration of the collected poems as "leaves" and "buds," and the natural refreshment they will provide to those who "unfold" the volume to read them.

At their most simple, lists in Whitman's verse are formed purely as series of individual words, predominantly nominal, with little supporting structure in the way of grammar or syntax. In these bare sequences principles of inclusion and order determine interrelations among component parts and between the list itself and the piece in which it appears. When, for example, the poet unfurls a series of place names of Native American origin—"Wabash, Miami, Saginaw, Chippewa, Oshkosh, Walla Walla" ["Starting from Paumanok," sec. 16; *W*, 186]—each item represents part of a cooperative effort to demonstrate the congruent assimilations of both the physical locale and its name into the landscape and language of America. In other words, the list celebrates the unique heritage of the nation and savors the sounds of native words incorporated into the lexicon.

Another such "simple" list is "the index from head to foot" (*W*, 249) that the speaker announces in "From Pent-up Aching Rivers" but actually chants in "I Sing the Body Electric" in precise anatomic clusters. This "divine list" tallies components, methodically dissecting limbs ("Upper-arm, armpit, elbow-socket, lower-arm, arm-sinews, arm-bones") and internal organs ("The lung-sponges, the stomach-sac, the bowels sweet and clean" [*W*, 257]). Harold Waskow has written that the sheer exuberance of this kind of nominal enumeration suggests that these things in and of themselves are miraculous. Merely stating their names is enough to achieve inspired communication, and their recitation suffices to convey both the beauty and the message that is generally elaborated by verse.[13]

Declaring the indivisibility of the word from the object designated calls into question the role of the poet in generating emotional responses: if the poet can communicate his sense of excitement, of "electricity," simply by naming things, without ornament or even supporting syntax, then this suggests that the "real poetry"

exists in the things themselves. The interpretation Waskow proposes recognizes Whitman's efforts to proffer objects in his verse
concretely and precisely. But while the enumerative technique does
favor a direct presentation of things, it does not signal the demotion
of the poet, for he is the one who frames the collections and, in ways
that are often overlooked, controls their development. In many
cases, the manner in which the list unfolds is more poetically expressive than its contents. Thus, even if it is simply a sequencing of
items, a poetic list can be seen to have a "path of disclosure" that is
appropriate to the work that contains it.[14]

Construction is important for a list's success or failure, and
though a Whitman list may appear to be instinctive and informal,
this is not to say that it actually is so. Lists that succeed do so because
they possess a suggestion of order. Buell elsewhere has described
the features necessary for a "good catalogue." His evaluation of the
success or failure of a catalogue includes the following: "As long as
the catalogue moves a certain amount in the direction of unity
upon close reading, that is all one should expect. If the quest for
unity seems useless, or if it is too easy, then the catalogue fails."[15]
Buell observes that an effective order is present in instances where a
perceptible modulation can be seen from item to item through the
list, or where the impression of a certain sense of shape is realized.

As we have seen, some system of organization directs the extension of a list by admitting chosen items into the series and rejecting
the overwhelming majority of possible candidates. When the compiler manipulates the sequential arrangement of members, the organization becomes more or less meaningful. The first magnitude
of order is the process of selection or omission that determines
membership within the list; the second is the fashioning principle
that determines the relative positions of the items included. In its
poetic mode, the list possesses a high degree of design whether that
design is apparent or not. Furthermore, there is a discernible corre-
lation between the pattern of items of a list in a poem and the role
the list plays there.

Not every Whitman compilation possesses an evident internal arrangement, however—indeed, some seem to celebrate disarrangement. Consider, for example, the difficulty of wading through this portion of the uneven "Song of the Broad-Axe":

> The Axe leaps!
> The solid forest gives fluid utterances,
> They tumble forth, they rise and form,
> Hut, tent, landing, survey,
> Flail, plough, pick, crowbar, spade,
> Shingle, rail, prop, wainscot, jamb, lath, panel, gable,
> Citadel, ceiling, saloon, academy, organ, exhibition-house,
>   library,
> Cornice, trellis, pilaster, balcony, window, turret, porch,
> Hoe, rake, pitchfork, pencil, wagon, staff, saw, jack-pane,
>   mallet, wedge, pounce,
> Chair, tub, hoop, table, wicket, vane, sash, floor,
> Workbox, chest, string'd instrument, boat, frame, and what
>   not . . . [sec. 9; W, 338]

Casting off Ovid's trees almost entirely, here Whitman concentrates instead on products, as America builds a new civilization out of its once-vast forests. As the forms tumble forth, noun after noun, with the punctuation paradoxically joining the items but disjoining the flow of the lines—which are already uneven in length—the reader is left wondering what to make of the odd assortment of elements. What progression can we see from pitchfork to pencil to wagon, or from string'd instrument to boat?

Nevertheless, even this list possesses a degree of order by specifying a broad family of items within each line, such as its sublists of tools and architectural structures. I must note, however, that I have cut off this enumeration at a chosen point. Whitman's list actually continues, adding larger objects—capitols, hospitals, and steamships. I have cropped it after the words "and what not" to create an intentional—though perhaps artificial—philological moment. According to the *Oxford English Dictionary,* "what not" is commonly used to conclude an enumeration and indicate that a variety of additional items might be mentioned. At the end of a long list, the elliptical phrase could be understood to refer to further unspecified items. However, a "whatnot" is a piece of furniture. Thus a whatnot, considered as a small set of shelves intended to hold miscellaneous things, may be suitable for inclusion in a sublist with other containers, such as a workbox or a chest. The whatnot serves as a suitable emblem for Whitman's poetics of the list: it reflects on what surrounds it, as both an open-ended epistemological instrument—an invitation to continue—and as an artifact for containing treasures.

As the preceding lists indicate, the nominal enumerative technique seems to reinforce the foregrounding of things, but it raises other complexities as well. Its use, for example, may demonstrate what Hayden White terms a "democracy of lateral coexistence." This proposes that there is an equivalence of valuation or weight between one item and the next.[16] Indeed, a purposeful paratactic structure, in which the poet arranges items side by side, may challenge other spatial and temporal relations if the context provides for some sort of parity between members. But a list is not always democratic; it is possible to arrange items according to a variety of rankings, from the top down or from the bottom up. A list is merely a repository: it is a container that compels relations between constituents to materialize within it, but does not dictate what those relations will be. Few lists can stand on their own as expressive statements without an external indicator or evident relation among contents to give context. It is possible to read a list as an egalitarian structure, with no difference in value or significance between members, or as a structure that reinforces hierarchical distinctions and separations. So, for example, the sequence 1, 2, 3, 4, 5, 6 has a different significance in the context of lottery numbers from its meaning in the designation of bus routes or in an order of operations or in the placement of athletes finishing a marathon.

A collection of items can be read sequentially, where there is a movement from one member to the next, or substitutionally, where there is an equivalence among members. Frequently in Whitman's verse the relation between list constituents is oblique, and the narrative of development through a series of terms is left to the reader. "Suggestiveness" is one of the key terms to use in describing Whitman's poetry, and one that, like "Indirection," distracts the focus from the poet's agenda and puts interpretation into the hands of the reader.

The list often requires participation; as Whitman wrote, reflectively, of *Leaves of Grass*, "I seek less to state or display any theme or thought, and more to bring you, reader, into the atmosphere of the theme or thought—there to pursue your own flight" ("A Backward Glance o'er Travel'd Roads," *W*, 667). Thus, the concrete, unadorned, nominal enumeration may force readers to create their own meaning. For Whitman words were loose, "floating and moveable," "ready to go this way or that," and their polyvalence was part of the poetic experience.

The short inscription "Beginning My Studies" provides one example of this oblique suggestiveness and captures succinctly the origin, method, and aim of the poet's list making:

> Beginning my studies the first step pleas'd me so much,
> The mere fact consciousness, these forms, the power of
>   motion,
> The least insect or animal, the senses, eyesight, love,
> The first step I say awed me and pleas'd me so much,
> I have hardly gone and hardly wish'd to go any farther,
> But stop and loiter all the time to sing it in ecstatic songs.
>   [*W*, 171]

As noted by William Dean Howells, "Mr. Whitman has summed up his own poetic theory so well in these lines, that no criticism could possibly have done it better."[17] Indeed, many readers, with the bulky inventories of *Leaves of Grass* in mind, have reproved the poet for his apparent predisposition to "stop and loiter all the time," hardly going beyond the "first step" of making the list, without perceiving that what appears as mere loafing is artistically productive.

"Beginning My Studies," as a prelude, stresses the enchantment of the initial celebration of facts, which the speaker accumulates and records in unique poetic products, in "ecstatic songs" that glorify phenomena by naming them.

Nevertheless, on closer examination the poem is less simply dealt with. How the items of the second and third lines interrelate is open to question. Clues to help the reader clarify the intent of the sequence are conspicuously absent. That the burden of interpretation might not always fall so heavily upon the reader, Whitman frequently made use of categorical shifts to maneuver an unfolding list in a particular direction. He usually developed these shifts through modulation among criteria (moving, for example, from factory to farm to steamship in a catalogue of occupations) or through grammatical manipulations. The clustering of items found in "Body Electric" or the syntactical connections that organize "Starting from Paumanok" are strategically omitted here.

The sequence begins with "mere fact consciousness" and concludes with "love." Without the direction of a specifying context, without markers or guideposts, the meaning of the list is open to interpretation. It may be intended to indicate a movement from one view to another, or perhaps an equation of one with the other. That is, it may represent a progression where recognition of external objects *leads* to sympathy and love for them, or it may represent a conceptual redefinition in which to recognize *is* to love. A third possibility is that there is no development or relation between items; rather, love is just another thing to be conscious of, another component to sing about. Ultimately, the list can be either processive or distributive, and the series of items in the third line can be understood accordingly. It may be decoded to mean that the creature or phenomenon, when recognized by the senses, will be loved, or it may not be intended to have a narrative of interrelation at all. It could be an impartial pronouncement of equal possibilities.

The ambiguity of interpretation of the relation between constituents illustrates one of the ways the literary list differs from its practical counterpart. The pragmatic list has a single clear meaning for at least one individual: the computer programmer writing a code or the postal clerk determining the time it will take for a parcel to be delivered to different locations. The literary list, however, is unfixed; its components need not rigidly adhere to the rubrics that order information and make practical lists useful. Unlike a phonebook, the literary list need not present entries as expected, with a formula of regularity.

Coexistent with deviation from systematized principles of organization is a concurrent freedom in what constitutes a list item. In the phonebook, the alphabetized list of names may contain the vagaries of initials or nominations for second lines, but representations such as anagrams, phonetic spellings, or descriptive portraits in rhymed couplets are not appropriate. While we package information for inclusion in pragmatic lists according to rules that are strictly enforced, our literary compilations possess a far greater flexibility. Borges's celebrated Chinese catalogue, which mixes nominal and descriptive terms with substanstives having various modalities of specificity, illustrates the possibilities that the convention invites, revealing both the kinds of items to be included and the ways they can be shaped for inclusion: "Animals are divided into: (a) belonging to the Emperor, (b) embalmed, (c) tame, (d) suckling pigs, (e) sirens, (f) fabulous, (g) stray dogs, (h) included in the present classification, (i) frenzied, (j) innumerable, (k) drawn with a very fine camelhair brush, (l) *et cetera*, (m) having just broken the water pitcher, (n) that from a long way off look like flies."[18] Whitman's poetic listings likewise demonstrate a free arrangement of component parts. The elements in a list often color each other, but some lists prevent such seepage. Section 15 of "Song of Myself," for example, presents the intriguing proximate juxtaposition of a prostitute with the president. Is the connection phonetic? Or is it a political commentary? or a reminder of the extremes of American lives? Does the speaker intend to indicate parity or disparity, the equality of citizens or the inequality across the span of society? No "correct" relation can be specified, for the elements seem to reside in sealed compartments.

This particular survey, kicked off with "The Pure contralto sings in the organ loft," also includes fragments that show that the formatting of items with respect to lineation is pliant. Certain lines present more than one element,

> The floor-men are laying the floor, the tinners are tinning the roof, the masons are calling for mortar [*W,* 202],

while others furnish greater definition in expanded lines,

> The young sister holds out the skein while the elder sister winds it off in a ball, and stops now and then for the knots [*W,* 201],

or in parenthetical remarks,

> The lunatic is carried at last to the asylum a confirm'd case, (He will never sleep any more as he did in the cot in his mother's bed-room). [*W,* 200]

Still other items deliberately shift focus: when the "clean-hair'd yankee girl works with her sewing machine *or* in the factory *or* mill" (italics added) (*W,* 201), the intrusion of indefinite and possible images unexpectedly breaks the established pattern of precise ones. Is this intended to suggest the same figure in three activities, with the emphasis on the girl's work and ability, or is she a type, represented in three manifestations? Are these variations consistent with the "prosodic egalitarianism" Buell found in Whitman's lists, where every line and image bears equal weight?[19] Or are we to recognize a change in valuation coinciding with the change in representation? Is there a difference in sympathy corresponding to the difference in verbal exactitude? Ultimately, the relative qualification of entries acknowledges that there are a variety of ways to compound words in order to present images, and certain representations of life require greater or lesser definition. In this sense, the manner of the itemization (variation), coincides with the matter of the itemization (the varied population of America).

In contrast, in a poem like "These I Singing in Spring," in which the speaker collects and dispenses plants and flowers, the differences among modes of itemization reveal privileges of status. In this case, the most emotionally and sexually expressive item, the calamus root, is cached inside embracing parentheses that augment its symbolic value. This placement exposes the root's private significance while at the same time it allows the poem to seem to be withholding something of personal meaning:

> Here, lilac, with a branch of pine,
> Here, out of my pocket, some moss which I pull'd off a live-
>   oak in Florida as it hung trailing down,
> Here, some pinks and laurel leaves, and a handful of sage,
> And here what I now draw from the water, wading in the
>   pond-side,
> (O here I last saw him that tenderly loves me, and returns
>   again never to separate from me,
> And this, O this shall henceforth be the token of comrades,
>   this calamus-root shall,
> Interchange it youths with each other! let none render it
>   back!)
> And twigs of maple and a bunch of wild orange and
>   Chestnut,
> And stems of currants and plum-blows, and the aromatic
>   cedar ... [*W,* 272]

Variations of syntax, number, verb tense and active and passive verb choices are present throughout the lists of *Leaves of Grass,* as they are in the preceding example. Such alterations break any formal patterning that a list, generically conceived of as a series of consecutive entries, might invite. Whitman employs such modulations throughout his compilations, according them a shimmering vibrancy instead of a monotonous rigidity of format. Furthermore, Whitman's qualification of components with meticulously chosen descriptors often conveys a story or presents a particularly lucid detail that enriches the information given without too much distortion of the bare-bones list structure. Such narratival indirections seem to overhang the confines of the list container and act to brake an otherwise plunging momentum.

While Whitman claims in "Beginning My Studies" that he is going to "stop and loiter all the time to sing," his enumerations are frequently the site of much poetic work. This work is not just the generation of components in laborious acts of recording environments or populating the American landscape, but the careful arrangement of his poems to reinforce the psychological dramas they are intended to illustrate. Although the poet may appear to be letting sense data or an encyclopedia of forms wash over him, he is in part concealing the narrative development of the poem. For example, because of the sheer quantity of material presented in section 33 of "Song of Myself"—an instance of a kind of representative art that is organized in its ideal moments by what Allen Grossman identifies as "a taxonomy" whose "sorting index is mere being-at-all"—it is easy to overlook the alternating pattern of phrasal and clausal entries there, and the modulation of this pattern through the course of the section.[20] The phrasal entries, which contain no finite verbs, portray the speaker as a shifting figure in a continual present who seems to adapt easily to a series of situations:

> By the city's quadrangular houses—in log huts, camping with
>   lumbermen,
> Along the ruts of the turnpike, along the dry gulch and rivulet
>   bed,
> Weeding my onion-patch or hoeing rows of carrots and
>   parsnips, crossing savannas, trailing in forests,
> Prospecting, gold-digging, girdling the trees of a new
>   purchase,

Scorch'd ankle-deep by the hot sand, hauling my boat down
  the shallow river. [*W,* 219]

In contrast, the clausal entries include both subject and predicate,
and present vignettes from which the speaker is notably absent:

Where the panther walks to and fro on a limb overhead,
  where the buck turns furiously at the hunter,
Where the rattlesnake suns his flabby length on a rock, where
  the otter is feeding on fish,
Where the alligator in his tough pimples sleeps by the bayou,
Where the black bear is searching for roots or honey, where
  the beaver pats the mud with his paddle-shaped tail. [*W,* 220]

The alternation between passages of phrasal forms and passages of
clausal forms serves to focus attention alternatively on the self and
on the physical world. Though the length of the complete enumeration reminds us of the richness of both the creative faculty and the
multitudinous external world, the proportion of phrasal elements
indicates the superiority of the former. Whereas the "clausal world"
remains relatively stable, the "phrasal self" gains power and momentum as the speaker's expansive imagination places him in an
increasing number of situations, ultimately transporting him out
of time and space: "Walking the old hills of Judaea with the beautiful gentle God by my side. / Speeding through space, speeding
through heaven and the stars" (*W,* 223).

Despite the appearance of spontaneity and unedited immediacy presented by the relentless seriations, Whitman's speaker is
never, as he describes in section 4 of "Song of Myself," "Looking
with side-curved head curious what will come next." Although we
as readers may be "both in and out of the game and watching and
wondering at it," as we savor the possibilities of each additional entry or skim through the entries in search of embedded keys to their
purpose, Whitman's lists are deliberate, programmatic presentations. In "A Backward Glance o'er Travel'd Roads," Whitman set
out the philosophical purpose of his poetry: "The true use for the

imaginative faculty in modern times is to give ultimate vivification to facts, to science, and to common lives, endowing them with the glows and glories and final illustriousness which belong to every real thing, and to real things only" (*W*, 659). For a poet who has often been described as treating words as things and things as words, this statement is not as candid as it appears. Indeed, it may strike us as completely fictive, for it is the poems that glow and shimmer as they conjure "real things" before us even though they are in fact only written sequences of words.

The lists of *Leaves of Grass* do present things, facts, and "common" lives, but at the same time they present an illusion that often hides their ulteriorities. Whitman's work offers surfaces in what Muriel Rukeyser termed a "montage" of images that masks the deeper questions of the nature of reality and the relation of the self to the external world. Along with his principal endeavors of creating a new poetics, championing an inclusive, democratic equality, and celebrating sexuality and the body, Whitman has a phenomenological objective for his poetry as well—to affirm existence. His goal, as Roy Harvey Pearce puts it, is "to know that the world is there, and in the knowing, to know *he* is there."[21]

We can see this illustrated in "There Was a Child Went Forth," which documents a child's encounters with his environment as he develops his concept of self-identification and understanding of the world. Many of his encounters are described through lists:

> The early lilacs became part of this child,
> And grass, and white and red morningglories, and white
>   and red clover, and the song of the phoebe-bird,
> And the March-born lambs, and the sow's pink-faint litter,
>   and the mare's foal, and the cow's calf, and the noisy
>   brood of the barnyard or by the mire of the pond-side . .
>   and the fish suspending themselves so curiously below
>   there . . and the beautiful curious liquid . . and the water-
>   plants with their graceful flat heads . . all became part of
>   him. [*W*, 138]

The child grows as he gathers experiences: each new encounter exposes him to the multiform world, and allows him to progress through sequential stages of conceptual development. After a number of such experiences, the child can tentatively trust and anticipate the phenomena he encounters.

When there is a disjuncture between expected and actual conduct, for example the father's surprising violence followed by his dissimulated reconciliation ("the blow, the quick loud word, the tight bargain, the crafty lure" [W, 139]), it shakes the child's entire mental schema. With the disruption of his manner of interpreting experience and his perceptions, the enumeration falters. When the child perceives that the father can dissemble, doubt extends to all his other relations:

> The sense of what is real . . . . the thought if after all it should
>   prove unreal,
> The doubts of daytime and the doubts of nighttime . . . the
>   curious whether and how,
> Whether that which appears so is so . . . . or is it all flashes and
>   specks? [W, 139]

Whitman uses the enumerative technique to develop these questions in other poems as well. "Of the Terrible Doubt of Appearances" presents the case thus:

> May-be the things I perceive, the animals, plants, men, hills
>   shining and flowing waters,
> The skies of day and night, colors, densities, forms, may-be
>   these are (as doubtless they are) only apparitions, and the
>   real something has yet to be known. [W, 274][22]

In contrast to the concretizing enumeration of "Body Electric," here there is doubt about the ability of language to represent reality adequately: if the thing itself is not what it seems, then the terms used to identify it must be imprecise. But expressing doubt in this creative way, successfully communicating it to and sharing it with readers, validates self-realization; Whitman's articulation of doubt propels us to seek our own places in the world.

Whitman specifically uses lists in his verse to produce, as evidence for his poetic and philosophic themes, the illusion that a representative portion of the aggregate of all things has been paraded before us. Pearce reminds us that "the world is too large, too much, to have an imitable order or pattern. It is just there." Through their selections and motions, Whitman's lists document the interactions of a self (Whitman's self, any self) with a miscellaneous, multitudinous world, sometimes fraternally through what Grossman terms "an unprecedented trope of inclusion," and at other times with an intensified particularity of surroundings.[23]

In the first great enumeration of "Crossing Brooklyn Ferry," for example, which takes up the majority of section 3, Whitman seems to guide the inner eye of the reader through a graceful, ever-widening panorama to present a sensitive and detailed prospect. The poet directs what, how, and where the reader will see; the vista appears to be presented, like the flight of the seagulls, in "slow-wheeling circles . . . gradually edging toward the south." These are the kinds of lists that so frustrated Santayana, who wrote that he found in them only "swarms of men and objects rendered as they might strike the retina."[24] But while this enumeration seems to direct the observations of the reader like a tour guide pointing out what to notice, the poet frames the list in a specific way that represents something besides only looking forward. The progression of the list presents not only the environmental particulars in a controlled cinematic sweep but also a narrative of development that details the speaker's existential relation with external reality.

> I too many and many a time cross'd the river of old,
> Watched the Twelfth-month sea-gulls, saw them high in the
>   air floating with motionless wings, oscillating their bodies,
> Saw how the glistening yellow lit up parts of their bodies and
>   left the rest in strong shadow,
> Saw the slow-wheeling circles and the gradual edging toward
>   the south,
> Saw the reflection of the summer sky in the water,

Had my eyes dazzled by the shimmering track of beams,
Look'd at the fine centifugal spokes of light round the shape
    of my head in the sunlit water,
Look'd on the haze on the hills southward and south-
    westward,
Look'd on the vapor as it flew in fleeces tinged with violet,
Look'd toward the lower bay to notice the vessels arriving,
Saw their approach, saw aboard those that were near me,
Saw the white sails of schooners and sloops, saw the ships at
    anchor,
The sailors at work in the rigging or out astride the spars,
The round masts, the swinging motion of the hulls, the
    slender serpentine pennants,
The large and small steamers in motion, the pilots in their
    pilot-houses,
The white wake left by the passage, the quick tremulous
    whirl of the wheels,
The flags of all nations, the falling of them at sunset,
The scallop-edged waves in the twilight, the ladled cups, the
    frolicsome crests and glistening,
The stretch afar growing dimmer and dimmer, the gray
    walls of the granite storehouses by the docks,
On the river the shadowy group, the big steam-tug closely
    flank'd on each side by the barges, the hay-boat, the
    belated lighter,
On the neighboring shore the fires from the foundry
    chimneys burning high and glaringly into the night,
Casting their flicker of black contrasted with wild red and
    yellow light over the tops of houses, and down into the
    clefts of the streets. [W, 309–310]

By beginning with *I*, the enumeration significantly starts with the realization of the self, but abandons the pronoun after the first line. In the following lines, various verbs suggest the "action" of vision; like all verbs of sensation, these actions imply receptivity.[25] But they too shortly drop away. After the verbs of perception disappear, the disintegration of the self is complete, and only the external things remain in the list. While the enumeration presents a spatial progression in its panorama, and a temporal progression in detailing the darkening night, more importantly it accomplishes Whitman's version of that Emersonian feat expressed in *Nature,* in which "all mean egotism vanishes. I become a transparent eyeball; I am nothing; I see all; the currents of the Universal Being circulate through me; I am part or parcel of God" (*E,* 10).

In the poem's sister catalogue, section 9, the listed imperatives reveal the speaker's regained powers of poetic authority, illustrating an equilibrium of the self engaged with, not merely receptive to, the world. The sense of self-identity is fortified, and the poem celebrates both the things of the external world and the writer's ability to command and coordinate words to stage manage a spectacle of language for the reading audience, a skill that has been silently present all along.[26]

> Be firm, rail over the river, to support those who lean idly, yet
> haste with the hasting current;
> Fly on, sea-birds! fly sideways, or wheel in large circles high in
> the air;
> Receive the summer sky, you water, and faithfully hold it till
> all downcast eyes have time to take it from you!
> Diverge, fine spokes of light, from the shape of my head, or
> any one's head, in the sunlit water!
> Come on, ships from the lower bay! pass up or down, white-
> sail'd schooners, sloops, lighters!
> Flaunt away, flags of all nations, be duly lower'd at sunset!
> Burn high your fires, foundry chimneys! cast black shadows at
> nightfall! cast red and yellow light over the tops of the
> houses! [*W,* 313]

One major application of the literary list is as a tool to suggest order, by either reflecting a perceived order or enforcing a desired one. Against the unsympathetic vastness of space, we have often been compelled to attribute significance to existence by finding a meaningful arrangement in the universe. In so doing, we can make sense of our existence by making sense of the external environment, whether the arrangement genuinely reflects external reality or is merely a projection of what we hope to find in the face of insignificance. The arrangement of language provides an approximate, attainable imitation of the arrangement of matter. By creating a list, we transform chaos into cosmos. In "The World Below the Brine" and "Germs," Whitman uses the list format to delineate the cosmos. Each poem is composed primarily of a list, and the intention of each is to map out a cosmography. Despite the similarities of technique and aim, the poems suggest widely differing possibilities. The range of their effects derives directly from the potentiality inherent in the list form. The list's flexibility comes from its alterable, interchangeable sequencing of constituents so that the development may appear to be progressive on one hand and random on the other.

Whitman arranges the list in "The World Below the Brine" to suggest a movement of ascent through concentric layers:

> The world below the brine,
> Forests at the bottom of the sea, the branches and leaves,
> Sea-lettuce, vast lichens, strange flowers and seeds, the thick
>   tangle, openings, and pink turf,
> Different colors, pale gray and green, purple, white, and gold,
>   the play of light through the water,
> Dumb swimmers there among the rocks, coral, gluten, grass,
>   rushes, and the aliment of the swimmers,
> Sluggish existences grazing there suspended, or slowly
>   crawling close to the bottom,
> The sperm whale at the surface blowing air and spray, or
>   disporting with his flukes,
> The leaden-eyed shark, the walrus, the turtle, the hairy sea-
>   leopard, and the sting-ray,
> Passions there, wars, pursuits, tribes, sight in those ocean-
>   depths, breathing the thick-breathing air, as so many do,
> The change thence to the sight here, and to the subtle air
>   breathed by beings like us who walk this sphere,

The change onward from ours to that of beings who walk
other spheres. [*W*, 399]

Here the gradation begins with vegetation and rises by a sort of speciation through life-forms of increasing complexity (invertebrates
to vertebrates), pausing only momentarily at the human level (tan-
gentially expressed) before continuing toward further realms beyond the penetration of human awareness. Whitman pairs the phylo-
genetic advancement in the poem with a movement that progresses
from sea to land, and then by extension from land to whatever
sphere is "onward from ours." The suggestion of movement continues toward a further sphere that is as indiscernible to us as ours is to
the "dumb swimmers" below.

In *The Order of Things*, Michel Foucault considered the role of
resemblance in determining and sorting similarity and difference.
When items are arranged, they fall into relations that have meaning
and that may either suggest correspondence or demonstrate difference when seen in proximity to one another. In "The World Below the
Brine," Whitman brings the contents of the oceans into proximity
with the terrestrial realm to prove a resemblance between two similar,
adjacent domains, and by extension to a third, as yet hypothesized.
Adjacency, Foucault observed, creates the hinge where resemblance
comes to light. When a writer brings things into juxtaposition in the
rhetorical device of *convenientia*, "their edges touch, their fringes intermingle, the extremity of one denotes the beginning of the other."[27]
Similarity disperses across the interface, and the aim of the poem is to
point out this diffusion: in both domains, vegetation grows, light travels, life-forms exist. Certain forms even inhabit the boundary, like the
marine mammals that rely on the contents of one sphere—the air, for
respiration—while obligated to fulfill all remaining life functions
within the other. The corresponding interface between "this sphere"
of ours and that which is "onward from ours" is undetermined, but
the delineation of the actual place of contact is less important than the
equivalent diffusion of similarity that is posited to occur across it.

In any series, items are placed side by side and are therefore always orthographically adjacent. In "The World Below the Brine," the real things designated in the list (life-forms, the seafloor, light) demonstrate a network of adjacency by virtue of their copresence within the oceans: light passes over and across forms, fish swim through rushes and coral, and among, over, and beneath one another. Though these signified things exist in the manifest world in complex, three-dimensional, and ever-changing associations, Whitman's arbitrary array imposes a rigid order on the listed signifiers that compels us to recognize a more fixed relation. The biological advance of the poem, with a concurrent intimation of increasing intelligence (from unthinking vegetation to "dumb swimmers" to "sluggish existences" to "passions") suggests that the things of the world are linked together in a great chain. As Foucault wrote: "At each point of contact there begins and ends a link that resembles the one before it and the one after it; and from circle to circle, these similitudes continue, holding the extremes apart (God and matter), yet bringing them together in such a way that the will of the Almighty may penetrate into the most unawakened corners."[28]

Superimposed on this interconnectedness is a different system of likeness that enforces a concentricity of layers on the poem. In contrast to juxtaposition, which implies one object brought into abutment with another, this second type of similitude needs no contact. Like an object and its reflection in a mirror, the resemblance of *aemulatio* occurs across spatial separations: separated things imitate and duplicate one another. From this perspective, similitudes between the submarine and the terrestrial arise not from contiguity but from rivalry. As Foucault noted, one thing may be of a greater magnitude than the other, and the weaker may be more receptive to the influence of the stronger. Thus, in Whitman's poem, the forests of the seafloor are imitations of the ones on the earth's surface, complete with branch and leaf, and the intra- and interspecies struggles for life are characterized as "wars" between "tribes," reflecting human actions and organizations.

Whitman uses the list in "The World Below the Brine" to compile evidence of known correspondences and to foreground relations that can be figured as correspondences from observation of the two spheres. If the undersea world can be perceived as a reflection of our own, then ours too can be an imitation of some further sphere. Determining similitude between the different media of water and air, Whitman suggests the possibility of a congruent similitude between air and a further sphere that can only be conjectured. The coincidency of adjacency and emulation of "The World Below the Brine" presents two realms as analogous, postulating a further analogy with a realm "beyond." The poem's lists, which elaborate horizontally within categories and vertically between them, use similarity and difference to draw things together and keep them apart. The grid of the poem classifies objects and phenomena into distinct strata, showing both their interconnectedness and their distinction.

While "The World Below the Brine" is conscious of the boundaries of difference that keep things separated and prevent the assimilation of matter and antimatter into one homogeneous wholeness, the poem "Germs" uses a looser sequencing of listed items to collapse distinctions into pluripotential microcosm:

> Forms, qualities, lives, humanity, language, thoughts,
> The ones known, and the ones unknown, the ones on the
>   stars,
> The stars themselves, some shaped, others unshaped,
> Wonder as of those countries, the soil, trees, cities,
>   inhabitants, whatever they may be,
> Splendid suns, the moons and rings, the countless
>   combinations and effects,
> Such-like, and good as such-like, visible here or anywhere,
>   stand provided for in a handful of space, which I extend
>   my arm and half enclose with my hand,
> That containing the start of each and all, the virtue, the
>   germs of all. [W, 409]

Unlike the demarcation of the previous poem, Whitman composes here an itemization of components that resist empirical similarity and escape categorization: under what common rubric can we include forms, qualities, lives, humanity, language, *and* thoughts, other than as broadly conceived "ideas" or "words"? Whitman lists not only these conceptual constructs but others that are fantastical, literally otherworldly. Furthermore, many are "anti-items," given distinction as constituents of the list by the lack of distinction that possibility, but not certainty, entails; things, "whatever they may be," unknown and unshaped and therefore not demonstrably things at all, when granted membership in the list are provided space for existence. Whitman goes beyond giving mere possibility to the possible; he guarantees the inevitable certainty of every potentiality. The idea of "potential" arises even in the second line in the unspecified identifier "the ones" in which all possible referents lie dormant.

Whereas the poet generates his list in "The World Below the Brine" to detail the symmetry between two known spheres so as to posit a further symmetry with the unknown, the list in "Germs" incorporates the unknowns. Where one expression of the cosmos uses the list to describe parallel existences reiterated in the ordered stratification of the list, the other obliterates distinguishability by the absence of order and the absorption within the list of the known and the possible, "such-like, and good as such-like." "Germs" does more than recognize natural phenomena and draw analogies; the poem commands that the realities of worlds and universes be revealed. With gesture and articulation, the poem compresses all—all existing and all possible—and reenacts divine creation.

The listing of components mandates a relation between them and metaphysically joins them. In imitation of the creation of matter, the poet may assemble a list that is either ordered or random, wherein internal relations are formed in order to represent those relations perceived in reality. The list becomes a chart for ordering the constituents of the cosmos, approximating a tidy systemization or evoking an enigmatic jumble. The frame of the list thus acts as a grid, with horizontal and vertical coordinates that determine relations among the various parts. The position of the components determines their meaning and gives the compiler the power to make something first, last, or in the middle.

Because time is not static but progressive, we can subdivide its passage into discrete units that are as amenable to organization as space and matter. The list of dates that make up a history or the series of integers on a digital timepiece are two examples in which each component represents a separate point on a continuum and where relations across time are the important factors in coordination. Just as Whitman is skilled at parceling out components to his worlds, so too is he adept at treating the passage of time as the sequential unfolding of individual moments, which he can then select and manipulate. So, for example, in this passage from "When Lilacs Last in the Dooryard Bloom'd," a poem that elaborates and interweaves a number of subtle list structures with different agendas, the lines evoke a controlled advancement of time, though the listing of moments is camouflaged:

> O western orb sailing the heaven,
> Now I know what you must have meant as a month since I
>   walk'd,
> As I walk'd in silence the transparent shadowy night,
> As I saw you had something to tell as you bent to me night
>   after night,
> As you droop'd from the sky low down as if to my side, (while
>   the other stars look'd on,)
> As we wander'd together the solemn night, (for something I
>   know not what kept me from sleep,)
> As the night advanced, and I saw on the rim of the west how
>   full you were of woe,
> As I stood on the rising ground in the breeze in the cool
>   transparent night,
> As I watch'd where you pass'd and was lost in the netherward
>   black of the night,

> As my soul in its trouble dissatisfied sank, as where you sad
>   orb,
> Concluded, dropt in the night, and was gone. [sec. 8; *W*, 461]

This list marks a series of moments, each chronicled in a separate
line, that traces the relations among the speaker, the star, and time.
(Whitman's use of the star as an overt symbol for the great president—"O powerful western fallen star"—provides an additional
layer of meaning in this relation.) The poem conveys the lapse of
time through the changing relative positions between the speaker
and the star. Though time is inseparably linked to the rotation of
the planet, the external markers of its passage—here the star—
seem to move while the speaker maintains his fixity. This motion is
nevertheless retarded by the poet who, as Kenneth Price comments,
has a "pervasive desire to achieve temporal immediacy."[29]

It must be noted that there runs through these lines an overlay
of multiple measures of time. The arrangement illustrates the descent of the star, though Whitman notes the "rising ground" that
creates the illusion of descent. The setting of the star occurs at the
conclusion of the stanza, where it is "dropt in the night." The lines
suggest, however, that this movement takes place over several
evenings ("night after night"); the moments the poet brings into
alignment to represent this apparent arc may be a synthesis of several nights placed in a desired pattern. Here Whitman plays on the
substitutional positioning of items within the list: a period of time
is divisible into subunits, and those subunits are interchangeable.
The sequence given to us in the lines of the poem incorporates temporal subunits from many nights woven into a collage. Through the
artifice of arrangement, the poet indicates not only one time period
but several similar yet separate moments fused into one, "as so often
happens in the alembic of memory."[30]

In contrast to the movement of the star, the anaphora in these
lines interferes with the sensation of time passing. Repetition seems
to have an uncomfortable ambiguity about it with regard to this ad-

vancement. It suggests recurrence, which may entail a progression of sequential moments or the return of the original one. When anaphora initiates each line, we expect a continued parallelism in the rest of the line. Instead, while the beginnings of the lines are fixed in similarity by the repeated "As," by the time the conclusion of each line is reached, the star has made its further descent. Indeed, there is a marked tension between motion and stasis elaborated in these lines that is not overcome until the star disappears below the horizon. In part this is because the parallel construction of the beginnings of the lines hides the distinction between them: the focus is on the nocturnal sympathy between the speaker and the star, and the apparent orbit of the star escapes notice until the star passes from view.

Whitman recognized that the list could hold an arrangement of items, and from this skeleton, by subtle manipulation, he could achieve dramatic effects. As we have seen, the underframe of this kind of poetry can be constructed by setting items in succession, thereby creating series and inducing networks of connections to propagate among them, or by the use of supporting devices, such as anaphora, in which a vertical arrangement of repeated words becomes the vertebral column from which the poem depends. As Jakobson observed, "The essence of poetic artifice consists in recurrent returns" achieved by "phonological, grammatical and semantic structures in their multiform interplay." As one way of introducing parallelism, anaphora can be almost a numbering of components, such as occurs in the highly repetitive poem "Salut au Monde":

> I see mountain peaks, I see the sierra of Andes where they
> range,
> I see plainly the Himalayas, Chian Shahs, Altays, Ghauts,
> I see the giant pinnacles of Elbruz, Kazbek, Bazardjusi,
> I see the Styrian Alps, and the Karnac Alps,
> I see the Pyrenees, Balks, Carpathians, and to the north the
> Dofrafields, and off at sea mount Hecla . . . [sec. 4; W,
> 289]

In other instances this construction permits what Basil De Selin-court has described as "the feeling at each stage that more is added in discovery than is lost through the trouble of treading the old path":

> That I could forget the mockers and insults!
> That I could forget the trickling tears and the blows of the
>   bludgeons and hammers!
> That I could look with a separate look on my own crucifixion
>   and bloody crowning. ["Song of Myself," sec. 38; *W*, 231]

Frequently, however, Whitman modulated his anaphora, often be-ginning a series with one preposition and switching in the next few lines to another, and in the next to still another. A particularly beau-tiful instance of this is the opening verse paragraph of "Out of the Cradle Endlessly Rocking":

> Out of the cradle endlessly rocking,
> Out of the mocking-bird's throat, the musical shuttle,
> Out of the ninth-month midnight,
> Over the sterile sands and the fields beyond, where the child
>   leaving his bed wander'd alone, bareheaded, barefoot,
> Down from the shower'd halo,
> Up from the mystic play of shadows twining and twisting as if
>   they were alive,
> Out from the patches of briers and blackberries,
> From the memories of the bird that chanted to me,
> From your memories sad brother, from the fitful risings and
>   fallings I heard,
> From under that yellow half-moon late-risen and swollen as if
>   with tears,
> From those beginning notes of yearning and love there in the
>   mist,
> From the thousand responses of my heart never to cease,
> From the myriad thence-arous'd words,
> From the word stronger and more delicious than any,
> From such as now they start the scene revisiting,

As a flock, twittering, rising, or overhead passing,
Borne hither, ere all eludes me, hurriedly,
A man, yet by these tears a little boy again,
Throwing myself on the sand, confronting the waves,
I, chanter of pains and joys, uniter of here and hereafter,
Taking all hints to use them, but swiftly leaping beyond them,
A reminiscence sing. [*W,* 388]

Leo Spitzer's treatment of this passage in his "Explication de Texte"
is unsurpassed: "The proem, composed in the epic style of 'Arma
virumque cano . . . ,' consists of one long, 'oceanic' sentence which
symbolizes by its structure the poetic victory achieved by the
poet. . . . Out of the maze of the world, characterized by those numerous parallel phrases, introduced by contrasting prepositions,
which invite the inner eye of the reader to look in manifold directions . . . out of the maze of the world emerges the powerful ego, the
'I' of the poet, who has extricated himself from the labyrinth."[31]

Whereas a list can arrange space and time by positioning selected
components in a particular order in which sequence creates meaning,
merely gathering selected components into a list is a gesture of choice
which itself has artistic significance. Here also discrimination determines the admittance of items; membership is based on various
criteria determined by the compiler. Thematic arrangements of compilations can elaborate in a number of ways. As I have observed previously, compilations are generally arranged according to a principle.
Lists that can be titled "The Contents of Tom Sawyer's Pockets" or
"The National Scene of Mourning for the Death of President Lincoln"
by definition possess a thematic character. Whitman's notes provide
evidence for a thematic approach to poetic technique: "Whole poem.
Poem of insects get from Mr. Arkhurst the names of all insects—in-
terweave a train of thought suitable—also trains of words."[32]

So, for example, staying with "Lilacs" for a moment, the poet uses the list format in sections 5 and 6 to group and characterize the sympathies aroused by the journey of President Lincoln's coffin. The two listings document the responses his death evokes in the natural and human worlds.

5
Over the breast of the spring, the land, amid cities,
Amid lanes and through old woods, where lately the violets
    peep'd from the ground, spotting the grey debris,
Amid the grass in the fields each side of the lanes, passing the
    endless grass,
Passing the yellow-spear'd wheat, every grain from its shroud
    in the dark-brown fields uprisen,
Passing the apple-tree blows of white and pink in the
    orchards,
Carrying a corpse to where it shall rest in the grave,
Night and day journeys a coffin.
6
Coffin that passes through lanes and streets,
Through day and night with the great cloud darkening the
    land,
With the pomp of the inloop'd flags with the cities draped in
    black,
With the show of the States themselves as of crape-veil'd
    women standing,
With processions long and winding and the flambeaus of the
    night,
With the countless torches lit, with the silent sea of faces and
    the unbared heads,
With the waiting depot, the arriving coffin, and the sombre
    faces,
With the dirges through the night, with the thousand voices
    rising strong and solemn,
With all the mournful voices of the dirges pour'd around the
    coffin,
The dim-lit churches and the shuddering organs—where
    amid these you journey,
With the tolling tolling bells' perpetual clang,

Here, coffin that slowly passes,
I give you my sprig of lilac. [*W,* 460]

The second list contrasts markedly with that of the first. The lamentation of the citizenry is black and solemn, but nature brings forth the vibrant colors of burgeoning spring. These colors in their own way simultaneously both salute and ignore the passing hearse. The insensate flowers and blossoms, the "endless grass," represent the cyclical, eternal natural world, in contrast to finite human existence. Nevertheless, the natural world offers an outward display of respect to the funeral carriage through its show of color and by "every grain from its shroud in the dark fields uprisen," conveying the suggestion of both resurrection and deference.

The two stanzas contrast the journey through life with the journey through death, but the connections Whitman makes between them are crucial to the overall meaning of the poem. These connections derive not only from their proximity or from the chiasmus of "Night and day" and "day and night" that reinforces their relation by suggesting that one is the inversion of the other. Whitman makes a more overt connection by concluding the second list with the speaker offering a lilac sprig to the fallen Lincoln. This action takes a component from the first list and interposes it into the sorrow and solemnity of the second. The sequence of these stanzas—these lists—is crucial. The catalogue of the public responses details an increase in intensity, from the silent sea of faces to the forlorn dirges the "shuddering organ" to the highest national demonstration of public mourning, the tolling of the bell; it climaxes with the speaker offering the sprig of lilac. For these catalogues to be successful, the lilac must be the last item presented: the import of the stanza will be completely lost if the sequence is altered. For only through this sequence does the gesture take on profundity, revealing the speaker's awakened understanding of death in the face of nature's eternal indifference and public manifestations of mourning which are principally outward signs of grief.

In another Whitman list, the specific arrangement of "I Heard
You Solemn-sweet Pipes of the Organ" uses an alignment of items
to imitate a musical score:

> I heard you solemn-sweet pipes of the organ as last Sunday
>   morn I pass'd the church,
> Winds of autumn, as I walk'd the woods at dusk I heard your
>   long-stretch'd sighs up above so mournful,
> I heard the perfect Italian tenor singing at the opera, I heard
>   the soprano in the midst of the quartet singing;
> Heart of my love! you too I heard murmuring low through
>   one of the wrists around my head,
> Heard the pulse of you when all was still ringing little bells last
>   night under my ear. [W, 266]

The itemization in this instance does not flow horizontally as a
string of items spun out in sequence. Rather, it is vertical: each line
is composed of one element or family of elements meant to represent an instrument.

- pipe organ
- wind instrument
- voice
- percussion

Stacking the components allows the poet to duplicate musical composition in complex ways. He develops each line to present part of a polyphonic arrangement, elaborating the items in this catalogue of "things
heard" as a heterophony, a piece wherein each line presents the duplication of a basic melody with certain differences. Whitman, as De
Selincourt notes, "uses words and phrases more as if they were notes of
music than any other writer." Here the poet uses a catalogue to capture
the concept of counterpoint. A poem is experienced differently from a
piece of polyphonic music: there is an inescapable incompatibility
between individual versus synchronized progression through each
work, unless multiple readers are reading aloud. Nevertheless, Whitman's list re-creates the appearance of music as it is written.

De Selincourt is again helpful in making clear what is involved in this transcription: "The chief difference between musical and verbal expression, as a rule, is that words, carrying each their modicum of meaning, have done their part when they have delivered it, while notes, being meaningless except in combination, develop new meanings by presenting a single combination in varying contexts or with varying accompaniment. In fact, repetition, which the artist in language scrupulously avoids, is the foundation and substance of musical expression."[33] As in a musical score, there is a meaningful vertical relation between the lines and a horizontal independence within each line. So, for instance, each measure contains a version of "I heard you" plus a characterization of the instrument plus a temporal reference. The phrase "I heard you" and the variations "you too I heard," "I heard," "Heard" and even "heart" occur at different positions in each line, sometimes at the beginning, sometimes in the middle, much as different instruments might deliver variations of melody at different moments in a symphonic work.

In organizing this ensemble, Whitman unites sounds whose origins differ in time and space. The isolation is so precise that the voice of the soprano can be separated from "the midst of the quartet." The result is an alternating, embracing, interweaving of the instrumental and vocal music produced by humans and the metaphorical music of the sounds of the natural world. Again the poet is using language to suggest sensual occurrences.

This mode of sampling recalls Section 26 of "Song of Myself," where the poet claims, "Now I will do nothing but listen, / To accrue what I hear into this song, to let sounds contribute / Toward it" (*W*, 214). Yet what follows these lines is not the silence of someone thought to be earnestly engaged in the concentrated effort of hearing but the particularization of a sonic landscape transcribed into a language that summarizes and communicates sensation. Further, in this laboratory of language, in this recording studio, sounds can be separated:

> I hear the bravuras of birds, bustle of growing wheat, gossip
> of flames, clack of sticks cooking my meals

or merged

> I hear all sounds running together, combined, fused or
> following. [*W,* 214]

Ultimately, when words are inadequate to the task of transmitting the effect of certain sounds, such as the sublimity of an orchestra, Whitman's enumerative technique collapses, yielding instead this dramatic figurative description:

> I hear the train'd soprano (what work with hers is this?)
> The orchestra whirls me wider than Uranus flies,
> It wrenches such ardors from me that I did not know I
> possess'd them,
> It sails me, I dab with bare feet, they are lick'd by the indolent
> waves,
> I am cut by the bitter and angry hail, I lose my breath,
> Steep'd amid honey'd morphine, my windpipe throttled in
> fakes of death,
> At length let up again to feel the puzzle of puzzles,
> And that we call Being. [*W,* 215]

Countering the synchrony suggested by its schematized arrangement, "I Heard You Solemn-sweet Pipes" contains an element of temporal identification in each line. The overlay of form provides the framework of the poem, but the arrangement of the lines is more than just an attempt to imitate visually: there is also a defined advance through the list of sounds heard from the start to the end of the poem. In this way the series progresses from the distant to the near past, emphasizing a sequential rather than a choral development. This temporal aspect to the poem is significant because all but the final member of the list, heartbeat, are presumably single occurrences. That is, even if the speaker does not hear them, at some time the organ will stop playing, the wind will stop blowing, and the singers will stop singing. But the heart of the loved one will not stop, and does not stop even when "all [is] still."

Indeed, the beating heart, a metaphor for the constancy of love, *must* not stop or love, and more significantly the loved one, will die. The beating of the heart keeps the beat to life and marks time for all the other instruments. The metronomic function of the heart underlies these other instruments, and is therefore at the bottom of the list. Furthermore, though we can tell that the rhythm making of the heart is occurring in a living being, we can hear the actual sound only with a certain intimacy. When the speaker is in intimate contact with the loved one, the pulse is characterized, joyously, as "ringing little bells," suggesting a celebratory nuance that contrasts with the solemn and mournful sounds heard by the speaker on his walks alone.

The first stanza of "Starting from Paumanok" illustrates still another carefully crafted strain of catalogue modulation. This beautiful opening verse paragraph uses a list structure that challenges and disorients, in part because of its unexpected categorical shifts:

Starting from fish-shape Paumanok where I was born,
Well-begotten, and rais'd by a perfect mother,
After roaming many lands, lover of populous pavements,
Dweller in Mannahatta my city, or on southern savannas,
Or a soldier camp'd or carrying my knapsack and gun, or a
    miner in California,
Or rude in my home in Dakota's woods, my diet meat, my
    drink from the spring,
Or withdrawn to muse and meditate in some deep recess,
Far from the clank of crowds intervals passing rapt and
    happy,
Aware of the fresh free giver the flowing Missouri, aware of
    mighty Niagara,
Aware of the buffalo herds grazing the plains, the hirsute and
    strong-breasted bull,
Of earth, rocks, Fifth-month flowers experienced, stars, rain,
    snow, my amaze,

Having studied the mocking-bird's tones and the flight of the
    mountain hawk,
And heard at dawn the unrivall'd one, the hermit thrush from
    the swamp-cedars,
Solitary, singing in the West, I strike up for a new world. [W,
    176]

The passage takes a list skeleton in which attributes of the subject, the speaker, are itemized and elaborated. It is difficult to extricate the central list of the stanza (or at least to determine which attributes of the list refer to which referent), for though certain items appear to be applied as epithets or descriptions of one entity, either through proximity or subtle manipulation the identity of that entity is rendered ambiguous. Significantly, the poet withholds the grammatical subject and verb until the end of the stanza. As with many Whitman passages, this stanza contains only one sentence but has numerous balanced digressions, which move the focus away from the subject and then are brought back by a controlled return. In some instances, these digressions amplify, in others they reiterate.

The first line, "Starting from Paumanok where I was born," resists identification as a member of the list because, as the first line, it signals neither directly nor indirectly that a list is being unrolled. It is too early in the development of the stanza for its itemization of attributes to be established. However, as the list unfurls, and certainly by the time the concluding line is reached, the first line becomes recognizable as another attribute. It is the initiating attribute of departure from the recognized security of home into the new and unknown. The starting point of this excursion is the first line, though the speaker does not complete or resolve his act of setting out until fourteen lines later. The catalogue of attributes suspends the journey.

The list clearly begins to emerge in the second line, with the attributes of upbringing that refer to the antecedent *I* of the first line. As the poem progresses, Whitman uses the list to enumerate further attributes of his speaker. Lines 3–8 reveal that he went through a period of wandering and experience, though the itemization here is not simple. Line 3 suggests a range of experience achieved by "roaming many lands" and wandering along "populous pavements." Nevertheless, as the list continues to recount numerous specific manifestations of lives and places lived, the persona of the speaker seems less and less identifiable as a clearly delineated individual and more and more fractured into separate yet unified identities. Here the catalogue technique, as Buell observes, is especially appropriate: "Through it, the self can be sung in such a way as to incorporate, or seem to incorporate, all particular selves. . . . The method of the song mirrors the complex unity of the singer."[34] It is possible that the itemization is intended to represent the varied far-flung experiences of a single unique individual who has been a city dweller and an outdoorsman and a miner and a soldier, but Whitman problematizes this interpretation by the express use of the conjunction *or*.

Although *or* could be intended to identify the persona at different stages of his life—for example, at eighteen he was a soldier, at twenty-one a miner in California, at thirty living off the land in the Dakotas—we get the sense instead of lives lived in parallel. This list, then, rather than tracing one life, seems to generate possible alternate yet simultaneous lives, each with a different experience of the world. Nevertheless the passage appears to ascribe these experiences to the singular persona of the speaker. He seems to be, as Grossman beautifully writes, "released from the rational justice of the situation, inclusive of many places at once (here and also there) not as seeing is but as light is."[35] It is important to note, however, that though these separate selves suggest an equality, a validation of each individual's unique existence, there is a progressive expansion and elaboration of each subsequent alternative. In this respect, the lives are congruent but not identical. The progressive enhancement prepares the way for the remainder of the catalogue, specifically the attention paid to the natural world that will culminate in the persona's merging with it and asserting his intention to step out farther from it. The catalogue of lives progresses from a focus on residence (one's life as defined by where one lives) to a focus on profession (one's life defined by what one does) to culminate in a life which can withdraw from the world in order to take pleasure in consideration, meditation, and, most important, awareness.

Though these lines appear to display equivalent alternate lives, each is progressively refined and better developed, culminating in a persona that possesses a defined intellect and psyche. Indeed, it is this expansion of character from demographic definition into a thinking, considering, conscious being that allows the catalogue of attributes to continue by itemizing what the consciousness is aware *of*. In this way, one sort of list deftly passes to another with an almost imperceptible transition: what began as a listing of kinds of lives determined by location or profession becomes a list of external phenomena, the awareness of which enhances conscious existence, enhances life. This is a movement of definition of the self from what we are—what we do or where we live—to what we are not, to those things of nature that are external to us. And it is against these external realities—through perception and acknowledgment—that we come to full self-definition, the state that must be achieved before transcendence can occur.

Finally, and most important, the stanza presents in its last two lines the crucial merging of the hermit thrush, "the unrivall'd one," with the speaker. Whitman achieves this through the ambiguity of referent in the final line: both bird and speaker seem to be "Solitary, singing in the West." Ultimately this list presents a movement through a number of categorical transitions from the starting point of self-realization toward the momentary identification with another form. At its conclusion the speaker finds a version of himself in the external world, a being that generates beautiful songs freely, and naturally, compelled only by the force within it. Characterized by its trills, quaverings, and rapid modulations, the expression of both, the one instinctive and the other appearing to be so, is "controlled not by rules or method but by the intensely personal pulsations and periodicities" that govern the creative act, as Pearce describes it. "Such pulsations and periodicities are expressions of the energy of the creative self," he adds, "and they cannot be plotted in advance: they can only be released and followed out to their transformative end."[36]

Striking out for a new world of poetic form, Whitman likewise sang his characteristic songs, using variations of listing that seemed to have all the added grace of unpremeditated improvisation, poured spontaneously like the unrehearsed songs of the thrush. *Leaves of Grass,* as a volume of such songs, resonates with these undulating rhythms and with the new and unforeseen patternings he built around permutations of enumeration. The structures of these lists, however, are painstakingly deliberate, requiring intense concentration to achieve poetic dynamism rather than quiescent inventory.

Disposed in his signature elastic forms, Whitman's instances of poetic listing display a multiplicity of structural possibilities and serve a variety of purposes. Many elaborate particular ad hoc patterns through syntactical manipulations or experiments with lineation. Alternation of syntactical groupings and developments between groupings become significant features for poems containing particularly discursive catalogues or enumerations. Other listings take shape in unique linear patternings where the arrangement of items is configured in a deliberate fashion. In Section 6 of "Song of Myself," the child's question "What is the grass?" invites many fitting replies, given in the form of a list of suppositions. The section represents an isolated instance of patterning: the poet arranges stanzas of different lengths through an expanding sequence of 2 lines, 1 line, 3, 1, 4, 1.[37] Besides this mathematical design, the series of responses presents an arc that recapitulates the broader themes of the poem, a sequential consideration of the relations of the grass to the self, to God, to birth, to life, and to death.

> A child said *What is the grass?* fetching it to me with full
> hands;

How could I answer the child? I do not know what it is any
   more than he.

I guess it must be the flag of my disposition, out of hopeful
   green stuff woven.

Or I guess it is the handkerchief of the Lord,
A scented gift and remembrancer designedly dropt,
Bearing the owner's name someway in the corners, that we
   may see and remark, and say *Whose?*

Or I guess the grass is itself a child, the produced babe of the
   vegetation.

Or I guess it is a uniform hieroglyphic,
And it means, Sprouting alike in broad zones and narrow
   zones,
Growing among black folks as among white,
Kanuck, Tuckahoe, Congressman, Cuff, I give them the same,
   I receive them the same.

And now it seems to me the beautiful uncut hair of graves.
   [*W*, 192–193]

Sequencing is important throughout Whitman's work; the poet
constantly reconsidered the effects of arranging collections of individual items, lines, even entire poems. We see this in the shuffling
that differentiates the various editions of *Leaves of Grass:* the revision
of the sequences of poems from one edition to the next indicates a
continual effort by the poet to achieve an order of contents that, for
a particular moment at least, would convey a certain meaning that
could be expressed only in the "best" arrangement. For Whitman the
list offered opportunities to experiment with form, provided plat-
forms on which to display his broad sympathy with his fellow Amer-
icans, and facilitated the elaboration of different ways of conceiving
the relation of the individual to the surrounding world.

4
Melville

"There are some enterprises in which a careful
disorderliness is the true method"

Whitman's style is unquestionably unique, but there is
nevertheless a certain resemblance between *Leaves of
Grass* and Melville's *Moby-Dick* suggested by the long,
rhythmic lines, with their occasional ramifications, that are common to both works. In his Preface to the 1855 edition of *Leaves of
Grass,* Whitman wrote of how "the rhyme and uniformity of perfect
poems show the free growth of metrical laws and bud from them as
unerringly and loosely as lilacs or roses on a bush." His allusion to
natural subdivisions, and the implicit suggestion of the ease, confidence, and flawlessness with which they occur, aptly suits the
prose poetry of Melville as well. Melville even adopts the organic
metaphor on his own, writing at the beginning of one chapter of
Moby-Dick, "Out of the trunk, the branches grow; out of them the
twigs. So, in productive subjects, grow the chapters." A principal
characteristic of *Moby-Dick,* as one scholar has described it, is its
preference "for letting branches, even twigs, grow as they will."[1]

In certain passages of the novel, heavily laden branches of factual details abound; in others, Ishmael adds vigor to his arguments through bundled accumulations of rhetorical questions. Elsewhere the writing takes Rabelaisian flight, extending "the sin of rhapsody," as one reviewer phrased it, over "all manner of philosophic, philo-logic, physiologic, zoologic and metaphysic reveries as regards whales and whaling."[2] There is a broad diversity of structural forms of listing in *Moby-Dick,* and different techniques of compilation produce different effects, but the extensive practice of listing here fulfills a significant purpose in the the novel as a whole. The digres-sions and amplifications in Ishmael's narration, the breadth and plenitude of facts and details, and the proliferation of inner forms, by suspending the temporal advance of the plot, are integral to what makes *Moby-Dick* remarkable. More than a sea adventure elevated to Shakespearean grandeur, the novel defies both description and criticism in part because of the dexterity of its raconteur. As one reviewer phrased it during the Melville revaluation of the 1920s, *Moby-Dick* is "a glorious example of what can be done with words urged to their task by a willing spirit."[3]

The purpose of this chapter is to consider the list in *Moby-Dick.* Like Ishmael and his whales, I "shall not pretend to a minute anatomical description of the various species" (*MD,* 165). I find myself caught, as it were, between two notions best expressed by Melville himself. On the one hand, as Melville wrote in "Hawthorne and His Mosses," "It is hard to be finite upon an infinite subject, and all subjects are infinite." On the other, as Ishmael laments, "This whole book is but a draught—nay, but the draught of a draught. Oh, Time, Strength, Cash, and Patience!" (*MD,* 176).

Since the inception of the novel, writers have devised abundant occasions for lists, a practice that neither began nor ended with Melville. Lists of possessions, for example, which became increas-ingly common as national and international trade expanded, al-lowed writers to use listing as a method of characterization: indi-viduals were identified by the accumulation of things they owned. Frank Norris's *McTeague* paints its title character by listing the bargain furnishings of his dental parlors intermingled with signs of his unsophisticated tastes, including a canary, a concertina, and a "steel engraving of the court of Lorenzo de' Medici, which he had bought because there were a great many figures in it for the money." McTeague's connection to these objects runs throughout the novel, but while the engraving is cheaply comical, the concertina later becomes a fateful clue to Trina's whereabouts, and the canary, clumsily lugged through the California desert in its gilt cage, serves as a fitting symbol of the spirit imprisoned by insatiable avarice.

In *Uncle Tom's Cabin,* the "shiftless" state of the St. Claire kitchen, described by Harriet Beecher Stowe in all its "hurryscurryation" corresponds to the disruption of domestic economy caused by slavery, as Gillian Brown has shown.[4] Furthermore, the chaos described there is symptomatic of a greater malaise, an inverted state wherein men, women, and children are considered articles and commodities rather than human beings, a practice that prompted Stowe to originally subtitle her novel "The Man That Was a Thing." The inventory of *Tom Sawyer*'s whitewash takings, a humorous artistic excess, is indicative of Twain's fascination with children's play and is used by the author to set the greed and murder of the adult world into relief against the innocence of childhood.

Other instances abound: Gatsby's party guests, Dos Passos's depiction of the manifold "Unknown Soldier" in *U.S.A.,* the inventories of 7 Eccles Street, Dublin, in *Ulysses.* Inevitably, certain lists will be of more consequence than others for the work in which they are found. In *Robinson Crusoe,* for example, Defoe elaborates an extended list of the items that his eponymous castaway removes from his wrecked ship. The enumeration fulfills important novelistic functions, but it is not characteristic of the novel as a whole. This instance of enumeration, which runs for several paragraphs, is an isolated incident that is significant for specific contributions to the novel (in verisimilitude and plot, among others), not a structural device that the author turns to repeatedly. Nevertheless it is a celebrated instance of listing in novel genre, and one that we can compare with the different usages of the device found in *Moby-Dick*.

The list of things Crusoe salvages from the shipwreck is presented in a prose form interspersed with narrative; it is not a vertically stacked recapitulation of the objects the protagonist recovers. In this way, the list presents the items more or less as they are come upon, so that the passages serve to express both the actions of collecting (which occurs during a dozen trips to the wreck) and the items that are collected. The episode is important to the book because it serves to outfit the marooned man with provisions necessary for his survival. Crusoe secures food, tools, arms, and other supplies from the wreck, and they enable him to establish his dwelling and subsist despite his circumstances. It is necessary for the castaway to have some implements to survive, and if the author is to give Crusoe's achievement an air of verisimilitude, he must demonstrate to the reader both what implements were acquired and where from. The enumeration thus underpins the greater plot by establishing the source of the necessities, and in addition it attests to Crusoe's luck and resourcefulness. It is fortuitous that certain key items are present at all and that Crusoe is able to recover them, and significant that he has the foresight and determination to secure them for future use.

Nevertheless, this list has particular stylistic traits that fortify its interaction with the rest of the text. Thus, in addition to its explanatory role in demonstrating where certain necessary implements come from, the list is arranged in a manner that is useful to the encompassing narrative. It is an inventory, but it is not written as a pragmatic checklist. It summarizes provisions secured from several trips to the wreck, "in which Time [Crusoe] had brought away all that one Pair of Hands could well be suppos'd capable to bring." The incremental approach conveys Crusoe's practicality, as he determines what are the first necessities and what he can leave for later visits ("having consider'd well what I most wanted," he states early in his recollection). He does not take everything of value on the first trip but discovers some key items later, giving not a strict hierarchical order of priorities but rather a mixed arrangement determined by a blend of necessity, luck, and a pragmatic approach to the items' removal. This highlights the action of collecting, as Crusoe searches some areas twice or stumbles across previously unseen items.

In addition, Crusoe's memory is a factor; he recalls who on board the ship had what and where specific items might have been stored before the wreck. This directs him to certain key articles and thus helps define the list's sequence. The passage also lists various items that could have been of use but have now been lost or ruined (some of the grain was destroyed by seawater, some casks are cracked). Furthermore, one load of cargo tumbles irretrievably into the water. In establishing verisimilitude, this inclusion of what has been lost also serves to delimit Crusoe's fortune.

Overall, then, this enumeration serves practical purposes in and for the novel. It works as a statement of fact that establishes the manner of things Crusoe will have at his disposal, and it also helps define Crusoe's capabilities. It thus serves to establish setting and character for the adventure. It concludes, however, with a turn of purpose when Crusoe discovers some scattered coins and precious metals. The pieces of money are the last things removed from the wreck before it breaks up, and they initiate a moment of philosophical pause. The situation is rich in irony: the coins are obviously worthless on a deserted island, but Crusoe is nevertheless human, and—perhaps anticipating a future return to society, perhaps just plain unable to shake the deeply ingrained idea that money is a good thing—he takes the coins: "I found about Thirty six Pounds value in Money, some European Coin, some Brazil, some Pieces of Eight, some Gold, some Silver. I smil'd to my self at the Sight of this Money, O Drug Said I aloud, what art thou good for, Thou art not worth to me, no not the taking off of the Ground, one of those Knives is worth all this Heap, I have no Manner of use for thee, e'en remain where thou art, and go to the Bottom as a Creature whose

Life is not worth saving. However, upon Second Thoughts, I took it away."

Crusoe's salvaging efforts run for several paragraphs. They are exceptionally meticulous, and it is only by Defoe's contrivance of an approaching storm that the itemization is curtailed. (As Crusoe states, "Had the calm Weather held, I should have brought away the whole Ship Piece by Piece," and what a catalogue that would have been!) Nevertheless, to summarize in our own list the character of the *Crusoe* list, we might say that it is:

- more inclusive than exclusive because it incorporates all the things Crusoe might possibly have been able to use, including items that are lost or ruined;
- ordered according to when Crusoe recovers the items in the many trips to the wreck; disorder and randomness are not philosophically important features of this list, except as they reflect the manner in which the various things are encountered; and
- generally static in its developmental principles. It stays close to pure inventory by consistently recording what is removed, except for the brief rumination triggered by the discovery of the money, and the irony of that concluding turn.

Altogether, Defoe situates the list within the context of the novel in such a way that it advances plot and character development. We read through it in the same way we read through the rest of the narrative. Put another way, we could say that the enumeration is the narrative, rather than merely something inserted into it. Its overall effect is different from that of a straightforward checklist of things taken from the ship.

When Melville deploys enumerative forms in *Moby-Dick*, in contrast, the results are entirely different. Though Melville uses many enumerative strategies throughout the novel (rhetorical accumulations, tabulations, classifications), there are no instances of cataloguing that serve an inventorial purpose similar to that found in *Robinson Crusoe*. This is to say that there are no passages where individualized items are counted out simply to record the quantities of various materials on hand. One pragmatic reason for this is that the catalogue of items salvaged by Crusoe is precipitated by the sinking of the ship early in the book, whereas *Moby-Dick* ends with the sinking of the *Pequod*. The former shipwreck initiates the adventure narrative, creating a situation where the survival of the protagonist and his tale depend upon securing provisions. The latter sinking concludes Ishmael's narrative, annihilating cast and crew. In contrast to the property Crusoe is fortunate enough to salvage, here the only item recovered is Queequeg's coffin. While the casket that becomes a life-preserver is the capstone of a novel dense with emblems, nevertheless, one item does not a list make.

Melville had himself created marvelous opportunities for listing in his first novel, *Typee*, using the adventure-narrative platform to assemble lists of exotic sights and experiences, the expected staples of this popular genre. Nevertheless, under the influence of great texts available to him in Evert Duyckinck's library, he cultivated a broader conception of what a novel was to do and consequently conceived of other ingenious occasions in which to list. *Moby-Dick* eventually contained a multitude of permutations of listing. Some of these are strict inventories, but others take more complex forms.

One might read the reiterative oratory of Father Mapple's sermon as one variation of listing ("Woe to him whom this world charms from Gospel duty! Woe to him who seeks to pour oil upon the waters. . . . Woe to him. . . . Woe to him . . ." [*MD*, 75]), and Ishmael's vigorously propounded examples of whiteness as another ("by the Persian fire worshippers, the white forked flame being held the holiest on the altar; and in the Greek mythologies, Great Jove himself being made incarnate in a snow-white bull; and though to the noble Iroquois . . . " [*MD*, 224]). Similarly, some descriptive passages (such as the account of the legendary weapons on the wall of the Spouter Inn, or the catalogue of the bounty of the *Bachelor*,

with every conceivable container filled with sperm oil, or the graceful delineation of the rise and fall of the open ocean) share certain
listing characteristics with the Ishmaelean cetological classification
system: they particularize components and arrange them, sometimes for thoroughness, sometimes for comic effect.

Lists frequently lend humor to the novel, as when Ishmael's enthusiastic monologue mounts in stepwise increments, or when he
brings together a satirical assemblage of items. One amusing instance occurs in the chapter "Merry Christmas," when Captain
Bildad's send-off leads to a round of moral and economic instructions. His slight but farcical set of rules seems as attentive to the
health of the profit register as to the spiritual well-being of the crew:

> "Be careful in the hunt, ye mates. Don't stave the boats need-
> lessly, ye harpooneers; good white cedar plank is raised full
> three per cent. within the year. Don't forget your prayers, ei-
> ther. Mr. Starbuck, mind that cooper don't waste the spare
> staves. . . . Don't whale it too much a' Lord's days, men; but
> don't miss a fair chance either, that's rejecting Heaven's good
> gifts. Have an eye to the molasses tierce, Mr. Stubb; it was a lit-
> tle leaky, I thought. If ye touch at the islands, Mr. Flask, beware
> of fornication. . . . Don't keep that cheese too long down in the
> hold, Mr. Starbuck; it'll spoil. Be careful with the butter—
> twenty cents the pound it was." [*MD*, 134–135]

One might even consider the series of encounters the *Pequod* has
with other ships as a list with a deliberate order, having a consequence to its sequence. These gams, as Walter Bezanson has suggested, variously may indicate "a group of metaphysical parables, a
series of Biblical analogues, a masque of the situations confronting
man, a pageant of the humors within men, [and] a parade of nations," among other interpretations.[5]

Some passages take the form of lists when Ishmael engages in
ecphrastic exercises. In "Loomings," he performs what John Hollander calls a "notional ecphrasis," the description of a purely fictional artwork.[6] Ishmael depicts a dreamy romantic landscape,

with hackneyed elements distributed here and there: "There stand [the artist's] trees, each with a hollow trunk, as if a hermit and a crucifix were within; and here sleeps his meadow, and there sleep his cattle; and up from yonder cottage goes a sleepy smoke. Deep into distant woodlands winds a mazy way, reaching to overlapping spurs of mountains in their hillside blue" (*MD*, 26). (The vitalizing force yet to be tabulated, and the integrating center of the painting, is, of course, water.) Ishmael elsewhere executes a vivid representational ecphrasis of a painting that captures the staving of a boat by a sperm whale. Though forced to particularize the elements of the painting in the linear unwinding of his description, he reckons the fragments of the instant of the confused drama:

> A noble Sperm Whale is depicted in full majesty of might, just risen beneath the boat from the profundities of the ocean, and bearing high in the air upon his back the terrific wreck of the stoven planks. The prow of the boat is partially unbroken, and is drawn just balancing upon the monster's spine; and standing in that prow, for that one single incomputable flash of time, you behold an oarsman, half shrouded by the incensed boiling spout of the whale, and in the act of leaping, as if from a precipice. The half-emptied line-tub floats on the whitened sea; the wooden poles of the spilled harpoons obliquely bob in it; the heads of the swimming crew are scattered about the whale in contrasting expressions of affright; while in the black stormy distance the ship is bearing down upon the scene. [*MD*, 308–309]

In addition, Ishmael's impulsive tendency toward rhetorical amplification repeatedly emerges; as Richard Brodhead characterizes it, "Having half-said something, [his] urge is always to stop and say it again."[7] Ishmael will frequently say in three sentences what could be said in one, for example providing three metaphors in illustration or three enthusiastic statements of exaggeration. Reiteration and repetition are common, appearing when Ishmael revels in legal oratory in his intercession on behalf of whaling in "The Advocate" or in the philosophical near-hyperbole of "Fast-Fish and Loose-Fish": "What are the Rights of Man and the Liberties of the World but Loose-Fish? What all men's minds and opinions but Loose-Fish? What is the principle of religious belief in them but a Loose-Fish? What to the ostentatious smuggling verbalists are the thoughts of thinkers but Loose-Fish? What is the great globe itself but a Loose-Fish? And what are you, reader, but a Loose-Fish and a Fast-Fish, too?" (*MD*, 449).

In *The Order of Things,* Michel Foucault observed that it is "partial identities or resemblances that make a *taxonomia* possible."[8] But partial likenesses similarly enable *metaphora:* the relational systems of both taxonomy and metaphor are based on connecting the similarities between things that are different. Throughout *Moby-Dick,* Ishmael consistently favors the figurative application of comparison (as in the above passage), and resists its pedantic, scientific use. The antipathy toward the science of natural history frequently shows through, as when Ishmael complains in his splendid excursus on cetological taxonomy, "It is by endless subdivisions based on the most inconclusive differences, that some departments of natural history become so repellingly intricate" (*MD*, 168). Hence he champions his own bibliographical system of classification, one that is at once brilliantly simple (with size as its basis) and marvelously resonant in its consciously literary aspects.

In addition to near-redundancy, a more significant mode of literary repetition in *Moby-Dick* is Melville's echoing of literary precursors, manifested in the novel in allusions to other works, imitations of the styles of other writers, and outright quotations. Of the many possible examples, consider Ishmael's antagonism toward systematics, or the science of classification. In the brilliant "Cetology" chapter, Ishmael asserts that he takes "the good old fashioned ground that the whale is a fish" (*MD*, 166), although Linnaeus had separated whales and fish because of their morphological differences. Robert Southey's similarly sprawling, allusive, and opinionated work *The Doctor* had earlier proclaimed the whale's place among the fish, "so very like a fish it is,—so strongly in the odour of fishiness . . . whatever the Cyclopaedists may think." The narrator of *The Doctor* is as skeptical of the Classificationists as is Ishmael, and just as witty: "But whether Whale be fish or flesh, or if makers of system should be pleased to make it fowl, (for as it is like a Quadruped except that it has no feet, and cannot live upon land, so may it be like a bird, except that it has neither legs, wings, nor feathers, and cannot live in the air,) wherever naturalists may arrange it, its local habitation is among fishes, and fish in common language it always will be called" (chap. 82: "A wish concerning whales, with some remarks upon their place in physical and moral classification").

Melville's vast reading has been well documented, and many studies corroborate the influences of various works on *Moby-Dick*, highlighting Melville's adaptation of such diverse authors as Milton, Shakespeare, Browne, Rabelais, Carlyle, and Captain Scoresby. The influence of other writers detectable in Melville's work has been alternately praised and damned by his readers and critics. From its first appearance, for every review that complimented the digressions of *Mardi* or *Moby-Dick* as "examples of thoughtful writing, and very extensive reading, much in the manner of Sir Thomas Browne, and with a dash of old Burton and Sterne" (*London Examiner*, 31 March 1849), there have been less flattering responses. A reviewer for the *Boston Post* wrote, perhaps not inaccurately, that *Mardi* reminded him of "the talk in Rabelais, divested of all its coarseness, and, it may be added, of all its wit and humor" (18 April 1849). Another reviewer rejected the frequent comparison of Melville to Defoe, writing that "the charm of de Foe is his simplicity of style, and artistic accuracy of description; [Melville] on the contrary is, at times ambitiously gorgeous in style, and at others abrupt in his simplicity" (*Holden's Dollar Magazine*, January 1850).

Regardless of these assessments, *Moby-Dick* in essence begins with its own bibliography in the "Extracts." Since a single quotation could never adequately serve an epigraphic role for this novel, Melville provides a list of eighty instead. Voraciously allusive, the

novel opens by frankly collecting an extensive but seemingly disconnected series of quotations to gesture at its epic scope and to ac-
cord formal credit where credit is due. The "glancing bird's eye view
of what has been promiscuously said, thought, fancied and sung of
Leviathan" (*MD*, 12) gestures toward the historical and imaginative
background that infuses the greater text. (Note that in the first
British edition, entitled *The Whale*, the "Extracts" concluded the
novel; this led to a very different reading experience.) Although the
speaker is at this point anonymous, an unnamed "I" curiously attempts to shift responsibility for the collection to a third party, the
Sub-Sub-Librarian. The speaker clearly empathizes with the Sub-
Sub, who functions as a convenient stand-in for Melville in his research into all things cetological. Yet as if to distance himself from
the dusty and painstaking burrowing and grubbing of collecting—
and perhaps to shield himself from accusations that the tale that
follows is too dependent upon preexisting works—the controlling
voice dismisses the collector and modestly undervalues the role of
the "higgledy-piggledy" set of quotations.

Readers have been zealous in interpreting the arrangement of
this collection, speculating, for instance, on various meanings to
be found in the order of the quotations. Is it coincidental that the
thirtieth entry mentions monetary rewards given the first crew-
man to spot a whale, and there are thirty men in the crew of the *Pequod?* But to focus merely on the specific sequence of citations, I
believe, is misguided. Certainly the first extract, from Genesis, is
significant, since it derives from a privileged work of origination.
But though there is a general chronological development through
the complete set, the overall movement from one entry to the next
rather anticipates the shifting habits of the chapters that follow,
and the meandering of the whale ship across bleak seas. Besides
previewing and reviewing the broad scope of materials that will
be used in the text, this "pre-pendix" (part preface, part appendix)
fulfills other roles as well. It presents a literary-historical timeline
across which is spread the whole subject of the whale, reinforcing

its perpetuity throughout all periods of history and prefiguring the immortality and ubiquity of the Whale, Moby Dick. Further, it recapitulates the literary canon to which this novel will add itself. We might say that here Melville consumes his predecessors in his leviathanic work.

To retreat to the book's first pages for a moment, it is important to recall that the "Extracts" are actually the second collection of the novel, and the Sub-Sub Librarian the second subordinate nominally delegated to the task of compiling material. *Moby-Dick* in fact begins with the "late consumptive Usher" haunting the vestibule of the novel, the "Etymology," where the collecting figure fulfills the dual role of doorkeeper and assistant teacher. The encyclopedist Isadore wrote in his compendium *Etymologies*, "Omnis enim rei inspectio etymologia cognito planior est" (Any investigation of a thing is more plain once its etymology is revealed; vol. 1). Similarly, Leo Spitzer noted in his essay "Linguistics and Literary History" that "an etymology introduces meaning into the meaningless."[9] Melville's double-columned list, however, is fragmented into thirteen assorted entries, and, despite certain family resemblances, it makes clear that the singular "Etymon," or true name of the thing, will elude comprehension because of a Babel-like confusion of tongues:

חן,	*Hebrew.*
κῆτος,	*Greek.*
CETUS,	*Latin.*
WHÆL,	*Anglo-Saxon.*
HVAL,	*Danish.*
WAL,	*Dutch.*
HWAL,	*Swedish.*
HVALUR,	*Icelandic.*
WHALE,	*English.*
BALEINE,	*French.*
BALLENA,	*Spanish.*
PEKEE-NUEE-NUEE,	*Fegee.*
PEHEE-NUEE-NUEE,	*Erromangoan.* [*MD*, 11]

The investigation here is not made more plain; it is rather made more complicated by additional possibilities, particularly when the fiercely independent terms from the Tropics burst onto the linguistic scene with the declarative force of a whale's arching breach. These last entries are etymologically isolated but nevertheless claim their positions among the languages of the ancient and modern worlds, the first languages of literature, and the languages of nautical exploration and world dominion. By their enigmatic presentations, these tabulations force the reader to speculate upon their significance. Ultimately, both "Etymologies" and "Extracts" gesture toward the novel's complexity, and indicate the historical, philological, and imaginative continua through which and across which it will selectively operate.

Coincident with its unrestrained pleasure in verbal play, the narrative of *Moby-Dick* shifts through many literary forms and styles, with abrupt changes that seem to interrupt what might be considered the plot of a traditional sea narrative. Melville was not the first to assemble a compendium of forms and styles in a single work. Renaissance theorists considered Homer's foundational encyclopedic epics the source of all literary forms, as well as of all arts and sciences. Milton, in devising his own seventeenth-century comprehensive epic, interwove a multiplicity of literary forms with such extraordinary precision that, to paraphrase Barbara Lewalski, the movement from "less to more noble genres (or varieties within a particular genre)" within *Paradise Lost* could be seen to correspond to the movement in moral understanding that occurs within it.[10]

In *Moby-Dick,* digressions and intrusions take a variety of forms, including short stories, dramatic monologues, satire, zoological or legal treatises, encyclopedias, and manuals. As Ishmael assimilates the descriptive and expressive means of literary and subliterary genres—sermons, ghost stories, travelogues, tall tales, epics, lyric poetry, and drama—he enfolds his narrative in an ever more complex system of languages. It is further complicated by the narrator's personal advance through a series of stages (neophyte, armchair naturalist, yarner) and by the rendering of the various characters with speaking parts. Queequeg, Bildad, the Cook, Starbuck, Ahab, and Pip each has his own phraseologies, with unique vocabularies and grammatical peculiarities. The novel even incorporates what we consider nonliterary forms and makes them important contributors. "Whaling Voyage of One Ishmael" reads as an interlude on a Barnumesque playbill, situated between an election and a battle;[11] lost sailors are memorialized on the wall of the Whalemen's Chapel, their markers indicating their fates with a reductive single sentence; a nongrammatical list of goods fleshes out the practical but arcane management of a whaling fleet.

Although *Moby-Dick* bombards the reader with information, it is continually undermining the validity of that information. A major theme seems to be that what can be acquired from books is one remove distant from what can be experienced, which is at another remove from what actually is. Though Ishmael propounds at length, citing all manner of evidence regarding the whale, he is frequently evasive. He states, for example, that "the sperm whale, scientific or poetic, lives not complete in any literature" (*MD*, 164) or notes, "Unless you own the whale, you are but a provincial and sentimentalist in Truth" (*MD*, 385). He further mocks the inadequacy of representation and claims that "there is no earthly way of finding out precisely what the whale really looks like" (*MD*, 387). Even to consider a single aspect of the whale becomes too much: "The more I consider this mighty tail, the more do I deplore my inability to express it" (*MD*, 428).

It is the contradictory nature of the novel to discharge a barrage of information in an attempt to get readers to "know" the whale and at the same time to assert condescendingly that as readers they cannot know it: "Only in the heart of quickest peril; only when within the eddyings of his angry flukes; only on the profound unbounded sea, can the fully invested whale be truly and livingly found out" (*MD*, 507). In turn, even direct contact with the whale—face-to-face confrontation with Nature, with the Other—cannot make certain an understanding of what is not knowable. Ahab's drive to pierce through the "pasteboard mask" of materiality to the "inscrutable thing" behind is ambitious but impossible. His error, as Wai-Chee Dimock has phrased it, is his desperate effort to "reduce indeterminate text to determinate meaning."[12] He has obdurately interpreted directed malevolence, an offensive malice that has personally singled him out, from what is an unreadable blankness.

In "Hawthorne and His Mosses," Melville confessed that he valued the inspired articulations about truth that he found in Shakespeare, "those short, quick probings at the very axis of reality." In attempting to comprehend Moby Dick, both Ahab and Ishmael strive to reach truth, that is, to achieve a realization of ultimate reality. The whale, an ambiguous entity that might be malicious or indifferent or indeed central to the universe, therefore serves a dual role as an object of both physical and metaphysical capture. While Ahab single-mindedly endeavors to pierce to the ineffable center with the overdetermined hurl of his harpoon, Ishmael makes numerous small "stabs at truth." He accumulates as much information as possible, from as many vantage points as he can, always realizing that complete knowledge of the ineffable will escape him.

Both Ahab and Ishmael attempt to lead others to "know" the whale. Ahab commands the ship from Nantucket through the perilous oceans with this single purpose. Ishmael likewise strives to bring his readers into contact with Moby Dick; he attempts to introduce the audience to the immeasurable and ultimately unknowable crux the creature symbolizes. For Ishmael, the whale represents an essence that, though affording dim hints of its meaning, can never be completely comprehended, no matter how thoroughly probed, measured, and analyzed. As summarized by one reader, "While one may observe the living majesty of the whale and gain poetic insight from contemplating him, a definable totality eludes the rational intellect."[13] The subplot of the great chase involves this exploration of the limits of human knowledge and the inadequacy of human learning. "Dissect him how I may, then, I go but skin deep; I know him not, and never will" (*MD*, 428), Ishmael admits. "Nescio quid sit" (I do not know what it is) is an important theme repeated throughout the novel. It is an acknowledgment of human limitation that suggests that scientific methods of investigation can assess only the surfaces of things, leaving the deep meanings of the nature of reality (and the reality of nature) undiscovered.[14]

At the conclusion of the novel, the whale escapes transfixion by Ahab's harpoon and likewise eludes the reader's endeavor to pin it with certain and unambiguous meaning. On the level of plot, the deaths of Ahab and the crew end the pursuit, but significantly the sole surviving witness to the scene escapes by having been tossed from the boat. Ishmael, as the creative force of the imagination, survives because he is deflected from the single-minded determination to master the whale. By being dumped overboard, he is freed from the obligation of pinpointing for the reader what the whale ultimately signifies. Ahab's monomaniacal will to strike through to the hated inscrutable thing behind the pasteboard mask leads to his destruction. By contrast, Ishmael succeeds in attaining a better albeit dim approximation of the ultimate fact (that "dead, blind wall") by employing a multiplicity of approaches and being consistently uncommitted in his lengthy metaphrasis. It is Ishmael's unmethodical method of seeking truth that proves meaningful. This gives the novel its form even if at the end he provides no definitive articulation of that truth. "I try all things," Ishmael states; "I achieve what I can" (*MD*, 393), and Melville could have said the same of himself. The journey toward the whale is a journey through many literary genres, many authors. The novel's success is the success of Melville's particular imagination, a creative force that is broadly allusive and adopts a variety of vocabularies.

The dual purpose of Melville's novel is to portray these two journeys—Ahab's single-minded search for vengeance, directing the course of the *Pequod,* and Ishmael's circuitous pursuit of truth, producing the tale of its fated voyage.[15] The two are inseparable—

Ishmael has no story without Ahab's driving obsession, and Ahab cannot advance without an Ishmael to tell it. Both Ahab and Ishmael are directed toward their respective goals, but both require an array of provisions to effect their advances. While Ahab's undertaking requires a heterogeneous blend of ship, capital, manpower, skill, experience, and character, Ishmael's requires a variety of literary forms, inspired by Melville's studious reading and his personal experience.

On the second day of the chase, at the midpoint of the three-chapter sequence in which the action has finally broken free of the weighty fact, instruction, and diverting commentary, the narrative plunges headlong into a previously unsustained suspenseful style of writing. Here is a fitting description of the motley—and polysemous—*Pequod:* "They were one man, not thirty. For as the one ship that held them all; though it was put together of all contrasting things—oak, and maple, and pine wood; iron, and pitch, and hemp—yet all these things ran into each other in the one concrete hull, which shot on its way, both balanced and directed by the long central keel; even so, all the individualities of the crew, this man's valor, that man's fear; guilt and guiltlessness, all the varieties were wedded into oneness, and were all directed to that fatal goal which Ahab their one lord and keel did point to" (*MD,* 619).

With Ahab as lord and keel, both ship and novel keep to their pursuit of the whale. Ahab is unswerving in his intention, though he must take unnumbered tacks, endure untimely delays, and move in many directions—physically and psychologically—to come across Moby Dick again. Ishmael's narrative likewise moves in many directions, adopting different tones and even making extreme temporal shifts. The heterogeneity of form in the novel reflects the mixed quality of the crew. Mates, harpooneers, cooks, blacksmiths, carpenters, and various mad fools necessary to the operation of a whaling vessel each contribute special abilities and limitations to the enterprise. Similarly, Ishmael uses a variety of formal devices in his story, "all the varieties wedded into oneness." Because it is a compendium of many modes of writing, the text brings the reader closer to know-ing the complete whale than any single approach could.

In his undeviating attack on Moby Dick, Ahab is consumed, and he causes others to be consumed as well. In contrast to this doomed single-mindedness, Ishmael's method of getting close to the whale, at least in a metaphorical sense, requires the use of a more varied armamentarium. This includes many different ap-proaches to the specific whale known as Moby Dick, and to whales and whaling in general. The result is an account that is an accumu-lation of data composed of "fact"—sometimes verifiable, some-times erroneous, and sometimes fictive—story, myth, and what-ever other peculiar detail Ishmael might supply.

In considering how Ishmael writes this natural history, it is use-ful to again consult Foucault's *The Order of Things*. In its tracing of the history of natural histories, the elegant chapter "Classifying" de-scribes the evolution of the genre. "Until the time of Aldovandi," Foucault recounts,

> history was the inextricable and completely unitary fabric of all that was visible of things and of the signs of what had been discovered or lodged in them: to write the history of a plant or animal was as much a matter of describing its elements or or-gans as of describing the resemblances that could be found in it, the virtues that it was thought to possess, the legends and stories with which it had been involved, its page in heraldry, the medicaments that were concocted from its substance, the foods it provided, what the ancients recorded of it, and what travelers might have said of it. The history of a living being was that being itself, within the whole semantic network that con-nected it to the world. The division, so evident to us, between what we see, what others have observed and handed down, and what others imagine or naively believe, the great tripartition, apparently so simple and so immediate, into Observation, Document, and Fable, did not exist.

However, Foucault notes also that after Linnaeus the descriptive or-der intended for the natural history was of a very different character. According to this order, "everything dealing with a given animal should follow the following plan: name, theory, kind, species, attributes, use, and to conclude, litteraria. All the language deposited upon things by this time is pushed back into the very last category."[16]

Ishmael states at the beginning of "The Honour and Glory of Whaling," "There are some enterprises in which a careful disorderliness is the true method" (*MD*, 410). Melville's treatise on the whale, like the other great asymmetrical works he so clearly loved, resists the kinds of compartmentalization dictated by scientific authority in favor of eclectic heterogeneity. Indeed, this novel repudiates the ethos of systematism and embraces instead genuine inventiveness. While reading the novel, we become ever more convinced of the veracity of Comte Buffon's memorable statement, "Nothing really exists in nature except individuals[;] . . . genera, orders, and classes exist only in our imagination."[17]

Melville seems to have been haunted by *Robinson Crusoe* throughout most of his creative life. Like Defoe's great first novel, Melville's *Typee* similarly contains an early inventory of articles brought from a ship, a collection of items on which the narrator overdetermines the fate of his adventure to "very probably" depend. Although there is only a passing reference to *Crusoe* in that novel, Melville's early reviewers emphasized comparisons between the two. The young Melville was referred to as "the De Foe of America," "a modernised Defoe," and "the De Foe of the Ocean," and the "authenticity" of his writing was held in the same ambiguous regard as Defoe's classic—considered fiction so true it could be believed, but acknowledged as fiction nevertheless. "This book [*Typee*] has all the *vraisemblance* of Robinson Crusoe—we hope it is at least as true," read one review (*New York Daily and Weekly Mirror*, 4 April 1846). A more discriminating critic admitted that "everybody knows that *Robinson Crusoe*

is a tale of the imagination, yet nobody publicly acknowledges the fact," before judging Melville's second novel, *Omoo*, to be as "fascinating a production . . . [though] twenty times less probable" (*London Times*, 24 September 1847). His third book, *Mardi*, however, was considered by a majority of his critical readers a "*Robinson Crusoe* run mad" (*London Examiner*, 31 March 1849).

In *Mardi*, published only two years before *Moby-Dick*, Melville had demonstrated that he was capable of writing inventories of provisions in the mode of *Robinson Crusoe* or *Swiss Family Robinson*, and was willing to do so. There is, for example, this passage of practical enumeration that could have appeared in *Moby-Dick* as part of the effort to give the minute particulars of whaling life: "Now, previous to leaving the ship, we had seen to it well, that our craft was supplied with all those equipments, with which, by the regulations of the fishery, a whale-boat is constantly provided: night and day, afloat or suspended. Hanging on our gunwales inside, were six harpoons, three lances, and a blubber-spade; all keen as razors, and sheathed with leather. Besides these, we had three waifs; a couple of two-gallon water-kegs, several balers, the boat-hatchet for cutting the whale-line, two auxiliary knives for the like purpose, and several minor articles, also employed in hunting the leviathan" (*MA*, 32).

Mardi, a peculiar work, marked an important point in Melville's evolution as a writer. Melville began the novel as what he described as "a bona-vide [*sic*] narrative of my adventures in the Pacific, continued from 'Omoo.'" It strayed radically, however, from the authenticity that his publisher John Murray demanded. Murray had complained to Melville that as yet there had been no means to prove to the English public that his books were not "imitations of *Robinson Crusoe*." "'Tis this Feeling of being tricked which impedes their Circulat[ion] here," Murray added. In response, a defiant Melville wrote, "I will give no evidence. . . . Truth is mighty & will prevail—& shall & must."[18]

Murray refused to publish fiction, but nevertheless it became clear to Melville in writing the book that *Mardi* was changing, and changing him as well. Though accused of being "a romancer in disguise" by reviewers of his previous books, and with Murray requesting "documentary evidence" of his seagoing experience, Melville was ministering to his own creative needs. It was while working on *Mardi* that he plundered private and public libraries, borrowing many volumes of Rabelais and Sir Thomas Browne, Burton's *Anatomy of Melancholy,* and other books. As Merrell Davis characterizes it in his detailed study of *Mardi,* "During these first months of 1848, Melville was experimenting with a whole range of new voices which the opening world of books helped to provide."[19]

Melville gave greater latitude to his imagination and intellect in his writing, apprising Murray of these developments. In his letter of 25 March 1848 regarding the progress of *Mardi,* he wrote: "Proceeding to my narrative of facts I began to feel an incurable distaste for the same; & a longing to plume my pinions for a flight, & I felt irked, cramped and fettered by plodding along with dull common places." Transformed by this exhilarated creative freedom (frequently figured by Melville with imagery of soaring and diving throughout his letters and works), *Mardi* shifts from sea narrative to fantastical travelogue to philosophical symposium. Like *Moby-Dick,* the novel oscillates wildly and refuses to conform to conventional generic description. *Mardi* is indeed rather like a *Moby-Dick* in embryo, wherein one can see the early stages of development, the generation of fundamental tissues, and the primitive formation of systems of a unique, self-sustaining organism. Leslie Stephen once observed that in *Robinson Crusoe* Defoe saw an allegory of his own fate, and he added that many of the best novels ever written have in them "the autobiographical element which makes a man speak from greater depths of feeling than in a purely imaginative story."[20] Melville's books drew on his personal experiences sailing in Polynesia and working in the whaling fleet, but only *Moby-Dick* consistently represented a more exhilarating intellectual journey: only through the pursuit of the White Whale would the author perfect his conception of the universe with the concentration that he could not dramatize in leisurely metaphysical South Seas island-hopping.

Nonetheless, *Mardi* does contain some surprisingly indulgent passages, explosions of verbal pyrotechnics for which we are totally unprepared. In a chapter fittingly entitled "The Center of Many Circumferences," there is a passage that evinces the kind of word manipulation characteristic of a line of writing that runs from Rabelais to Joyce. Here the island's king, Donjalolo, rests in the heart of his palace, encompassed by mats as "innumerable as the leaves of an endless folio": "And here, in this impenetrable retreat, centrally slumbered the universe-rounded, zodiac-belted, horizon-zoned, sea-girt, reef-sashed, mountain-locked, arbor-nested, royalty-girdled, arm-clasped, self-hugged, indivisible Donjalolo, absolute monarch of Juam:—the husk-inhusked meat in a nut; the innermost spark in a ruby; the juice-nested seed in a golden-rinded orange; the red royal stone in an effeminate peach; the insphered sphere of spheres" (*MA*, 240). Not only is Donjalolo the center of the universe, he is also typographically the center of the paragraph, surrounded by epithets worthy of Homer on one side, and succulent metaphors on the other.

Melville presents the series of compounds as concentric circles, with the largest, universe-spanning ring the first and outermost, and the closest, innermost circle "indivisible" from Donjalolo himself. The figurations that follow, aided by the self-sealing chiasmus of the near repetitive "husk-inhusked" and "insphered sphere," progress toward a Zenlike calm. There are other self-conscious lists in *Mardi*, including a guide to the *Chondropterygii* (an order of fish, such as sharks, rays, and sturgeons, that have cartilaginous endo-skeletons) that anticipates the "Cetology" chapter of *Moby-Dick*; a comical inventory of the rarities of the antiquarian Oh-Oh; a bibliographic collection of Oh-Oh's "ancient and curious manu-scripts"; and a fantastical last will and testament of the sage Bar-dianna. None of them, however, can match the formal precision of this list.

The orderly arrangements that pragmatic formats provide (that is, the different divisions and subdivisions of groupings and itemizations) offer an author numerous opportunities to experiment with organizational patterns. Further, they create instances for a writer to invent a diverse number of items to be gathered. The imaginative possibilities available to Melville were seemingly infinite, though they were of minor significance to either the plot or the philosophical agendas of *Mardi*. Such lists, much like the novel itself, affirm the origins of the word *improvisation*. Their developments are unexpected, unforeseen, *improvisus:* you never know what you are going to get. Consider, for example, the following congeries of laxatives and poultices bequeathed to an overly concerned (and appropriately named) neighbor, who "called daily to inquire after the state of my [Bardianna's] health . . . and nightly made tearful inquiries of my herb-doctor, concerning the state of my viscera": "I do hereby give and bequeath to the aforesaid Lakreemo all and sundry those vegetable pills, potions, powders, aperients, purgatives, expellatives, evacuatives, tonics, emetics, cathartics, clysters, injections, scarifiers, cataplasms, lenitives, lotions, decoctions, washes, gargles, and phlegmagogues; together with all the jars, calabashes, gourds, and gal[l]ipots, thereunto pertaining; situate, lying, and being in the west-by-north corner of my east-southeast crypt" (*MA*, 583).

The finished *Mardi* illustrated Melville's urge to move his writing away from the linear narrative of events common to adventure literature and across an expanded range of genres instead, across a range that indeed included hybrid forms and forms that fit into no generic category. Melville's biographer Hershel Parker notes how the adventure of simply writing *Mardi* and getting it published seemed to Melville to have been "altogether more hazardous than the threat of cannibalism he described in *Typee* and the actual imprisonment he described in *Omoo*."[21] Melville did not wish to be known as the modern Defoe but rather to be free to pursue "his own peculiar vein." As he wrote to Richard Bentley, the publisher who eventually lost money on *Mardi,* "Some of us scribblers, My Dear Sir, always have a certain something unmanageable in us, that bids us do this or that, and be done it must—hit or miss."

A peek into how Melville himself reevaluated "literature" can be seen in his review of J. Ross Browne's *Etchings of a Whaling Cruise.* This passage indirectly acknowledges the kind of writing Melville wished to avoid, and additionally suggests the personal regard with which he held the open sea as a source of inspiration: "From time immemorial many fine things have been said and sung of the sea. The days have been, when sailors were considered veritable mermen; and the ocean itself, as the peculiar theatre of the romantic and wonderful. But of late years there have been revealed so many plain, matter-of-fact details connected with nautical life that at the present day the poetry of salt water is very much on the wane. . . . Mr. J. Ross Browne's narrative tends still further to impair the charm with which poesy and fiction have invested the sea. It is a book of unvarnished facts."

It is important here to make the distinction between the "facts" of a novel as its narrative sequence of events (the plot), and the historical, scientific, and literary facts that a novel might make use of. In *Moby-Dick,* Melville composed a splendid "narrative of facts" in Ahab's chase of the White Whale, but he also compiled a vibrant assembly of facts of the latter sort as well. Indeed, one might argue that some of the novel's finest writing results when such facts, as isolated fragments of raw material, are subjected to what Newton Arvin artfully described as Melville's "imaginative anabolism." As Arvin characterized him, Melville was "almost incapable of leaving any piece of information in its raw state of unresonant factuality."[22]

Numerous readers have commented on how the catalogues of whaling knowledge add "ballast" to the novel. They enjoy the supply of detail, noting how Melville skillfully provides a wealth of particulars to establish an appropriately epic scope and efficiently prepare the uneducated mainlander in advance for the novel's fast and furious climax. Henry Pommer notes that it is a basic requirement of an epic that the author "turn a mass of confused splendors into a grand design, forcing parts to obey a single presiding unity of purpose." Others have observed that in his enthusiastic accumulation of whaling lore (particularly in the chapter "The Affidavit"), Ishmael amasses evidence for the veracity of the encounter with Moby Dick, and the unlikely event of locating one particular whale in all the world's wide waters. The novel's digressiveness has also been seen to defer the terror of the final encounter, and the relentless insertion of material variously to simulate the occasional periods of inactivity experienced in long voyages and to build suspense for the work's resolution.[23]

In an early essay about *Moby-Dick*, Van Wyck Brooks wrote of "Melville's insecure artistic control," noting that the author "forgets his story, [and] loses himself in the details of cetology" (*New York Freeman*, 26 October 1922). His later reappraisal, entitled "A Third Look at Melville," reflects a reconsideration regarding the incorporation of all this data into the text: "The book is an epic, and an epic requires ballast. Think of the catalogue of ships in Homer, the mass of purely historical information in the *Aeneid*, the long descriptions in *Paradise Lost:* how immeasurably these elements add to the density and the volume of the total impression, and how they serve to throw into relief the gestures and activities of the characters! This freight of inanimate or partially inanimate material gives *Moby-Dick* its bottom, its body, in the vintner's phrase; and I am convinced that Melville knew exactly what he was about" (*Freeman*, 16 May 1923).

Although it is much more than an encyclopedia of whaling information, *Moby-Dick* does indeed assemble a great number of facts. Lewis Mumford once observed that almost all the important works of the nineteenth century respected observations and facts, and in *Moby-Dick* Melville gives this kind of information almost material substantiality. Nevertheless, Melville's undertaking was twofold, and he progressed with one eye on the visible world, and the other on the invisible. The intent of the novel, as Arvin astutely wrote, was "to do justice both to 'visible objects' and to the immaterial reality that, as [Melville] believed, lies behind them."[24]

With the *Crusoe* listing once again in mind, we can consider how Melville handles similar material in *Moby-Dick*. The straightforward inventory Ishmael provides in the chapter "The Decanter" serves as a good illustration. The list is supposedly taken from a "Low Dutch book," and details the provisions necessary to outfit a fleet of whalers:

400,000	lbs. of beef.
60,000	lbs. of Friesland pork.
150,000	lbs. of stock fish.
550,000	lbs. of biscuit.
72,000	lbs. of soft bread.
2,800	firkins of butter.
20,000	lbs. Texel & Leyden cheese.
144,000	lbs. cheese (probably an inferior article).
550	ankers of Geneva.
10,800	barrels of beer. [*MD*, 499]

While the *Crusoe* inventory is integral to establishing the setting for the narrator's survival, Ishmael's list is borrowed, peripheral to his passage aboard the *Pequod*, and dropped into one of his many digressions. Thus its relevance to the plot is in sharp contrast to the cataloguing of necessities acquired by Crusoe. Ishmael is several removes from the materials itemized here, whereas Crusoe's survival (and the contingent narrative of that survival) depends upon the physical presence of what is close at hand. Ishmael is not unloading ships; rather, he is telling us what goes into them in one of his frequent digressions. His commentaries are precipitated by plot events but do not advance the action of the tale. In this instance, the connection between the plot and the uprooted inventory is convoluted indeed. The *Pequod* has just crossed paths with the emblematic *Samuel Enderby,* another whaler whose captain has had the misfortune to encounter Moby Dick. Unlike Ahab, however, pursuit and vengeance do not interest him, and though he avers that the glory of conquest would be great, he prefers to leave well enough alone. But the connection between plot and inventory is yet further distant, for it relies on Ishmael's memories of good cheer, feasting, and drinking from a visit to this same ship that supposedly occurred at some time subsequent to the events that conclude the novel.[25] Curious about why English whalers are so hospitable, he chances to find the tabulation amid his "Leviathanic" researches.

Thus, if the actual listing appears to be a straightforward inventory, the approach to it, the narrative course that brings us to it, is exceedingly complex. To get to the tabulation from the deck of the *Pequod* requires the pursuit of several tangential threads and numerous temporal leaps. It is one point along the path blazed by the author, whose narrative freedom leads Ishmael to meander, sometimes clumsily, in order to connect a seemingly designless array of data. The material of Melville's book was literally and metaphorically "blubber." As he wrote to Richard Henry Dana, "Tho' you may get oil out of it, the poetry runs as hard as sap from a frozen maple tree;—& to cook the thing up, one must needs throw in a little fancy, which from the nature of the thing, must be as ungainly as the gambols of the whales themselves."

In this way the excerpted inventory can be seen as one fact that Ishmael essays to incorporate into his text, chosen from an infinitude of possibilities. Indeed, he presents much of the cetological material as a series of discrete units of information, seemingly random and noncontinuous, interspersed with narrative, that in aggregate culminate to give fullness to the specific whales met in the text and to the idea of the whale in general. Nonetheless, these units of information actually may be statements of verifiable physiological and historical fact, or they just may appear to be when they really have no basis other than the author's inventive imagination.

On the one hand, the "Low Dutch" inventory is just another

piece of esoterica—genuine or fabricated minutia scattered by Ishmael in his desire to prove himself "omnisciently exhaustive." This comprehensiveness is more random than thorough, however. It touches serendipitously on far-flung particulars instead of handling the matter in depth, and in this way conforms to the undisguised acknowledgments of incompletion Ishmael makes elsewhere ("God keep me from ever completing anything" [*MD*, 176]). Nevertheless, we must recall also that Melville was a consciously literary writer, and his Ishmael a rampantly allusive narrator. Though he pleads as "unlettered Ishmael," this narrator knows how to turn quotation to his own inexplicable purpose, as when he makes Macbeth's expression of grief a curt and dismissive witticism. After appending to his System "a rabble of uncertain, fugitive, half-fabulous whales," he excludes a set of "uncouth names . . . suspecting them for mere sounds, full of Leviathanism, but signifying nothing" (*MD*, 175).

For Ishmael, the dietetic inventory of the whaling fleet likewise becomes an occasion for joking. Recall what Emerson wrote in "The Poet": "Bare lists of words are found suggestive to an imaginative and excited mind" (*E*, 455). Although Melville may not be answering that claim directly, he does use the itemization as a creative jumping-off point. With Gargantuan appetite Ishmael punningly consumes the entire inventory, perhaps at Emerson's expense: "At this time I devoted three days to the studious digesting of all this beef, beer, and bread, during which many profound thoughts were incidentally suggested to me, capable of a transcendental and Platonic application" (*MD*, 499). This particular excited mind is inspired to make tabulations and calculations, and to exert his freedom to digress. Again it is the "incidentals," and their eclectic heterogeneity, that declare the work's originality; Ishmael's digressions and interjections paradoxically solidify the novel as they interrupt it. It is this discontinuity, as Wai Chee Dimock tellingly describes, that enables it "to set itself apart, to transcend mimesis, to rest within an impervious tissue of words."[26]

The *London Atheneum* (25 October 1851) called *Moby-Dick* an "ill-compounded mixture of romance and matter-of-fact." The *Boston Post* (20 November 1851) described it as "a crazy sort of affair, stuffed with conceits and oddities of all kinds, put in artificially, deliberately, and affectedly, by the side of strong, terse and brilliant passages of incident and description." Nevertheless, the cetological material interacts symbiotically with the narrative of the chase. If at one moment we are lowering in turbulent seas to harpoon our first whale—and by the brilliant passages of incident and description brought into proximity with Leviathan in a way that only fiction can effect—at the next we are learning the importance of whalebone to the fashion industry, or the role of the whale in mythology, or how much of the whale's life eludes our examination in the depths of the sea. The interconnectedness of all this material, radiating from the centrality of the whale to its most peripheral, most minor detail, confirms one reading of Ishmael's statement that "Nothing exists in itself" (*MD*, 80).

The simplicity of this phrase, however, belies its more profound consequence for the novel. It is the distillation of Ishmael's existential inquiry (a parallel to Ahab's hunt), and it oscillates between two different though not incompatible interpretations: 1) Everything exists in relation to everything else (and is of consequence or interest); 2) Nothingness, the state of nonexistence, exists. In the chapters that intercalate with the pursuit of the White Whale—those parts of the novel that Melville referred to as "shanties of chapters and essays"—*Moby-Dick* manages to juggle both the everything and the nothing. "The Whiteness of the Whale" addresses the gnawing anxiety about the actuality of nothingness, but the many digressions of the novel elaborate the importance of every particular and incidental thing. In terms of relevance to the pursuit of the White Whale, the inventory of "The Decanter" is just such an incidental. Nonetheless, as Mumford affirmed, the truth is that such "irrelevancies are an essential part of [*Moby-Dick's*] form, and had Melville attempted to reduce the bounds of his universe to the scene required for a slick story of the sea, that universe would not have been the multitudinous and terrible thing he sought to create."[27] As Ishmael states, "Some certain significance lurks in all things, else all things are little worth, and the round world itself but an empty cipher" (*MD*, 483).

Nevertheless, the trivial facts and details about whales and whaling have complicated roles in the novel. They may be accurate or erroneous, documented by actual observation or things that someone once said, conjectured, or fabricated. The observations of methodical naturalists compete with seamen's lore; the words of Linnaeus are set against the words of Charley Coffin. What is verifiable and what is fictive intermingle, and both are treated equally as "fact." Like all narrators, Ishmael acts as a kind of filter, allowing certain things to enter the narrative while obstructing others. (Bezanson dubs this the "Ishmael membrane.") "In behalf of the dignity of whaling," Ishmael claims in chapter 25, "I would fain advance naught but substantiated facts" (*MD*, 143). But one objective of fiction is to persuade, and this requires the use of other rhetorical tactics: "But after embattling his facts, an advocate who should wholly suppress a not unreasonable surmise, which might tell eloquently upon his cause—such an advocate, would he not be blameworthy?" (*MD*, 143). Which "facts" are true is difficult to ascertain, since even Ishmael is not above distortion and outright invention. Who knows? The purported source of "The Decanter"'s itemized list might never have existed. Certainly, Ishmael never finds it, since he is a fiction. Melville himself, even in his prodigious preparation, may never have come across this particular piece of information. He may have found something similar to it and altered it to suit his purposes, or he may have made it all up, and its translator, Dr. Snodhead, too. This is all to say that what Ishmael states is fact may not necessarily be true; sometimes it may be "a not unreasonable surmise."

As we can see from Melville's efforts in *Moby-Dick,* prose lists may often be built from a diverse collection of accumulated "facts."

This is an open category, to be sure. It includes a broad variety of particularized details; as Ishmael has shown us, these components can be any variety of scientific, practical or historical fact—or, as seems to better suit Melville's narrator, factoids. Ishmael possesses an astounding ability to accumulate and synthesize trivia, which he disperses throughout his text in sometimes discrete, sometimes ornate mosaics.

Melville's great novel is a remarkable demonstration of whaling scholarship, as we might call it, and Ishmael, Melville's stand-in, clearly labored in his study. In preparation for the actual telling of his tale, Ishmael evidently initiated his researches into all things cetological some time after the sinking of the *Pequod,* and the intermittent references in *Moby-Dick* to the course of this investigation suggest an approach to the subject matter that is as far-ranging, circuitous, and haphazard as a Nantucketer's hunt for whales.

One curious digression occurs late in the novel when Ishmael recounts his discovery of a well-preserved full-length whale skeleton on an island in the Arsacides. He describes his finding there as "a wondrous sight," and it serves as an opportunity to assemble a collection of details. Firsthand observation is the most reliable source of information, and this discovery affords him a rare opportunity to "seize the privilege of Jonah alone" and discourse upon "the joists and beams; the rafters, ridge-pole, sleepers, and underpinnings, making up the frame-work of leviathan" (*MD,* 501). Not anticipating such fortune, on the spur of the moment this amateur naturalist devises a novel manner of recording the skeletal features: "The skeleton dimensions I shall now proceed to set down are copied verbatim from my right arm, where I had them tattooed; as in my wild wanderings at that period, there was no other secure way of preserving such valuable statistics" (*MD,* 504–505).

What is striking in this otherwise minor episode is not merely Ishmael's compulsion to record the measurements, but the lengths to which he goes to do so. He is not content merely to see the skeleton; his dedication to the creation of a useful written record of the

findings extends as far as self-mutilation. Many critics and histori-
ans have observed that the careful documentation of such seemingly unimportant facts as these, or as the ones Thoreau amassed in
his writing indicated the developing interest in scientific research
that occurred in the mid-nineteenth century. Mumford described
how this respect for facts played out in the literature of the period:

> One of the finest love-poems of the nineteenth century, Whit-
> man's "Out of the Cradle Endlessly Rocking," is expressed in
> such an image as Darwin or Audubon might have used were
> the scientist as capable of expressing his inner feelings as of
> noting "external" events: the poet haunting the sea-shore and
> observing the mating of the birds, day after day following their
> life, could scarcely have existed before the nineteenth century.
> In the seventeenth century, such a poet would have remained
> in the garden and written about a literary ghost, Philomel, and
> not about an actual pair of birds: in Pope's time, the poet
> would have remained in the library and written about the
> birds on a lady's fan. Almost all the important works of the
> nineteenth century were cast in this mode and expressed this
> new imaginative range: they respect the fact: they are replete
> with observation: they project an ideal realm in and through,
> not over, the landscape of actuality.[28]

But what is even more interesting than Ishmael's enthusiasm for
documentation here—and more peculiar—is the complicated tension between fact and fiction that this *Mardi*-like episode reveals,
for Melville goes to some pains to state that these prized statistics,
which I conceive of as a listed set of numbers, must nevertheless
contend for space against a poem in progress: "But as I was crowded
for space, and wished the other parts of my body to remain a blank
page for a poem I was then composing—at least what untattooed
parts might remain—I did not trouble myself with the odd inches;
nor indeed should inches at all enter into a congenial admeasurement of the whale." In contrast to the "new imaginative range" of
detail and phenomena that Mumford suggested natural history
made available for poetic treatment, the competition for space be-

tween Ishmael's field notes and his verse is indicative of a conceptual disjunction that nevertheless effectively partitions science and
poetry.

Ishmael's variegated body is a brilliant trope for it is emblematic of the novel as a whole: in both, elements of the science of natural history accompany elements of poetry, as they interdigitate in
his writing and across his person. And in this sense, while he is not
like Moby Dick the whale, Ishmael is not unlike *Moby-Dick* the text.
Nonetheless, since it seems that Ishmael wishes to segregate his
measurements from his poetic composition—they may be adjacent to it but must not interfere with it—consequently, there must
be some kind of qualitative difference on which to make a distinction between what is fact and what is fiction.

Turning to the *Oxford English Dictionary,* we can find a succinct
means of differentiating the one from the other. A fact is defined
there as "something that has really occurred or is actually the
case . . . hence a particular truth known by actual observation or
authentic testimony." A fact is distinguished from "what is merely
inferred, or [from] a conjecture or fiction." Accordingly, the dimensions Ishmael provides derive from "actual observation," at least
within the narrative framework of the novel. In contrast, a fiction is
"imaginatively invented," a "feigned existence, event, or state of
things."[29] If Melville is our point of reference, then Ishmael is of
course a fictive construct. Subsequently, any empirical data that he
relates are also fictional representations, or, if they are derived from
real-world fact or Melville's own experience, they become slightly
colored when they are attributed to their secondhand owner.

The Melville-Ishmael relationship is intriguing in its own right,
but has been well handled elsewhere. Here I wish to limit my discussion to the general division between fact and fiction, between
science and poetry, according to the above definitions. In so doing,
I am making a broad distinction between representations of "actual
observations" and imaginative or creative literature in general. It is
in the writings of Thoreau that these categories tend to break down

as the facts of observed phenomena become the elemental units in the creation of "poetic" prose catalogues.

Notwithstanding that when undertaken at sufficiently accomplished levels, both science and poetry are means by which we endeavor to better comprehend our world, the two have all too often been considered immiscible, if not in direct opposition. Although it is possible to broadly conceptualize both poetry and science as essentially similar activities that, as George Levine succinctly puts it, "work out in different languages the same project,"[30] it seems that a reigning division separating them has commonly held, at least since Coleridge set down his "final definition of a poem" in *Biographia Literaria:* "A poem is that species of composition which is opposed to works of science, by proposing for its immediate object pleasure, not truth."

Given the apparent incongruity of mission that this formulation implies, it is to be expected that there is commonly a friction "along the boundary where the exact sciences border upon those which are not 'exact' in quite that sense," as Elizabeth Sewall writes at the beginning of *The Orphic Voice.* In her illuminating study of the relation of poetry to natural history, Sewall notes that this friction is only worsened where there is a mutual distrust between science and poetry, and they are set against each other. "We have the scientist setting science against poetry and seeing in the latter a loose, vague, drunken activity, liable to mislead thought by procedures which are easier and less exacting than those of science, neither disciplined nor in contact with reality. . . . [The poet], on the other hand, speak[s] of science as hostile to poetry, obsessed with an exactitude which is quantitative, mechanical, niggling, pedestrian, and unfortunately for the poet's argument, vulgarly successful."[31]

This opposition aptly characterizes Ishmael's dilemma. As the wild wanderer he would like to pretend to be, he has the looseness (though perhaps not the intemperance) that the scientist suspects of the poet, and as the "mere painstaking burrower and grub-worm of a poor devil" that on one level he so clearly is, he demonstrates a zealous preoccupation with details that the poet faults in the scientist. In his apportionment of epidermal space, however, Ishmael's decision to rate the "valuable statistics" beneath a vacant area reserved for the anticipated poem (which, incidentally, is never made public if indeed it is ever written), is ultimately a consequence of his being forced to choose in this "frictional" zone. The loss of precision of his numbers is an additional compromise, though he rationalizes this away. It further betrays a willingness to blunt the sharp edge of the exact sciences.

Ishmael's outward surface is an overprinted patchwork figuratively reprising *Moby-Dick*'s patchwork of literary genres, but the divisions that set the whale's dimensions apart and separate quantification from decoration and epigraph are superficial and do not represent an impermeable division between his different intellectual abilities. Ishmael provides his measurements of the whale's head and ribs in the subsequent chapter, "Measurement of the Whale's Skeleton": "In length, the Sperm Whale's skeleton . . . measured seventy-two feet. . . . Of this seventy-two feet, his skull and jaw comprised some twenty feet, leaving some fifty feet of plain back-bone. . . . The ribs were ten on a side. The first, to begin from the neck, was nearly six feet long; the second, third, and fourth were each successively longer, till you came to the climax of the fifth, or one of the middle ribs, which measured eight feet and some inches. From that part, the remaining ribs diminished, till the tenth and last only spanned five feet and some inches" (*MD*, 507). Ishmael's presentation of data here is really quite elegant, particularly as he sketches out the incremental expansion and then diminishment of the whale's ribs. It is not, however, the bare statistical list of measurements we have been anticipating; Ishmael promised, almost boasted, to give them "verbatim" from his right arm. Surely this is not how, word for word, he recorded the dimensions. If it is, it is no wonder that he has few unmarked areas remaining.

While the objection here may seem trivial, this breach is one of many such instances where the narrator plays fast and loose in the telling of his tale. And it is this particularly slippery narrative voice that Melville chooses that sets the diverting tone for what could otherwise be a murderous, bloody novel. Ishmael's terminological inexactitude here, his inaccuracy, combined with his other exaggerations and concoctions throughout the book, are symptomatic of the personage of the yarn-spinner. Indeed, one senses that Ishmael is most himself not when he is the insignificant, anonymous mariner about his sailorly business but when he is the center of attention evolving tales for willing listeners. A more suitable role for him is the genial fabler lounging among friends on the piazza in Lima, as depicted in the interlude of "The Town-Ho's Story," rather than the sober student of natural history. This humorously noisy taking of liberties falls into the same general camp as Ishmael's claims to "possess the only extant copy" of the works of an old writer ("The Carpet-bag"); his outright denial that Moby Dick is anything other than factual, and that only ignorant landsmen could interpret his words as a "monstrous fable, or still worse, and more detestable, a hideous and intolerable allegory" ("The Affadavit"); his declaration that the great genius of the sperm whale "is declared in his doing nothing to prove it" ("The Prairie"); and perhaps most flabbergasting, his claim that "from the heads of all ponderous, profound beings . . . there always goes up a certain semi-visible steam, while in the act of thinking deep thoughts" ("The Fountain").

The relation between fact and fiction, or reality and imagination, is not unlike the relation between being and nothingness. While fact has hard, firm truth to support it, fiction has nothing. One of the great questions regarding creation is "Where does it all come from?" Did Dr. Snodhead spring ex nihilo? The "void," then, of blankness is really quite a fertile place, indeed, infinitely so. This silent, paradoxical nothingness—the whiteness of the whale—is the central concern of *Moby-Dick*. It underlies the entire novel, metaphysically and physically, with regard to both its abstract philosophical questions and its actual printed pages of black on white. *Black,* we should remember, is one of the many descendants of the Indo-European **bhel,* along with *blank, bleak, bleach,* the French *blanc* (white), and many others. The seemingly contrarious relation between black and white underlies the entire text of *Moby-Dick,* determining both the text and the subtext of the novel.

The inscrutability of whiteness has stimulated writers as various as Milton, Emerson, Poe, and Beckett, but one of the most remarkable, and haunting, of all the analyses is Ishmael's extended meditation on whiteness in "The Whiteness of the Whale." Like Poe's *Narrative of Arthur Gordon Pym of Nantucket,* Melville's novel is partly a straight adventure and partly a metaphysical quest, one in which whiteness plays a significant role. Although Ishmael has previously spoken of the perils of whaling, with precision detailing X, Y, and Z, it is in this chapter that he strives to articulate the "vague, nameless horror" (*MD,* 499) that distinguishes Moby Dick as more than a powerful and deadly creature but something altogether menacing.

Many chapters of the novel detail specific information in order to make the tale of the White Whale credible. Some document the existence of other beasts given "the rights, privileges and distinctions of a name" (*MD,* 240). Others explain with careful and elaborate detail the whale's immense size, its unique anatomy, its habits, or the fact that so much of its life remains hidden. Nevertheless, Ishmael's digression on whiteness is the psychological center, the heart of all the material presented. "It was the whiteness of the whale that above all things appalled me," the narrator states plainly, though the reasons for this are considerably more difficult for him to articulate: "But how can I hope to explain myself here; and yet, in some dim, random way, explain myself I must, else all these chapters might be naught" (*MD,* 223).

While Moby Dick is powerful, nevertheless, "aside from those more obvious considerations . . . which could not but awaken in any man's soul some alarm," his whiteness is the whale's most significant quality, the attribute that has the most chilling effect on the narrator. It is here that Melville's novel, so full of life and character and motion and humor and the grand compass of things, reveals itself as a profoundly disturbing expression of nihilism. For the White Whale, paradoxically, represents the absence of meaning, symbolizes the meaninglessness of the universe: Moby Dick is the verification that "Nothing exists in itself." The blankness of white is unreadable not because it is too complicated to be deciphered, like the intricate tattoos of Queequeg, but because the white field bears the imprint of Nothing. The attempt to interpret the unmarked is a confrontation with nothingness. The unreadable makes apparent the limitations of human discernment and, conversely, the frightful prospect of the lack of meaning in the world. Once introduced, the influence of the meaningless is corrupting: if it can exist at one point, it can exist at all points, beneath whatever colorings Nature lays upon the world, fooling us with "allurements," or, alternatively, beneath those colorings we project upon the world, fooling ourselves. The White Whale is the site where meaninglessness enters the Melvillean universe, with immense confrontational force, indestructible and terrifying.[32]

"The Whiteness of the Whale" is Melville's effort to articulate the existentially horrifying prospect of nothingness. Though he provides many illustrations, the chapter is clearly not an attempt to delineate degrees of whiteness. It progresses from a great number of examples wherein white is invested with meaning to the bleak supposition that it is the "dumb blankness" underlying all things. This is not the "Unity" that Emerson proposed lay "under the undermost garment of Nature." This is the blankness that Mumford describes as "the colorless, unintegrated, primal world that underlies and antedates that which we know through our senses, our feelings, our experiences."[33] It is upon whiteness that deceitful Nature paints, misleading us into complacency. As Paul Brodtkorb writes, white "makes vibrantly visible as a presence the nothingness with which all existence is secretly sickened."[34] These analyses make clear how Melville's conception of whiteness differs from those of Emerson or Milton.

For Emerson it is we *ourselves* who blanch the excellence of the external world through human defects of character: "The ruin or the blank that we see when we look at nature, is in our own eye. The axis of vision is not coincident with the axis of things, and so they appear not transparent but opake" (*E*, 47). For Milton, by contrast, we do not see *enough* white, since the "Eternal Coeternal beam" loses its singular perfection as it descends to earth, and the objects gross that intervene in our distance from God keep out his light. Milton's blindness has an ironic benefit, then, as the handicap serves instead to identify the poet more closely with the redeemed:

> But clouds instead, and ever-during dark
> Surrounds me, from the cheerful ways of men
> Cut off, and for the Book of knowledge fair
> Presented with a Universal blanc
> Of Nature's works to me expung'd and ras'd. [*Paradise Lost*,
>   3.45–49]

The challenge to Melville in this chapter is to oppose the positive and well-known usages of white as a symbol. He must undermine confidence in societally accepted emblems of purity, honor, justice, and divinity and instill doubt in their place. The task is to render the symbolic overlays transparent, and to query the cause of our instinctive revulsion. This intention is manifested in the asymmetry of the chapter: a cultural and religious survey, catalogued in a single paragraph, is followed by a series of illustrations and explanations that attempt to say what cannot be said directly. As James Guetti describes it, although these efforts to define "with language . . . that which is beyond language [fail,] Ishmael's failures, in their suggestiveness and ultimate inconclusiveness, become the evidence for the existence of what is beyond them, something expressed because it is not expressed, which we can only call the ineffable."[35]

In the discussion of whiteness, Melville is clearly echoing Rabelais and the officious cataloguing of white as an indicator of joy and pleasure, "not at random but by unimpeachable authority," that occurs in the first book of *Pantagruel*. The listings of Rabelais are almost always irrepressible, but this particular sixteenth-century prototype exuberantly expresses the rollicking happiness of a proud new father as he emblematically clothes his son in white and blue to signify his delight. It confidently cites biblical and historical sources and even extemporizes far-fetched conclusions from insubstantial evidence. The narrator puts to use all manner of material without concern for challenge or question. The listing is so jubilant that it co-opts even death, careering into an itemization of individuals who have perished from excessive joy. In a few pages Rabelais accomplishes an unforeseen and dizzying maneuver, moving from joy occasioned by birth to death occasioned by joy. Though certainly more haunting, Melville's series of citations moves in a similarly unpredictable manner. More important, it addresses the penetrating question that Rabelais asks but never satisfactorily answers: "What moves, impels or induces you to believe what you do?"

Ishmael's aim is to counter the benevolent associations and applications of whiteness, but not merely by presenting contrary examples. To set "good" against "bad" would be to illustrate the polarity of meanings that human beings have lent to the color white, but it would not be a way of elucidating the disturbing qualities of whiteness. That approach would not provide an answer to why white is "at once the most meaning symbol of spiritual things . . . and yet . . . the intensifying agent in things the most appalling to mankind." Ishmael acknowledges that his efforts to explain will be indirect, which is why he is at great pains to set whiteness apart from other characteristics that make a thing terrifying. A shark or a bear or a squall is impressive enough, but when it is white as well the effect is magnified: "But though without dissent this point be fixed, how is mortal man to account for it? To analyse it, would seem impossible. Can we then, by the citation of some of those instances wherein this thing of whiteness—though for the time either wholly or in great part stripped of all direct associations calculated to impart to it aught fearful, but nevertheless, is found to exert over us the same sorcery, however modified;—can we thus hope to light upon some chance clue to conduct us to the hidden cause we seek?" (*MD*, 227).

Although he presents a large number of counterexamples, these are not representations of whiteness as "un-holiness" or "injustice" or "impurity." Ishmael sets them not as contradictions to his positive illustrations but as images calculated to induce a visceral recoil in the reader, a repulsion that reverberates through the chapter. Whiteness becomes increasingly dreadful with each successive repetition, as it ceases to be a benign, positive symbol and converts into a malign, negative one. The reiteration enhances the power of whiteness as a "vital force." The "incantation of whiteness" that Ishmael attempts to solve—and this is an inexact figure for it that is somehow just right—is presented in a form that is itself an incantation, a formula of words that produces a magical effect.[36]

Ishmael's method here resembles a collage more than an organized encyclopedia, or taxonomy, of whiteness. The piling up of examples and the different ways of presenting them betoken the urgency of his statements. But the narrative of connection between each successive attempt is loose indeed. Certainly, when a subject is infinite any method of presentation will be seen to be arbitrary, but here Ishmael's efforts seem haphazard. His shifting tactics suggest desperation. As Harry Levin argues, though Ishmael "richly heaps up illustrations, the essential quality becomes more and more elusive as he undertakes to define it, until it finally seems to fade away into an appalling sensation of panic before the unknown and the unknowable."[37]

The presentation of examples as insistent questions further augments the agitation of the chapter. Melville has used this relentless questioning on other occasions in the novel, especially when Ishmael feels pressed to justify his opinions. Who could possibly disagree with him, if one could get a word in edgewise, as he ventilates in "Loomings"?

Were Niagara but a cataract of sand, would you travel your thousand miles to see it? Why did the poor poet of Tennessee, upon suddenly receiving two handfuls of silver, deliberate whether to buy him a coat, which he sadly needed, or invest his money in a pedestrian trip to Rockaway Beach? Why is almost every robust healthy boy with a robust healthy soul in him, at some time or other crazy to go to sea? Why upon your first voyage as a passenger, did you yourself feel such a mystical vibration, when first told that you and your ship were now out of sight of land? Why did the old Persians hold the sea holy? Why did the Greeks give it a separate deity, and make him the own brother of Jove? [*MD*, 27]

Or in "The Advocate"?

Why did the Dutch in De Witt's time have admirals of their whaling fleets? Why did Louis XVI. of France, at his own personal expense, fit out whaling ships from Dunkirk, and politely invite to that town some score or two of families from our own island of Nantucket? Why did Britain between the years 1750 and 1788 pay to her whalemen in bounties upwards of £1,000,000? [*MD*, 139]

Or in the brief (but still misleading) "Postscript"?

What kind of oil is used at coronations? Certainly it cannot be olive oil, nor macassar oil, nor castor oil, nor bear's oil, nor train oil, nor cod-liver oil. What then can it possibly be, but sperm oil in its unmanufactured, unpolluted state, the sweetest of all oils? [*MD*, 143]

As Longinus observed of the use of rhetorical questions in discourse, such an "impassioned rapidity" of questioning increases the realism and vigor of the writing. Furthermore, Longinus noted that rhetorical figurations are most persuasive when the reader is unaware of their use. The deployment of a rapid succession of questions is effective: it seems to be offering to give up control, by saying to the reader "What do you think?" when it really is doing no such thing. The successive questions bowl through the reader's opposition, on the one hand beseeching a response while on the other denying the opportunity of making one. Although Ishmael continues to remind us that he hasn't yet uncovered the answer to the enigma of white, he will present instead another example where the mysterious effect is posited to occur in what Buell terms "a barrage of linked analogies."[38] Indeed, the use of the technique in "The Whiteness of the Whale" is somewhat manipulative, in that Ishmael presents a cogent and frightening analysis of whiteness in the chapter's final paragraph, stripping off the layers that deceitful Nature paints upon the undercoat of nothingness.

The threatening theme of the chapter, however, is intricately related to a restorative theme that has a greater place in the novel. Whereas the sinister aspect of whiteness may escape "the common apprehension," the key to comprehending Ishmael's peroration is imagination: "Without imagination no man can follow another into these halls" (*MD*, 228). To "get" Ishmael (and this is akin to Ishmael's efforts to prepare his readers to "know" the whale), one must follow him by imagining what Ishmael cannot state outright. His examples appeal to the imagination and require that the reader be willing to look into the abyss: we must have the imaginative capacity to conceive the horror of which Ishmael is speaking. To our intellectual endeavors meaninglessness is a repugnant conception, and insight into the absence of meaning necessitates an imaginative ability that makes us vulnerable. But imagination not only allows us to contemplate what to less creative minds would be unthinkable, it also provides some protection, indeed some hope in the face of nothingness. As Edgar Dryden argues, although the "confrontation with whiteness is a positive and direct encounter with blankness," fiction can, paradoxically, put "man in touch with Truth while protecting him from it."[39]

Nevertheless, Ishmael's refusal to figure whiteness with its most obvious image—a blank page—is suspicious, especially as he has elsewhere been so conscious of the figurative use of the physical aspects of books, swimming through libraries, bibliographically classifying whales, suggesting that the narwhal's horn is an appropriate page turner for pamphlets. If whiteness is the ultimate unreadable text, it is consequently terrifying to the writer who wishes to be read. A meaningless unreadability, or an unreadable meaninglessness, has the potential to puncture a text. Except for Sterne's invitation to the readers in *Tristram Shandy* to pencil in their own illustration of the Widow Wadman, few narrators are willing to relinquish control of where their story goes or how it gets there.

Ishmael's words mark the blank page, marring the uniform whiteness and making meaning upon it even when the expressions cannot communicate intentionality without ambiguity, but in the whiteness beneath he sees his own dissolution as a fictional character, a state in which he will cease to exist. In this way whiteness is much like the self-projected white shadow that Pym sees at the Pole: both share, as John Irwin writes, "that condition of indeterminacy in which the observer in part creates the phenomenon he observes."[40] In an effort to hold nonexistence at bay, Ishmael must speak, talk, write. And with the pressure of annihilation continually threatening to rend a seam in his narration, he endeavors to establish a bulwark against that inevitability by throwing whatever he can into the gap. Hence Ishmael's tendency to ramble: his words upon the page protect him from nonexistence, though his defense is fragile. Seen in this light, it is no wonder that Ishmael is so prolific—he maintains himself only by elaborating his "impervious tissue of words."

To Ishmael, the terrifying aspect of whiteness—and his obsession with it is almost pathological, almost "Ahabistic"—is the prospect of having nothing to say. For the garrulous narrator, this aspect is indeed horrifying, though it is never addressed directly or admitted outright. This is not to say that at times Ishmael does not say that he cannot express something in words, for he often avers that he is unable to describe a particular thing well enough. What really frightens Ishmael is the prospect of being silenced. Hence his rapidly constructed collage of "citations" and inability to adhere to a systematic approach. The collage includes, for example, this paean, an effort to out-do Rabelais by including a uniquely American example:

> Most famous in our Western annals, and Indian traditions is that of the White Steed of the Prairies; a magnificent milk-white charger, large-eyed, small-headed, bluff-chested, and with the dignity of a thousand monarchs in his lofty, over-scorning carriage. He was the elected Xerxes of vast herds of wild horses, whose pastures in those days were only fenced by the Rocky Mountains and the Alleghenies. . . . Nor can it be questioned from what stands on legendary record of this noble horse, that it was his spiritual whiteness chiefly, which so clothed him with divineness; and that this divineness had that in it which, though commanding worship, at the same time enforced a certain nameless terror. [*MD*, 225–226]

Another pattern is provided by a sequence of connected images, as in this progression from the dead to their ghosts to the pale rider himself:

> It cannot well be doubted, that the one visible quality in the aspect of the dead which most appals the gazer, is the marble pallor lingering there; as if indeed that pallor were as much the badge of consternation in the other world, as of mortal trepidation here. And from that pallor of the dead, we borrow the expressive hue of the shroud in which we wrap them. Nor even in our superstitions do we fail to throw the same snowy mantle round our phantoms; all ghosts rising in a milk-white fog— Yea, while these terrors seize us, let us add, that even the king of terrors, when personified by the evangelist, rides on his pallid horse. [*MD*, 227]

Ishmael also betrays a certain suggestibility, which he tries to pass on to the reader, when he conjures chilling aspects of whiteness in things that merely bear the name white. Through this purely semantic connection, Ishmael links things that have no substantive common visual qualities. Playing on such associations, he then al-

lows his imagination to generate his tenuous arguments, as he in-
sists on his own interpretation of things:

> To the unread, unsophisticated Protestant of the Middle
> American States, why does the passing mention of a White
> Friar or a White Nun, evoke such an eyeless statue in the soul?
>   Or what is there apart from the traditions of dungeoned
> warriors and kings (which will not wholly account for it) that
> makes the White Tower of London tell so much more strongly
> on the imagination of an untravelled American, than those
> other storied structures, its neighbors—the Byward Tower, or
> even the Bloody? And those sublimer towers, the White Moun-
> tains of New Hampshire, whence, in particular moods, comes
> that gigantic ghostliness over the soul at the bare mention of
> that name, while the thought of Virginia's Blue Ridge is full of
> soft, dewy, distant dreaminess? Or why, irrespective of all lati-
> tudes and longitudes, does the name of the White Sea exert
> such a spectralness over the fancy, while that of the Yellow Sea
> lulls us with mortal thoughts of long lacquered mild after-
> noons on the waves, followed by the gaudiest and yet sleepiest
> of sunsets? [*MD*, 228]

Melville has searched the universe to compile his examples, moving
from the tops of snow-covered mountains to the depths of the sea,
from the faith of religion to the fiction of fairy tales. As a matchless
figurative construct, whiteness expresses a range of thought and
emotion. Further, it fuses a variety of opposites across a moral spectrum from bridal innocence to murder. Indeed, white invites a
characterization that surprisingly affirms nonpresence: from absence of evil to absence of good.

Despite his numerous attempts to define what it is about whiteness that is so disturbing, the conclusion ultimately evades Ishmael;
likewise, every reader brings away his or her own meaning from the
blankness. Whiteness is a trap that invites many interpretations but
refuses to validate any of them. An apt symbol for cosmic inscrutability, Ishmael's white is infinitely suggestive of meanings and
endlessly elusive, like the uncapturable White Whale. As Khalil

Husni recounts, since the Melville revival of the 1920s, "almost every critic has left his reflected hue on the whiteness of the whale."[41] For Richard Chase, whiteness symbolizes an "inviolable spiritual rectitude" that cannot be found in the imperfections of this fallen world. For Ronald Mason, whiteness is Melville's vision of "Nothing replacing whatever God he had previously worshipped as Lord and Creator of his universe." To Charles Feidelson, indefiniteness is the "ultimate horror of whiteness." Lost in it are whatever marks might distinguish or differentiate one thing from another; "the merging of distinctions . . . destroys individuality."[42] In other words, whiteness brings about a loss of distinction, merging all things and blotting out the things that a list so precisely delineates.

5
Thoreau

"These statistics, however accidental and therefore uninstructive they may appear, as they have a certain completeness, have a certain value also"

In my introduction I observed a distinction between literary and pragmatic lists. When it comes to authoritatively ordering the variety of things in the world, the scientific categorization of natural history is perhaps the epitome of the pragmatic list. The work of Linnaeus and others in classifying the components of the living world by means of language enabled an astounding variety of literal listings. Every species in Noah's Ark could be named, and subsequently the natural world could be gathered in professional and scientific ways. The scientific method of classification introduced a new modality into the practice of compilation. Finely distinguished categories, with the official validation of science, could be shuffled and arranged with analytical precision. Melville played with such subcategories in the "Cetology" chapter of *Moby-Dick*, but the writer who most seduously embraced the language of systematic natural history was Thoreau.

Thoreau's interest in nature, his delight in etymology, and his background in classical languages all led to his easy use of this kind of accountancy. But though he acquired considerable skill in these fields, Thoreau nevertheless considered himself neither a naturalist nor a botanist but a writer first and foremost. The languages and techniques of science were tools to be utilized for self-expression— "Here I have been these forty years learning the language of these fields that I may better express myself," he wrote in his journal (20 November 1857)—and they served him well in the creation of some of the most delicate prose listings in American literature.

If he never achieved commercial success in his lifetime, Thoreau was nevertheless committed to the craft of writing, even desperately so, as Daniel Peck has pointed out.[1] Listing was only one of his techniques, but, like Melville's, his lists appear in a variety of manifestations. The budgetary accounts of *Walden* are well known, as are the measurements, charts, and tables of the journals. Rhetorical lists exist as well, such as the impassioned, incremental rant against the "owner" of Flint's Pond, that "unclean and stupid farmer . . . who never *saw* it, who never bathed in it, who never loved it, who never protected it, who never spoke a good word for it, nor thanked God that he made it" (*T,* 479). (Apparently Thoreau had at first hoped to build his cabin on the banks of Flint's Pond but was denied permission to do so.) There is also in *Walden* a spartan inventory, a list that calls to mind the staggeringly short itemization of a family's possessions that James Agee provided in *Let Us Now Praise Famous Men:* "My furniture, part of which I made myself, and the rest cost me nothing of which I have not rendered an account, consisted of a bed, a table, a desk, three chairs, a looking-glass three inches in diameter, a pair of tongs and andirons, a kettle, a skillet, and a frying-pan, a dipper, a wash-bowl, two knives and forks, three plates, one cup, one spoon, a jug for oil, a jug for molasses, and a japanned lamp" (*T,* 374). (Thoreau, however, is boasting of his lack of possessions whereas Agee is using it to horrify readers by itemizing the depths of the family's poverty.)

Thoreau creates a more compelling list when he defends his solitary tendencies in "Solitude." "I have a great deal of company in my house," he begins, "especially in the morning when nobody calls." Following this faintly misanthropic opening, he propounds a series of examples that link him to a world in which separation and independence, rather than sociability, are the norm, and singleness makes one part of a greater unity:

> Let me suggest a few comparisons, that some may convey an idea of my situation. I am no more lonely than the loon in the pond that laughs so loud, or than Walden Pond itself. . . . The sun is alone, except in thick weather when there sometimes appear to be two, but one is a mock sun. God is alone,—but the devil, he is far from being alone; he sees a great deal of company; he is legion. I am no more lonely than a single mullein or dandelion in a pasture, or a bean leaf, or sorrel, or a horse-fly, or a humble-bee. I am no more lonely than the Mill Brook, or a weathercock, or the north star, or the south wind, or an April shower, or a January thaw, or the first spider in a new house. [*T,* 431]

What interests me here, to begin with, is a particular species of listing—a prose catalogue of reported "facts"—that occasionally appears in Thoreau's writings. These gatherings derive from Thoreau's observations of nature and his meticulous record keeping as much as Whitman's great chants derive from democratic aspirations or Melville's collections derive from the possibilities of the mock encyclopedia. In such listings, Thoreau takes account of various entities, generally flora and fauna, frequently either by compiling surveys of diverse populations he has encountered or by composing detailed scenic panoramas of his surroundings at a particular instant. This report from "The Ponds" exemplifies the survey:

> There have been caught in Walden, pickerel, one weighing seven pounds, to say nothing of another which carried off a reel with great velocity, which the fisherman safely set down at eight pounds because he did not see him, perch and pouts, some of each weighing over two pounds, shiners, chivins or

roach (*Leuciscus pulchellus*), a very few breams, and a couple of
eels, one weighing four pounds,—I am thus particular because the weight of a fish is commonly its only title to fame,
and these are the only eels I have heard of here;—also, I have a
faint recollection of a little fish some five inches long, with sil-
very sides and a greenish back, somewhat dace-like in its character, which I mention here chiefly to link my facts to fable. . . .
These are all very firm fish, and weigh more than their size
promises. The shiners, pouts, and perch also, and indeed all the
fishes which inhabit this pond, are much cleaner, handsomer,
and firmer fleshed than those in the river and most other
ponds, as the water is purer, and they can easily be distinguished from them. Probably many ichthyologists would
make new varieties of some of them. There are also a clean race
of frogs and tortoises, and a few muscles [*sic*] in it; muskrats
and minks leave their traces about it, and occasionally a travel-
ing mud-turtle visits it. . . . Ducks and geese frequent it in the
spring and fall, the white-bellied swallows (*Hirundo bicolor*)
skim over it, and the peetweets (*Totanus macularius*) "teter"
along its stony shores all summer. I have sometimes disturbed
a fishhawk sitting on a white-pine over the water; but I doubt if
it is ever profaned by the wing of a gull, like Fair Haven. At
most, it tolerates one annual loon. These are all the animals of
consequence which frequent it now. [*T*, 469]

The textual context for this catalogue provides the criteria for
inclusion, and, by default, exclusion as well. In a chapter that relates
all the virtues of Walden Pond and its neighbors, the purpose of this
list is, ostensibly, to count out the creatures that inhabit their waters. In the first half of the catalogue, Thoreau casts a wide net, and
brings to the surface all the fish that otherwise escape detection beneath the water. The introductory phrase "There have been caught"
initiates the momentum of the list, with *caught* as the operative
word. Earlier in the chapter Thoreau had observed how the practice
of fishing, by literally hooking us back into reality, brings our
thoughts down from other "cosmogonal themes in other spheres"
to link us again to nature. The first part of this passage is a list of the

fish caught in the pond; it is therefore not an exhaustive survey of the pond's aquatic inhabitants but rather a collection of the select few that fulfill this function of reconnecting. Fishing is useful, both as a diversion and as a means of providing for oneself, and in this list the fish are prioritized as food. Here record sizes figure prominently to demonstrate the superior quality of Walden's waters. Thoreau capitulates with the common perceptions of value, in that fish are commonly valued according to weight. To identify Walden as a special place, Thoreau celebrates it according to the superiority of its fish, fish that are indeed so superior that they no doubt would merit special treatment in the hands of systematizing professionals.

The second half of this list continues to reckon "the animals of consequence which frequent it now." What maintains the thematic continuity of this passage, however, is something other than its censuslike quality, for Thoreau here gives preference to a certain irregularity that challenges the strict orderings characteristic of more objective scientific record keeping. Thoreau mingles forms of designation, occasionally dropping in Latin names and shifting among seasonal appearances. This irregularity, minor as it may seem, is intentionally provocative, intended to strengthen Thoreau's claim as an amateur, a classifier who refuses to conform to the expected standards of "serious" literature and science.

This is evident from the opening lines of the passage where the first sentence extends the bounds of conventional grammar and syntax in its series of diversions, a sequence of deflections that almost have the character of asides. The listing of the fish is disrupted by one tall tale, one scientific reference, one interjection, and one significant addendum. As I mentioned previously, lists can always take on new members, so the presence of an addendum is nothing remarkable in itself. In this case, however, because Thoreau provides a minute description uncharacteristic of the other members of the list, the addition that closes out the sentence hints at a further feature of this list of facts assembled by Thoreau, namely the linking of facts and fable. Facts and mythmaking are often intertwined.

In contrast to the survey, the other frequently occurring species of prose catalogue in Thoreau's writing is the scenic description. If the passage from "The Ponds" unites natural entities separated in time and space, the scenic description captures the particulars of an instant. A model scenic description occurs in *A Week on the Concord and Merrimack Rivers:*

> The banks had passed the height of their beauty, and some of the brighter flowers showed by their faded tints that the season was verging towards the afternoon of the year; but this sombre tinge enhanced their sincerity, and in the still unabated heats they seemed like a mossy brink of some cool well. The narrow-leaved willow lay along the surface of the water in masses of light green foliage, interspersed with the large white balls of the button-bush. The rose-colored polygonum raised its head proudly above the water on either hand, and, flowering at this season, and in these localities, in the midst of dense fields of the white species which skirted the sides of the stream, its little streak of red looked very rare and precious. The pure white blossoms of the arrowhead stood in the shallower parts, and a few cardinals on the margin still proudly surveyed themselves reflected in the water, though the latter, as well as the pickerel-weed, was now nearly out of blossom. The snake-head, *chelone glabra,* grew close to the shore, while a kind of coreopsis, turning its brazen face to the sun, full and rank, and a tall dull red flower, *eupatorium purpureum,* or trumpet weed, formed the rear rank of the fluvial array. The bright blue flowers of the soap-wort gentian were sprinkled here and there in the adjacent meadows, like flowers which Proserpine had dropped, and still further in the fields, or higher on the bank, were seen the Virginia rhexia, and drooping neottia or ladies'-tresses; while from the more distant waysides, which we occasionally passed, and banks where the sun had lodged, was reflected a dull yellow beam from the banks of tansy, now in its prime. In short, nature seemed to have adorned herself for our departure with a profusion of fringes and curls, mingled with the bright tints of flowers, reflected in the water. [*T,* 18–19]

Emerson might well have complained about the atomizing of nature in such a passage, which here Thoreau attains by the enumeration and careful delineation of various species of flowers. In contrast to Thoreau, Emerson steadfastly opposed the cataloguing of particulars. He affirmed this anticataloguing disposition in *Nature:* "When I behold a rich landscape, it is less to my purpose to recite correctly the order and superposition of the strata, than to know why all thought of multitude is lost in a tranquil sense of unity" (*E*, 43). Rather than settle for the eye's proclivity to select individual objects, Emerson promoted a higher level of "aesthetic seeing," a method of apprehending that Sherman Paul describes as a "diffusion of focus into a blur of relatedness." Emerson distinguished this elevated "distant" vision from particularizing, or "proximate," vision, in which the beholder's field of sight was limited by the eye's convergence upon a single, central object.[2]

Thoreau, however, wrote in *A Week* that he admired Goethe because he "was satisfied in giving an exact description of things as they appeared to him, and their effect upon him" (*T*, 266). To achieve this fidelity required an eye that did not blur, one that was acute enough to analyze, dissociate, and distinguish. Indeed, one of Thoreau's strengths as both an observer and a writer derives from his ability to pronounce names, both botanical and common. Knowing the name of something implies a measure of mastery over it, and this sense of power influences the degree to which we as readers accept the probability of lists like this.

Lawrence Buell has noted that although Thoreau had limited formal knowledge of art, he did like to see land as landscape.[3] Creating a scene such as the description of the riverbanks requires careful attention to such elements of composition as color, texture, and framing. Coloration, spatial relations, and temporal relations with regard to the various stages of blooming or decaying are all finely communicated here. In this passage, Thoreau transforms a visual landscape into a landscape of words in which the superposition of various species sentence by sentence substitutes for their commingling in real life. The true appearance of the banks must be transcribed into text, not translated onto a canvas. As a comprehensive ordering of perceptions, the unitary representation of the flowers by kind prevents the verbal chaos that would ensue from a complete rendering of individual blossoms. In striking a compromise between particularizing each individual flower and reducing the entire view of the banks to a generic description, Thoreau achieves a position halfway between "proximate" and "distant" vision. Ultimately, however, the landscape is imbued with a meaning that is fully explicit: nature has readied itself in sympathy for this occasion, in the spirit of Ovid (note the reference to Proserpine). Furthermore, the description of this moment is itself but a portion of Thoreau's valedictory to his companion traveler, his brother John—only one paragraph in the memorial that *A Week* essentially constitutes.

Thoreau has been described as a "preternaturally accurate observer of phenomena," and this assessment seems most fitting when we recall the scrupulous attention to detail given to the pond and its inhabitants in *Walden* or his other careful descriptions of wildlife. In his uncommon concern for accuracy, Thoreau went so far as to correct the reported findings by the state of Massachusetts that the local perch had seven transverse bands. This fastidiousness, however ("the number . . . is very variable, for in some of our ponds they have nine and even ten"), was less an instance of pedantry than a testimony to his sharp-eyed interaction with nature, an engagement in which regard for particulars, such as size, shape, number, color, and time, mattered: "I would know even the number of their fin-rays," he declared, "and how many scales compose the lateral line."[4]

Nevertheless, to describe Thoreau as preternatural is not without consequence, in that its connotations of "extraordinariness" and existence literally "beyond nature" reinforce the indefinable

separation that forever kept Thoreau on the outside of nature, as
it were. Further, Thoreau's naturalist ambitions of completeness
seem to have kept him a social outsider as well. Not only was
Thoreau's work solitary and labor intensive, but its worth was mis-
understood by his contemporaries; even Emerson underestimated
it. Whereas Emerson became increasingly social, Thoreau became
more absorbed in the solitary study of natural history. Emerson
could only lament what he considered wasted opportunity, and he
expressed his feelings in his eulogy for his friend: "Had his genius
been only contemplative, he had been fitted to his life, but with his
energy and practical ability he seemed born for great enterprise and
for command; and I so much regret the loss of his rare powers for
action, that I cannot help finding it a fault in him that he had no
ambition. Wanting this, instead of engineering for all America, he
was the captain of a huckleberry party."[5]

Thoreau's collection of particulars and the accumulations of
data that came to occupy an increasingly large portion of his journal in later years should not be seen as evidences of antisocial tendencies, however, nor as indications of the Sisyphean inexhaustibil-
ity of his project. Rather, they are testaments to the extent of his
commitment to his work. In his early essay "The Natural History of
Massachusetts," which Daniel Peck identifies as Thoreau's first
public declaration of his lifelong endeavor to translate facts into
"truths," Thoreau predicted the degree of investment that would be
required: "We must look a long time before we can see. Slow are the
beginnings of philosophy."[6]

Emerson had commissioned the "Natural History" essay for the
Dial in 1842, although he later came to have reservations about it.
Written as a review of the studies of biological diversity requested by
the state of Massachusetts, the essay illustrates the intersection of
science and poetry. In his review Thoreau suggested that the volumes of the state study were imperfect and spiritually limited because of their reliance on fact. This is not to say that he disputed their
findings, although he did discreetly point out that they included

several errors. Impressed with the thoroughness of the reports, Thoreau acknowledged the diligence and labor with which they had been compiled and noted that they adequately fulfilled the purposes for which they were commissioned. The state wanted complete catalogues of the region's natural riches, and that's what it got.

In reading "The Natural History of Massachusetts" it is nevertheless obvious that Thoreau lamented the fact that utilitarian concerns came at the expense of both enthusiasm for the task and any pleasurably affirmative rendering of the results. They were not enjoyable to read nor did they capture any of the pleasure Thoreau thought should accompany such endeavors. Thoreau felt that mere lists of species, which the reports essentially were, could not adequately express the resources of the state. He summarized the worth of the studies, as he saw it, at the end of his essay: "The volumes deal much in measurements and minute descriptions, not interesting to the general reader, with only here and there a colored sentence to allure him, like those plants growing in dark forests, which bear only leaves without blossoms. But the ground was comparatively unbroken, and we will not complain of the pioneer, if he raises no flowers with his first crop. Let us not underrate the value of a fact; it will one day flower in a truth."[7]

This assessment is a curious reworking of an earlier journal entry that similarly dealt with facts and their relation to truth. "How indispensable to a correct study of natural history is a perception of her true meaning—the fact will one day flower out into a truth. The season will mature and fructify what the understanding had cultivated. Mere accumulators of fact—collectors of materials for the master-workmen, are like those plants growing in dark forests, which 'put forth only leaves instead of blossoms'" (16 December 1837). The passages share a sense that the pregnant meaning of natural facts will be demonstrated in the future, but there is a significant difference between them.

Thoreau omits the reference to the "true meaning" of natural history from the *Dial* essay precisely because he has determined that the projects were undertaken without "correct" intentions to begin with—they were conducted with "more labor than enthusiasm." The state's investigators had worked to collect their data but failed to represent their findings in an enticing way, one that might use the creative capacities of language to stir readers. As Thoreau wrote in his journal, "The man of science, who is not seeking for expression but for fact to be expressed merely, studies nature as a dead language" (10 May 1853). Furthermore, Thoreau omits from the review his original formulation that it is the "mere accumulators of fact" who collect materials for the "master-workmen." Such collectors fail to bloom because they fail to produce anything of beauty. A master workman like Thoreau has an investment in both the facts and the literature that can be made from them.

In this essay Thoreau uses facts to arrive at his own reading of nature, transforming what in the hands of others was dry tabulation into poetic prose. From a mass of particulars, he arranges a distinctly shaped catalogue. Though he would himself assemble detailed and extensive lists of facts in his journals, his response in this essay is this effort to produce a more meaningful flowering truth:

> The nut-hatch and chickadee flitting in company through the dells of the wood, the one harshly scolding at the intruder, the other with a faint lisping note enticing him on; the jay screaming in the orchard; the crow cawing in unison with the storm; the partridge, like a russet link extended over from Autumn to Spring, preserving unbroken the chain of summers; the hawk with warrior-like firmness abiding the blasts of winter; the robin and lark lurking by warm springs in the woods; the familiar snowbird culling a few seeds in the garden or a few crumbs in the yard; and occasionally the shrike, with heedless and unfrozen melody bringing back summer again:
>
> > His steady sails he never furls,
> > At any time o'year,
> > And perching now on Winter's curls,
> > He whistles in his ear.[8]

As the passage unfolds, it catalogues its birds freely. It is evident, however, that this is neither a statistical census nor a detailed accounting of a singular moment. In fact, its coherence is somewhat forced by the writer. The passage is rather an irregular compilation of a number of situations: before our eyes birds flit, while off in the distance another is heard; a storm arises; the seasons shift, then shift again; calm comes with a snapshot of backyard foraging; finally, and with a dramatic flourish, there is a shift to an invocation in verse. In contrast to the state survey, what Thoreau puts together here is a reckoning of the many ways wildlife is apprehended, sometimes peripherally, sometimes prophetically. The insistence on sounds and songs reinforces the fact that we experience and taxonomically identify many creatures by hearing rather than sight. A characteristic song is one signature of a bird, and it indicates to the listener a proximate presence, even if the bird is not in sight. Routinely such signals are considered clues rather than proof because hearing is usually given lesser credence than sight—seeing, we say, is believing. By reminding us of nature's auditory aspects, Thoreau here makes an effort to democratize the sensual experience of our world.

Another feature of this compilation is something that frequently recurs in Thoreau's writings: his predilection for using facts of nature in a manner that intentionally counters the findings made by natural science. In opposition to scientific research, Thoreau often uses his observations to mythologize. As Thoreau renders it above, the shrike possesses a power that brings about the turn of seasons: "with heedless and unfrozen melody bringing back summer again." Although we are assured otherwise by science, there is still a modicum of truth to this claim, for animal behavior does anticipate global seasonal change. Innate and ingrained patterns of behavior (migration, mating, nesting) coordinate with annual changes of season. We now understand these connections as encoded features of evolutionary adaptation, but in the past the mysterious relations in the web of nature were given other meanings, although they were not considered coincidental. The correspondences were attributed to an invisible supernatural agency: the arrival of birds brought spring, rather than merely being a sign of spring. In its appeal to the imagination, Thoreau's depiction opens conceptual possibilities that the state documentation determinately ignores. If his relation is not categorically accurate, it is nevertheless "alluring" for the reader.

That the overall rendering of the passage is more poeticized than based in fact is irrelevant; for Thoreau the important thing is the manner of documentation. He strives to write poetically about an environment that is experienced poetically. He had alluded to a similar process in *A Week,* noting that from "the bald natural facts" of a reference work one could extract "the pleasure of poetry." In communicating his surroundings poetically, in part through proper poetic structures, Thoreau creates something akin to prose poetry. As Steven Monte notes, "When the essence of poetry is no longer felt to reside in its external features but rather in the intensity of the response it elicits in the reader, the possibility exists for something like the prose poem."[9]

We need to make an important qualification here, however. Genre studies assert that true prose poetry must be short. Beyond a certain length, "the tensions and the impact are forfeited and [the prose poem] becomes—more or less—poetic prose." Mindful of this distinction, Buell notes that the Transcendentalists were able to do impressive things with the idea of plenitude that the catalogue format facilitated, at least "in the more elementary units of composition," like the paragraph or passage. When they extended themselves further, Buell writes, they lapsed into sheer itemization. Considered in isolation, selected passages of Thoreau's writings may bear similarities to instances of prose poetry, but they properly exist as indissoluble constituents of something else. This is one reason why the extraction of Thoreau's lists is somewhat more difficult than singling out those of Whitman or Melville. As Walter Harding noted, what is impressive about *Walden* is that it is "tightly constructed, each sentence, each paragraph and each character is in its carefully chosen niche and cannot be moved or removed without severe damage to the artistry of the whole."[10]

Although Thoreau's major works are considered prose, they nevertheless challenge such a designation. The hybridized cast of his writings, published and unpublished, resists categorization, and his literary expressions sit uneasily in the old literary forms. Like some of the finest aggregating paragraphs found in Melville, Thoreau's prose can possess listed nests and subnests that call to mind the organic clusterings of Whitman. The bunches and groups caught in the intermittent eddies of the following passage, for instance, are as pleasurable as the paragraph's own riverine meanderings:

> It is worth while to make a voyage up this stream, if you go no farther than Sudbury, only to see how much country there is in the rear of us; great hills, and a hundred brooks, and farmhouses, and barns, and hay-stacks, you never saw before, and men everywhere; Sudbury, that is *Southborough* men, and Wayland, and Nine-Acre-Corner men, and Bound Rock, where four towns bound on a rock in the river, Lincoln, Wayland, Sudbury, Concord. Many waves are there agitated by the wind, keeping nature fresh, the spray blowing in your face, reeds and rushes waving; ducks by the hundred all uneasy in the surf, in the raw wind, just ready to rise, and now going off with a clatter and a whistling, like riggers straight for Labrador, flying against the stiff gale with reefed wings, or else circling round first, with their paddles briskly moving, just over the surf, to reconnoiter you before they leave these parts; gulls wheeling overhead, muskrats swimming for dear life, wet and cold, with no fire to warm them by that you know of; their labored homes rising here and there like haystacks; and countless mice and moles and winged titmice along the sunny, windy shore; cranberries tossed on the waves and heaving up on the beach, their little red skiffs beating about among the alders;—such healthy natural tumult as proves the last day is not yet at hand. And there stand all around the alders, and

birches, and oaks, and maples full of glee and sap, holding in
their buds until the waters subside. . . . You shall see men you
never heard of before, whose names you don't know, going
away down through the meadows with long ducking guns,
with watertight boots, wading through the fowl-meadow
grass, on bleak, wintry, distant shores, with guns at half cock;
and they shall see teal, blue-winged, green-winged shelldrakes,
whistlers, black ducks, ospreys, and many other wild and noble
sights before night, such as they who sit in parlors never dream
of. You shall see rude and sturdy, experienced and wise men,
keeping their castles, or teaming up their summer's wood, or
chopping alone in the woods, men fuller of talk and rare adventure in the sun and wind and rain, than a chestnut is of
meat; who were out not only in 1775 and 1812, but have been
out every day of their lives; greater men than Homer, or
Chaucer, or Shakespeare, only they never got time to say so;
they never took to the way of writing. Look at their fields, and
imagine what they might write, if they ever should put pen to
paper. Or what have they not written on the face of the earth
already, clearing, and burning, and scratching, and harrowing,
and plowing, and subsoiling, in and in, and out and out, and
over and over, again and again, erasing what they had already
written for want of parchment. [*T*, 8–9]

In the episode discussed in the previous chapter in which Ishmael
discovers the whale's intact skeleton, we could observe that Melville's Ishmael is someone who can draw conclusions from his
collected "valuable statistics." These conclusions amount to a kind
of Emersonian metaphysics of cetology deriving from a fluidity of
thought between the dissimilar modes of factual and poetic thinking. Ishmael's remarks in the osteological analysis of "A Bower in
the Arsacides," however, ultimately concede limitation rather than
knowledge. His measurements of the bones actually diminish the
stature of the whale, and Ishmael is abashed. "How vain and foolish,

then, thought I," he laments, "for timid untravelled man to try to comprehend aright this wondrous whale, by merely poring over his dead attenuated skeleton, stretched in this peaceful wood" (*MD*, 507).

Of course, if there ever were a figure in American letters who seemed capable of extrapolating broader comprehension through the observation of natural phenomena in peaceful woods, it was Melville's contemporary Thoreau. With seemingly tireless steps, Thoreau incrementally advanced his discovery of the world. Each new observation, each new piece of data, triggered in miniature the awakening he continually signaled in *Walden*. "It is only necessary," he noted in his journals, "to behold the least fact or phenomenon, however familiar, from a point a hair's breadth aside from our habitual path or routine, to be overcome, enchanted by its beauty and significance" (11 December 1855). Such curiosity and drive for investigation led Thoreau to record the following detailed structural examination of the body of an unusually large dead mouse. The description complements the skeletal analysis of Ishmael's cetacean: "Entire length, 8 inches; length from head to *base* of ears, 1 inch; body 3 (?); tail, $3\frac{1}{2}$ . . . hind legs longest, *say* $1\frac{1}{4}$; fore $\frac{3}{4}$; hind foot more than $\frac{3}{4}$ inch long . . . ears *large*, almost bare, thin, slaty-colored, $\frac{5}{8}$ inch long on outside; upper jaw $\frac{1}{4}$ + inch longer than lower . . . longest mustachios $1\frac{3}{8}$ inches" (16 February 1855).

In comparing the cetological and rodential quantifications, I must first acknowledge that there is more involved here than merely contrasting two exercises in comparative anatomy, inasmuch as the passages derive from two very different modes of writing. It is important to note the genre distinction between them because differences that affect the way the measurements are intended to be received have an influence on how they are produced.

The most fundamental difference is that Ishmael is Melville's fictive creation, and his primary purpose is commercial—broadly, the entertainment of readers. If he could not maintain readers' interest he would quickly be forgotten.[11] Whatever important articulations might be embedded in the text—philosophical, social, and moral dicta, allegories, or what have you—would disappear, like the *Pequod*, without a trace. Given the imperative of keeping the novel afloat, so to speak, Melville easily dispatches Ishmael's "valuable statistics": he offers them in a palatable prose that smoothly maintains the forward impetus of the novel.

Thoreau's journals constitute a different kind of document altogether. Although he drafted them with great care and occasionally shared them with acquaintances, Thoreau did not ever think that a publisher would want to distribute them in their entirety. (This, however, is not to deny that he put an enormous amount of creative energy into them; the work of the journals became for Thoreau his principal literary endeavor.) Notations such as those anatomizing the mouse typify a personal investigation of the world; they are documents of the development of the self in its interaction with nature. As such, they are not simply a set of reports upon the world Thoreau inhabited but are also reports upon himself and his relations to that world.

That the two excerpts were written with entirely different agendas and audiences in mind is as clear as the fact that the passages survey creatures as dissimilar as possible. One is huge, the other small; one is marine, the other terrestrial; one is reduced to a bleached skeleton, the other is recently deceased and free of evident necrosis. Furthermore, the specimens seem apt symbols for their respective examiners. Whales have an exotic cachet attached to them and course widely across the expanse of the globe, like Melville in his early years; mice remain in one area, like the "untravelled" (though not timid) Thoreau, and though they are taken for granted because they are so common, they have valuable information for those who know how to observe them properly.

Besides these obvious differences, Thoreau's meticulous statistics have an almost clinical thoroughness that well surpasses Ishmael's measurements. Thoreau's list reveals much about the sort of observer he was. The notations capture for the reader a mental image of an investigator manipulating the mouse's body and limbs to determine their lengths carefully and exactly, as if to uncover some truth of nature that the relative proportions insist on. This attitude contrasts with that of Whitman, who late in life cautions in *Specimen Days*, "You must not know too much, or be too precise or scientific about birds and trees and flowers and water craft; a certain free margin, and even vagueness—perhaps ignorance, credulity—helps your enjoyment of these things, and of the sentiment of feathered, wooded, river or marine Nature generally. I repeat it—don't want to know too exactly, or the reasons why."[12] Finally, whereas Ishmael is struck by a powerful sense of humility while strolling though the whale bower, in effect stunned by the sublimity of the natural world, Thoreau displays a kind of mastery over it, albeit limited. Represented on a small scale, the discipline of his technique here indicates a forceful engagement with the world, an attitude that can even demonstrate a kind of whimsy, as is evident in the deadpan final measurement.

Like his recording of snow depths, temperatures, tree rings, and the like, Thoreau's measurements here are certainly—echoing Elizabeth Sewall's phrasing—quantitative, mechanical, niggling, and pedestrian, though they are very much in contact with reality. They represent a kind of exact knowledge that enriches rather than robs the imagination. If they do not indicate an attitude Emerson would have approved of since he felt that our relation to truth was "not to be learned by any addition or subtraction or other comparison of known quantities" (*E*, 43), the notes do confirm a different variety of the valued "untaught sallies of the spirit" because, despite their nearly pedantic exactitude, they complete a higher philosophical purpose. For Thoreau the measurements record an unearthed *point d'appui*, a solid foundation on which to build. If Ishmael retreats from the whale's bleached bones, overcome by evidence of significances beyond his grasp, Thoreau converges upon his mouse skeleton to declare, "This is, and no mistake." The notes are documentary evidence of the kind of piercing concentration he argued for most powerfully in the manifesto "Where I Lived, and What I Lived For":

> Let us settle ourselves, and work and wedge our feet downward through mud and slush of opinion, and prejudice, and tradition, and delusion, and appearance, that alluvion which covers the globe, through Paris and London, through New York and Boston and Concord, through church and state, through poetry and philosophy and religion, till we come to a hard bottom and rocks in place which we can call *reality*, and say, This is, and no mistake; and then begin, having a *point d'appui*, below freshet and frost and fire, a place where you might found a wall or a state, or set a lamp-post safely, or perhaps a gauge, not a Nilometer, but a Realometer, that future ages might know how deep a freshet of shams and appearances had gathered from time to time. [*T*, 400]

As this wonderfully excavational passage suggests, digging its way through the interweaving layers of humanmade and therefore artificial impedimenta that separate us from truth, it is only the substantial reality of the natural world that at bottom affords us the bedrock of ontological security. In the nineteenth century, natural science was considered one means of undertaking this search for truth (although it is curiously omitted from Thoreau's collection of obstructions), but it was an approach that was becoming increasingly professionalized in terms of method and language. Thoreau conducted his natural studies at a particular point in American history, a transitional moment when the differentiation between amateur and professional scientist was being codified. The appointment of the respected scientist Louis Agassiz at Harvard in 1846 and the publication of Asa Gray's *Manual of Botany* in 1848 were but two events that significantly influenced the stature of natural history. As John Hildebidle characterizes it in *Thoreau: A Naturalist's Liberty*, Thoreau stood just before this irrevocable moment and made "a last effort to refuse to accept the split."[13]

But though the nascent boom in comprehensive and accurate

biological and botanical study invigorated Thoreau and his own researches, the absence of a meaningful philosophy underlying most
of the scientific investigation undertaken in the nineteenth century
had become increasingly distressing to Thoreau's Concord neighbor and sometime friend Emerson. Emerson had expressed his an-
noyance at the shallow, mechanical isolation of mere quantitative
scientific measurement from the other important "experiences" of
life in *Nature:* "The problems to be solved are precisely those which
physiologist and naturalist omit to state. . . . I cannot greatly honour minuteness in details, so long as there is no hint to explain the
relation between things and thoughts; no ray upon the metaphysics
of conchology, of botany, of the arts, to show the relation of the
forms of flowers, shells, animals, architecture, to the mind, and
build science upon ideas" (*E*, 43).

The gathering of facts that had been undertaken by science and the organized collections that Emerson had seen in Paris
had demonstrated a control of truth. "The use of natural history is
to give us aid in supernatural history," he wrote in *Nature* (*E*, 20).
But as Sherman Paul describes it, for Emerson the result would
prove to be the dead end of science, for it was a mechanical science
that collected facts but "failed to find them, as he did, raw and insignificant without the teleological presence of God." It was an attitude, Paul writes, that "searched piecemeal into a nature no longer
spiritually intimate with man."[14] (Asa Gray, an empiricist, held a reciprocal hostility toward Transcendentalism, and kept his distance
from it.)

The naturalism of the serious amateur offered its own rewards,
minus the accolades, to the layman. In its conclusion, the "point
d'appui" passage from *Walden* continues to affirm that the individual willing to engage the phenomena of the natural world, the
individual willing to "see," will achieve a seemingly antithetical

objective, one that is astonishingly revelatory anu transformative. Thoreau concludes that in an instant, in an illuminating moment of truth, the committed observer perfects a vaguely defined but teleological understanding: "If you stand right fronting and face to face to a fact, you will see the sun glimmer on both its surfaces, as if it were a cimeter, and feel its sweet edge dividing you through the heart and marrow, and so you will happily conclude your mortal career" (*T*, 400).

In his extraordinary book *The Senses of "Walden,"* Stanley Cavell directly links this fronting of facts (as exemplified in the study of the mouse) to the act of writing. Cavell reads Thoreau's appeal for engagement with the sharp edge of fact as an affirmation of a kind of writing that assumes responsibility for the meaningfulness of language, "totally [and] systematically." Provocatively, Cavell extends Thoreau's urging of the perception of truth in the unimpeded interface with reality to a call for an allegiance to the production of truth. For him, Thoreau's intention is "conviction," and *Walden* is "an accounting" in an absolute sense, where every line is "a mark of honesty." This represents Thoreau's conviction to the obligation of writing itself, for the actual notation of written words works only when every mark means something "in its look and in its sequence."[15]

Cavell astutely segregates Thoreau's prominently displayed budgets, however, as parodies of the customary conception of what it means to be honest. If the transparency is valid, according to this conception, then the credits and debits of one's account will compute in an irrevocably linear grammar:

My whole income from the farm was $23 44.
Deducting the outgoes   14 72½
There are left $ 8 71½. [*T*, 366]

It is significant, however, that the ledgers of addition and subtraction, perhaps Thoreau's best-known lists, are set apart from the more substantial text of *Walden* not only by their surrounding

white space but by their spirit as well. Our words and how we use them, Cavell's argument concludes, show "how we count phenomena, what counts for us,"[16] and the entire "Economy" chapter works to admonish us for our pecuniary concerns and material possessions. Regarding such things, we are richer with fewer and poorer with more, and a "Spartan simplicity of life" in conjunction with "an elevation of purpose" can provide the cure.

Cavell points out that Thoreau plays upon this accountable kind of writing, in which "words and their orderings are meant by human beings," and "the saying of something when and as it is said is as significant as the meaning and ordering of the words said." (These comments on ordering and sequence are especially resonant for a consideration of literary lists.) In the "ecstasies of exactness" of such writing, the committed writer's sentences "must at each point come at to an edge." According to Cavell's rendering, facts are significant because rather than confining the imagination, they release it; "left to its own devices," he writes, the imagination "will not recover reality, it will not form an edge."[17] Extending this reading, we might posit that where there is a deficiency of fact we will have an imprecise or ambiguous picture. A celebrated instance of this, an occasion in which Thoreau threw a "veil over his experience" as Emerson described it, is the enigmatic formulation of "I long ago lost a hound, a bay horse, and a turtledove . . . " (T, 336). (Readers have speculated on this little parable for decades, but its indeterminacy is precisely what is so attractive about it. As Emerson belatedly judged, Thoreau's "riddles were worth reading," adding that "if at any time I do not understand the expression, it is yet just.")[18]

At the other extreme, in contrast, at times Thoreau's prose can almost crystallize with a surfeit of fact: "In 1845 Walden froze entirely over for the first time on the night of the 22d of December, Flint's and other shallower ponds and the river having been frozen ten days or more; in '46, the 16th; in '49, about the 31st; and in '50, about the 27th of December; in '52, the 5th of January; in '53, the 31st of December" (T, 520). And as the freezing of the pond is chroni-

cled, so is its thawing: "In 1845 Walden was first completely open on the 1st of April; in '46, the 25th of March; in '47, the 8th of April; in '51, the 28th of March; in '52, the 18th of April; in '53, the 23d of March; in '54, about the 7th of April" (*T,* 564). These instances of record keeping, as precise as they are with regard to dates, and as strict as they are in their ordering of years, days, and months, nonetheless bring to the fore the changeability of nature: with each repetition of the seasonal pattern there is variability. But if the second list gives a particular data value of half of the freeze-thaw cycle, the collection is used by Thoreau only as a starting point from which to describe the breaking up of the ice and the vernal thawing of the sand and clay banks that encircle the pond.

A few pages later the depiction of the thaw, in all its liquidity, becomes itself a "foliaceous mass." In contrast to the crispness of the collected dates, the representation of the thaw is fluid, letters oozing into words ("The radicals of lobe are *lb,* the soft mass of the *b* . . . with a liquid *l* behind it pressing it forward" [*T,* 566]), words into sentences, and sentences into paragraphs with a freely organic inevitability, like spring, which refuses to be confined within a tabular form. Here Thoreau's writing, like the living earth it describes, "is not a mere fragment of dead history, stratum upon stratum like leaves in a book . . . but living poetry like the leaves of a tree" (*T,* 567).

Rebirth begins with the thaw, and as evidence of spiritual renewal here Thoreau counts "the first tender signs of the infant year," the newly emerging wildflowers: "life-everlasting, golden-rods, pinweeds . . . cottonwoods, cattails, mulleins, johnswort, hard-hack, meadowsweet" (*T,* 569). At the end of the chapter he tells over the other signs of the waxing year: the visits of the loon to the pond and the phoebe to the cabin, the songs of the woodthrush, the whippoorwill, the brown-thrasher, the veery, the wood-pewee, the chewink. If he is one to pass on the old ascetic adage that "a man is rich in proportion to the number of things which he can afford to let alone" (*T,* 387), Thoreau is also one to exclaim unrestrainedly,

"We can never have enough of nature" (*T*, 575). The inventories in "Economy" are Thoreau's mockeries; throughout *Walden*, the journals, and the other writings, he takes stock of his important things in an entirely different way.

Thoreau's journals and his other writings, like *Moby-Dick*, contained meticulous observations of the world held intimately alongside fragments of verse and prose. Thoreau's close scrutiny of patterns or peculiarities in nature often led him to set down reflections upon human nature. In other instances his documentation of phenomena was just that—the notations of an individual interested enough in his surroundings to record them. In this way his writings are inseparably both a recording of the world as one man saw it and an intriguing memoir of an individual who unconsciously selected, pursued, and represented choice fragments from the multitude impressing themselves upon him. The later journals, however, hold extensive listings of flora and fauna seen on Thoreau's various excursions, the kind of inventories that eventually made Thoreau himself philosophically uncomfortable. As he confided in his journal on Christmas Day, 1851, "What sort of science is that which enriches the understanding, but robs the imagination?"

The rather ticklish relation between science and poetry that Ishmael's methodological comments had suggested in *Moby-Dick*—that "facts" should be kept separate from "poetry"—was also confronted by Thoreau. In contrast to Ishmael's predicament of how to adjudicate between facts on the one hand and poems on the other, however, Thoreau's problem was to elide the difference between them. For the true amateur naturalist—that is, the living as opposed to the fictional one—it was not only possible but common for science and poetry to be united: "I have a commonplace book for facts and another for poetry, but I find it difficult always to preserve the vague distinctions which I had in mind, for the most

interesting and beautiful facts are so much the more poetry and
that is their success. They are *translated* from earth to heaven. I see
that if my facts were sufficiently vital and significant,—perhaps
transmuted more into the substance of the human mind,—I
should need but one book of poetry to contain them all" (Journal,
18 February 1852).

Thoreau here states explicitly what had been implicit for
Melville in the writing of *Moby-Dick:* it is not so much that science
and poetry are two irresolvable essences set in opposition to each
other—"this portion of my blank page I devote to my statistics
(which have significance for me because of their basis in fact), and
this other portion to my verse"—but rather that it is possible to en-
vision a reformulation that voids the schism between the two and to
conceive of facts *as* poetry and vice versa. In his sweeping *American
Renaissance,* F. O. Matthiessen provided an apt description of the
individual who was capable of this feat of interconversion: "The
different forms of his experience—of observation and of poetry, of
judgment and of fancy, of science and of faith—were not sundered
but so close together that he could pass freely from one to another
and make use of all in each."[19] (Although this description was intended for Thoreau, we should note that it might apply equally to
the author of *Moby-Dick,* for it is in just this way that the many scientific and historic facts function cooperatively with the pure fiction, in a sense unified in the "one book of poetry" that Melville's
encyclopedic novel essentially is.)

Nevertheless, Thoreau's confession of difficulty makes apparent his unease at always acting as arbiter. Maintaining a clear line of
demarcation between facts and poetry was not always possible because, as Hildebidle points out, Thoreau sensed that there was
"something beyond the facts which must always be kept in sight."[20]
This sensitivity to extrafactual significance in his careful observations tended to cloud the distinction between the two options. In a
sense, Thoreau's sensitivity could have been an externalization of
his inability to categorize himself satisfactorily. Thoreau had been

an admirer of Linnaean nomenclature, which was a system that he considered particularly "poetic." Nevertheless, when he applied this classification system to himself, he found himself relegated to a catch-all designation. "According to Linnæus's classification," he wrote in his journal, "I come under the head of the *Miscellaneous Botanophilists*,—'Botanophili sunt, qui varia de vegetabilibus tradiderunt, licet ea non proprie de scientiam botanicam spectant,' either one of the *Biologi (panegyrica plerumque exclamarunt)* or *Poetae*" (17 February 1852).

Such a self-assessment suggests that Thoreau probably wanted to remove from consideration any idea of a division between science and poetry, though he does not state this directly. Linnaeus's Latin here roughly translates, "Lovers of botany are those who have handed down various things about plants, although they look at these things not exclusively concerning the knowledge of botany." The discriminating characteristics of the self-categorization here, the key features that make Thoreau stand apart from the ordinary school of naturalists, are the words "various things" and "not exclusively concerning." There is implied in this phrasing the separation of a holistic comprehension of a subject from mere knowledge of it, a distinction that would have appealed to Thoreau since such "Miscellaneous Botanophilists" could communicate something more than the identification of plants based on their taxonomic features. This comprehension indicates a curiosity about botanical variation that does not totally subdue other human intellectual capabilities (figuration, abstraction, theological and philosophical speculation, societal criticism, awe, humility) beneath the study of process and differentiation. Rather, these two modes of thinking—logical and imaginative—though distinct, are allied.

Until Thoreau's time it seems to have been a common assumption that the observation of nature was inherently a spiritual and moral enterprise that did not conflict with the tasks of science. Consequently, Thoreau was free not to "let the practical offices of science, its classification, its measurements, its numerations, take precedence over other forms of understanding," as Lewis Mumford has described it. Hildebidle concurs but in addition posits that something more than lack of intelligence or ability kept Thoreau from the ranks of the professional naturalists, manifestly his certainty that there are "states of consciousness concerning which science has no relevance, and to which science contributes little insight."[21] That Thoreau could not easily choose between the categories of the "biologi" and the "poetae" is obvious, since his self-defining journal entry concludes in a state of irresolution between "either" and "or."

Still, while he claimed elsewhere that he looked at nature with no intention of having any "communication to make to the Royal Society,"[22] nevertheless, the choice between science and poetry was not quite as clear-cut for him as for someone like John Ruskin. Ruskin had set the botanist and the poet in opposition, distinguishing them, with evident bias, in his preface to the second edition of his *Modern Painters:* "This is the difference between the mere botanist's knowledge of plants, and the great painter's or poet's knowledge of them. . . . The one counts the stamens, and affixes a name, and is content; the other observes every character of the plant's colour and form; considering each of its attributes as an element of expression, he seizes on its lines of grace or energy, rigidity or repose. . . . He associates it in his mind with all the features of the situation it inhabits, and the ministering agencies necessary to its support. Thenceforward, the flower is to him a living creature, with histories written on its leaves, and passions breathing in its motions." Such a simplification—not to mention the overt imbalance between "mere" botanist and "great" painter or poet—proved disappointing to Thoreau, and he took the book to task in his journal: "I have just read Ruskin's 'Modern Painters.' I am disappointed in not finding it a more out-of-door book, for I have heard that such was its character, but its title might have warned me. He does not describe Nature as Nature, but as Turner painted her, and though the work betrays that he has given a close attention to Nature, it appears to have been with an artist's or critic's design. How much is written about Nature as somebody has portrayed her, how little about Nature as she is, and chiefly concerns us, i.e. how much prose, how little poetry!" (6 October 1857). Recalling the interconversion of facts and poetry, when Thoreau writes, "how little poetry," we may with some justification interpret him as meaning "how little fact," in defense of the kind of "botanist's knowledge" that characterizes the naturalist.

One of the chief ironies here is that Thoreau's own creative gifts inclined toward finer and finer expression in prose, with a concurrent diminution in his production of poetry, both in quantity and quality. He began to feel disappointment rereading poetic works he had previously found inspiring. Nonetheless, as we have already glimpsed, throughout his writings Thoreau consistently used references to poetry in a metaphoric rather than a literal sense. He employed poetic representation especially to describe the beauty of nature or his subjective encounters and experiences. Ultimately, he considered himself a creator of poetry, though not necessarily a writer of it. As he described himself in *A Week,* he was "an unskilful rhymer" to whom even the muse spoke in prose, yet also an individual who produced a "true poem" that was "not printed on paper." This true poem was one that was coincident with his life, "*what he ha[d] become through his work.*" Ironically, Thoreau found expression for this sentiment in a couplet: "My life has been the poem I would have writ, / But I could not both live and utter it" (*T,* 279). His copious output (fourteen volumes of journals alone), gives ample evidence that he was capable of literary production. The couplet is all the more ironic since much of this output involved the documentation of his life.

I have digressed. To conclude what started as a consideration of Thoreau's lists that compile, often poetically, the facts of nature, we

must further examine the nature of fact. It may be difficult for readers to reconcile the image of Thoreau the statistician or the exacting
anatomist, ruler in one hand and pen in the other, with the writer
who elsewhere avowed, "I would fain set down something besides
facts" (Journal, 9 November 1851), for certainly the seasonal history
of the pond or the measurements of the mouse amount to "particular truths known by actual observation," as the *Oxford English Dictionary* defines facts. Thoreau's attitude toward facts, occurrences
of natural phenomena observed and recorded, seems inconsistent
until we probe carefully into his own interpretation of a fact. Indeed, Thoreau's personal definition of what constitutes a fact is radically different from and opposed to the use of facts in the worlds of
science and society and is one of the major underpinnings of both
his personal philosophy and the theory of literature he employed.

In the essay "Persecution and the Art of Writing," Leo Strauss
argues that writers who possess unorthodox views must develop a
particular method of writing, "writing between the lines," to convey
their messages to their intended audiences. As a writer whose opinions were frequently critical of and contrary to those of the majority, Thoreau qualifies as a member of this class. Indeed, *Walden*
largely fits Strauss's definition of a type of literature addressed to
"trustworthy and intelligent readers only." This literature is based,
Strauss writes, on the principle that "thoughtless men are careless
readers, and only thoughtful men are careful readers. Therefore an
author who wishes to address only thoughtful men has but to write
in such a way that only a very careful reader can detect the meaning
of his book."[23]

Many readers have noted that Thoreau seems to write on two
levels at once. Thoreau encoded his writings to reach a select audience within his general reading public in a way that required em-
bedding one level of discourse within another. As Steven Fink describes it, Thoreau wrote on one level to interest ordinary readers
and on another "to satisfy the rare extravagant reader capable of going out-of-doors for wilder meanings."[24] Just as it takes a careful

reader to catch all Thoreau's punning wordplay, so too must one read mindfully to fully appreciate his distinctive definitions and the frisson these definitions generate when considered alongside their popular significations. When Thoreau announces in *Walden*, for example, that "the cost of a thing is the amount of what I will call life which is required to be exchanged for it" (*T*, 128), he is not only subverting the language of business—a feat he sustains throughout the "Economy" section of *Walden*—he is further reappropriating language so that its service to him will transcend its conventional use. The firm assertion places the definition within himself: it is "the amount of what *I* will call life" that is important. Georg Simmel defined the worth of an item thus: "Economic value as such does not inhere in an object in its isolated self-existence, but comes to an object only through the expenditure of another object which is given for it."[25] For Thoreau, cost is the expenditure of living, a trade-off of time that would otherwise be spent in different pursuits.

When Thoreau states in his journal what "facts" will signify for him, he is similarly appropriating common terminology to fulfill his own idiosyncratic purposes. "Facts," he declares, "should only be as the frame to my pictures; they should be material to the mythology which I am writing; not facts to assist men to make money, farmers to farm profitably, in any common sense; facts to tell who I am, and where I have been or what I have thought: as now the bell rings for evening meeting, and its volumes of sound, like smoke which rises from where a cannon is fired, make the tent in which I dwell. My facts shall be falsehoods to the common sense. I would so state facts that they shall be significant, shall be myths or mythologic. Facts which the mind perceived, thoughts which the body thought,—with these I deal" (9 November 1851).

If *Walden*'s "cimeter" passage is meant to stir readers to engage the "hard bottom and rocks" of "reality" rather than the murky "alluvium," this journal entry is intended to show the world that he is so engaged. Smoke seen rising from a cannon indicates that it has been fired; sound heard resonating from a bell indicates that it has been struck. Similarly, his deliberate documentation of facts is the natural conclusion to his encounter with individual entities. As Cavell reminds us, "A fact is not merely an event in the world but the assertion of an event, the wording of the world."[26] The recording of a fact indicates that the mind has, with a spark of consciousness, registered a "thing." For Thoreau registered facts leave the record of his experience, his observation of particular objects of nature and particular occurrences. As he writes in one of his earliest journals, in 1841, his recordings are "gleanings from the field which in action I reap." They are facts that tell who he is, and he defines himself in relation to these external things. Nonetheless, this smoke-sound-tent complex is fragile and ephemeral. As the sound fades and the smoke dissipates, so too the connection to a natural fact passes. But with a fertile and varied landscape other connections can be made in a seemingly endless series. It is such encounters with individual facts of nature that are underappreciated in Thoreau's journals. Though he cannot reside in any single instance as he would in a castle or a fortress, the journals house him, ascetically and peacefully, in page after page of documentation and, necessarily, self-documentation.

Thoreau also deliberately associates his facts with the improbable and the inexpedient at the expense of the practical. The facts are "falsehoods" used to establish the "myth" of himself; they are exercises in self-fashioning. Marking the trail he has left, the facts will tell a story of events that serves to explain who he is, how he came to be the individual he is. But additionally the facts build the mythology of the external world; they constitute his mythopoeia, his way of understanding the world. Elizabeth Sewall describes mythmaking as characteristic of both science and poetry, "activities in which thinker and instrument combine in some situation which is passionately exciting because it is fraught with possibilities for discoveries."[27] Pulling together these four elements—science and poetry, nature and myth—Thoreau links his facts to fable and links himself to the world. "If I am overflowing with life," he records, "[if I] am rich in experience for which I lack expression, then nature will be my language full of poetry,—all nature will *fable*, and every natural phenomenon be a myth" (Journal, 10 May 1853). As Emerson writes in *Nature*, "To the wise . . . a fact is true poetry, and the most beautiful of fables" (*E*, 48).

The conjunction of nature and myth in Thoreau's writings can be explicit. In the opening of the "Baker Farm" chapter of *Walden*, he catalogues trees in a manner that echoes the passage from book 10 of the *Metamorphoses*, as assembled by the great recorder of myth, Ovid:

> Strong trees came up there—the Chaonian oak,
> The Heliad's poplar, and the lofty-branched
> Deep mast-tree, the soft linden and the beech,
> The brittle hazel, and the virgin laurel-tree,
> The ash for strong spears, the silver-fir,
> The ilex bent with acorns and the plane,
> The various tinted maple and with those,
> The lotus and green willows from their stream,
> Evergreen box and slender tamarisks,
> Rich myrtles of two colors and the tine,
> Bending with green-blue berries: and you, too,
> The pliant-footed ivy, came along
> With the tendril-branching grape-vines, and the elm
> All covered with twist-vines, the mountain-ash,
> Pitch-trees and arbute-trees of blushing fruit,
> The bending-palm prized after victories,
> The bare-trunk pine of tufted foliage,
> Bristled upon the top, a pleasant sight
> Delightful to the Mother of the Gods.[28]

Thoreau inverts Ovid's great catalogue, however. It was important to him to know the specific location of plants and trees in Concord, and so, whereas Ovid records the trees drawn to Orpheus by his song, *Walden* catalogues the trees that the author himself seeks out:

> Sometimes I rambled to pine groves, standing like temples, or
> like fleets at sea, full-rigged, with wavy boughs, and rippling

with light, so soft and green and shady that the Druids would have forsaken their oaks to worship in them; or to the cedar wood beyond Flint's Pond, where the trees, covered with hoary blue berries, spiring higher and higher, are fit to stand before Valhalla, and the creeping juniper covers the ground with wreaths full of fruit; or to swamps where the usnea lichen hangs in festoons from the white-spruce trees, and toad-stools, round tables of the swamp gods, cover the ground, and more beautiful fungi adorn the stumps, like butterflies or shells, veg-etable wrinkles; where the swamp-pink and dogwood grow, the red alder-berry glows like eyes of imps, the waxwork grooves and crushes the hardest woods in its folds, and the wild-holly berries make the beholder forget his home with their beauty, and he is dazzled and tempted by nameless other wild forbidden fruits, too fair for mortal taste. Instead of call-ing on some scholar, I paid many a visit to particular trees, of kinds which are rare in this neighborhood, standing far away in the middle of some pasture, or in the depths of a wood or swamp, or on a hill-top; such as the black-birch, of which we have some handsome specimens two feet in diameter; its cousin the yellow-birch, with its loose golden vest, perfumed like the first; the beech, which has so neat a bole and beautifully lichen-painted, perfect in all its details, of which, excepting scattered specimens, I know but one small grove of sizable trees left in the township, supposed to have been planted by the pigeons who were once baited with beech nuts near by; it is worth the while to see the silver grain sparkle when you split this wood; the bass; the hornbeam; the *celtis occidentalis*, or false elm, of which we have but one well-grown; some taller mast of a pine, a shingle tree, or a more perfect hemlock than usual, standing like a pagoda in the midst of the woods; and many others I could mention. These were the shrines I visited both summer and winter. [*T,* 483]

Regardless of who is in motion, regardless of who or what remains fixed, both compilations parade a variety of species before the eyes of the reader. But notable here is the determined pantheism that permeates Thoreau's passage. As his "shrines," Thoreau depicts these trees as sacred, in a manner that evokes a surprising number of belief systems: the "temples" are fit worshiping places for Druids; the trees are worthy of standing before Valhalla; they are used by "swamp gods"; they have tempting "forbidden fruits." If such a sweep does not encompass enough, the trees also take their origins from local myth; they were planted by pigeons baited nearby.

In his study of Thoreau's journals Leonard Neufeldt has concluded that of all the metaphors Thoreau employed to describe his "journalizing"—gleaning, harvesting, gathering, collecting, storing, preserving—the most fitting is "anthologizing."[29] *Anthologia,* Neufeldt reminds us, before it came to refer to a collection of lyric poetry, literally meant "flower gathering." Familiar with this classical connection, and using a trope exquisitely tailored to his botanical interest, Thoreau figured the facts inscribed in his journals as flowers plucked from the field. The inscribed fact took the place of the perceived specimen: Thoreau took the specimens from the wild and bunched them together. "Mere facts & dates & names communicate more than we suspect," he noted, "whether the flower looks better in the nosegay—than in the meadow where it grew—& we had to wet our feet to get it." Recording the sighting of a flower in the anthology enhances the beauty of the physical flower, both preserving it in an assembled nosegay and conserving it in the wild. Given Thoreau's lifelong interest in language and etymology, it is clear that when he allied his facts with flowers he was aware of the third line of the syllogism. If the facts could be handpicked flowers, and a collection of flowers resembled a collection of lyrics, then the facts, by a transitive chain, could be like lyrics.

As repositories of facts, Thoreau's journals act like a writers' warehouse in which he indexes his stored observations.[30] Here is a typical list:

It occurs to me that these phenomena occur simultaneously,
say June 12th, viz.:
Heat about 85 at 2 P. M. True summer.
Hylodes cease to peep.

Purring frogs (*Rana palustris*) cease.
Lightning-bugs first seen.
Bullfrogs trump *generally*.
Mosquitoes begin to be really troublesome.
Afternoon thunder-showers almost regular.
Sleep with open window (10th), and wear thin coat and ribbon on neck.
Turtles fairly and generally begun to lay. [15 June 1860]

In addition to their function as storage, the journals constitute a complex of processing plants as well, where the notations become descriptions, meditations, ruminations, judgments, and other types of studies: "From all points of the compass, from the earth beneath and the heavens above, have come these inspirations and been duly entered in the order of arrival in the journal. Thereafter, when the time arrived, they were winnowed into lectures, and again, in due time, from lectures into essays" (1845–1847). In short, in the journals Thoreau negotiates the transformation of facts into forms of written expression that have entirely different orders of resonance; they are where he undertakes what we might call the synthesis of "poetry" from science. Poetry, as he formulated it, "puts an interval between the impression & the expression—waits till the seed germinates naturally" (23 July 1851). This was frequently a two-step procedure, a reporting of specifics followed by a second look: "I would fain make two reports in my Journal, first the incidents and observations of today; and by tomorrow I review the same and record what was omitted before, which will often be the most significant and poetic part" (27 March 1857). It would seem that setting aside particulars and allowing for an incubation period are necessary for the most meaningful yields: later returns to the details may uncover new, previously unseen material or allow for a ripening of thought to arise from the original matter.

Thoreau's work here calls to mind the methods Goethe described when asked about the secret of his art. "I let objects produce their effects on me, in all patience and quietness, then I observe

these effects and take pains with myself to give them back or repro-
duce them, true and undistorted." "This is the whole secret of what
people are pleased to call genius," he added. Elaborating on the
strengths—and limitations—of genius, Goethe exposed the not so
mysterious manner by which it produces art. In seeming contradiction to its etymological derivation (from Latin, *gignere,* "to beget"),
genius for Goethe was not a quasi-divine faculty that endowed its
possessor with the ability to bring forth creations ex nihilo but
rather a wholly human, finely tuned capability of the imagination
to make use of matter reserved from previous experience. With a
straightforwardness that coordinates well with Thoreau's, Goethe
explained that genius retained observed phenomena; it preserved
facts: "The very greatest genius would not get very far if it had to
bring forth everything out of itself. What is genius if it is not the capacity to make use of everything that it meets with? . . . Everything
I have ever seen, heard, or taken notice of I have stored up and
turned to good account."[31]

For Thoreau the most veracious recorder was the stream ("for
every higher freshet and intenser frost is recorded by it"), a genius
that kept "a faithful and a true journal of every event in its experience" (Journal, 5 July 1852). At times he strove for similar accuracy,
and his efforts at fidelity and completion led to him to compose his
most significant contribution to New England botany, a detailed
list of plants organized into zones, which he recorded during an ascent of Mount Washington in 1858. This was the most thorough accounting that had been made for the location, and it was not super-
seded until the twentieth century:

> To sum up (omitting sedges, etc.) plants prevailed thus on Mt.
> Washington:—
>   1st. *For three quarters of a mile:* Black (?) spruce, yellow
> birch, hemlock, beech, canoe birch, rock maple, fir, mountain
> maple, red cherry, striped maple, etc.
>   2d. *At one and three quarters of a mile:* Spruce prevails, with
> fir, canoe and yellow birch. Rock maple, beech, and hemlock

disappear. (On Lafayette, lambkill, *Viburnum nudum,* nemo-panthes, mountain-ash.) Hardwoods in bottom of ravines, above and below.

3d. *At three miles, or limit of trees* (colliers' shanty and Ravine Camp): Fir prevails, with *some spruce* and canoe birch; mountain-ash, *Alnus viridis* (in moist ravines), red cherry, mountain maple, *Salix* (*humilis*-like and *Torreyana*-like, etc.), *Vaccinium Canadense, Ribes lacustre, prostratum,* and *floridum* (?), rhodora, *Amelanchier oligocarpa,* tree-cranberry, chio-genes, *Cornus Canadensis, Oxalis Acetosella,* clintonia, gold-thread, *Listera cordata, Smilacina bifolia, Solidago thyrsoidea, Ranunculus abortivus, Platanthera obtusata* and *dilatata, Oxyria digyna, Viola blanda, Aster prenanthes* (?), *A. acuminatus, Ar-alia nudicaulis, Polystichum aculeatum* (?), wool-grass, etc.

4th. *Limit of trees to within one mile of top,* or as far as dwarf firs: Dwarf fir, spruce, and some canoe birch, *Vaccinium uligi-nosum* and *Vitis-Idaea, Salix Uva-ursi,* ledum, *Empetrum ni-grum, Oxalis Acetosella, Linnaea borealis, Cornus Canadensis, Alsine Graenlandica, Diapensia Lapponica,* gold-thread, epi-gaea, sorrel, *Geum radiatum* var. *Peckii, Solidago Virgaurea* var. *alpina,* S. *thyrsoidea* (not so high as last), hellebore, oldenlan-dia, clintonia, *Viola palustris,* trientalis, a little *Vaccinium an-gustifolium* (?), ditto of *Vaccinium caespistosum, Phyllodoce taxifolia, Uvularia grandiflora, Loiseleuria procumbens, Cas-siope hypnoides, Rubus triflorus, Heracleum lanatum,* arch-angelica, *Rhododendron Lapponicum, Arctostaphylos alpina, Salix herbacea, Polygonum viviparum, Veronica alpina, Nabalus Boottii, Epilobium alpinum, Platanthera dilatata,* common rue, *Castilleja septentrionalis, Arnica mollis, Spiraea salicifolia, Salix repens, Solidago thyrsoidea,* raspberry (Hoar), *Lycopodium an-notonium* and *Selago,* small fern, grass, sedges, moss and lichens. (On Lafayette, *Vaccinium Oxycoccus, Smilacina trifo-lia, Kalmia glauca, Andromeda calyculata,* red cherry, yellow (water) lily, *Eriophorum vaginatum.*)

5th. *Within one mile of top: Potentilla tridentata,* a very lit-tle fir, spruce, and canoe birch, one mountain-ash, *Alsine Graenlandica,* diapensia, *Vaccinium Vitis-Idaea,* gold-thread, *Lycopodium annotinium* and *Selago,* sorrel, *Silene acaulis, Sol-*

idago Virgaurea var. *alpina,* hellebore, oldenlandia, *Lonicera caerulea,* clintonia, *Viola palustris,* trientalis, *Vaccinium angustifolium* (?), a little fern, *Geum radiatum* var. *Peckii,* sedges, rush, moss, and lichens, and probably more of the last list.

6th. At apex: Sedge, moss, and lichens, and a little alsine, diapensia, *Solidago Virgaurea* var. *alpina* (?), etc. [Journal, 19 July 1858]

This is a very serious list indeed. It is determined in its accuracy and comprehensiveness. For this undertaking, humor and poetry are inexpedient: both are absent from the botanical tabulation, making the list difficult to get through. Though a testament to Thoreau's vigor and his careful, unremitting attention, this expedition up Mount Washington, plant by plant, is not for the faint of heart. If anything, what this compilation suggests to nonbotanists is that perhaps there are trips with Thoreau that are just too demanding for us, too laborious. What relief we find upon reaching the summit, but we are not sure that we want to do it again.

Thoreau realized his own limitations, and his compulsion to view the world as a student of natural history took its toll. Wishing he could enjoy nature rather than observe it, he confided to his journal, "I feel that I am dissipated by so many observations. . . . I have almost a slight, dry headache as the result of all this observing" (23 March 1853). He recognized a certain philosophical discomfort caused by his systematic approach to nature and desired "a true sauntering of the eye" (13 September 1852), in which "the walker does not too curiously observe particulars, but sees, hears, scents tastes, and feels only himself" (30 March 1853).

Thoreau knew that neither he nor his journals could sustain the level of faithful recording the stream could achieve. One of his principal challenges was "how to render an account of something that is unaccountable," as Hildebidle finely phrases it.[32] In reference to his *Walden* budgets, Thoreau noted that their completeness gave them value, though whether the recorded expenses squared with the actual amounts is irrelevant. The itemizations of expenses, like the itemization of observations, however thorough, are necessarily incomplete. If objects and experiences can be particularized and collected, tabulated in lists or poetic catalogues, certain things, Thoreau knew, still eluded such representation. He recognized that many of the phenomena and experiences of life could not be captured by any conventional system of notation. "Perhaps the facts most astounding and most real are never communicated by man to man," he wrote in the "Higher Laws" chapter of *Walden* (*T,* 495), suggesting the inadequacy of all means of expression, spoken as well as written. Turning to the indeterminacy of nature's infinite gradation—which in truth resists our measures of scaling—Thoreau found the most fitting analogue with which to represent the value of a life lived, really a valuelessness that is incapable of being estimated or computed. "The true harvest of my daily life," he wrote, "is somewhat as intangible and indescribable as the tints of morning or evening" (*T,* 495).

Extracts

A List of Literary Lists

"Another secret, my dear. I have added to my collection of birds."

"Really, Miss Flite?" said I, knowing how it pleased her to have her confidence received with an appearance of interest.

She nodded several times, and her face became overcast and gloomy. "Two more. I call them the Wards in Jarndyce. They are caged up with all the others. With Hope, Joy, Youth, Peace, Rest, Life, Dust, Ashes, Waste, Want, Ruin, Despair, Madness, Death, Cunning, Folly, Words, Wigs, Rags, Sheepskin, Plunder, Precedent, Jargon, Gammon, and Spinach!"

CHARLES DICKENS, *Bleak House*

"I wonder, now, if I was divided up and inventoried," said [Augustine St. Claire] as he ran over the paper, "how much I might bring. Say so much for the shape of my head, so much for a high forehead, so much for arms, and hands, and legs, and then so much for education, learning, talent, honesty, religion! Bless me! there would be small charge on that last, I'm thinking."

HARRIET BEECHER STOWE, *Uncle Tom's Cabin*

"Shif'less!" said Miss Ophelia to herself, proceeding to tumble over the drawer, where she found a nutmeg-grater and two or three nutmegs, a Methodist hymn-book, a couple of soiled Madras handkerchiefs, some yarn and knitting-work, a paper of tobacco and a pipe, a few crackers, one or two gilded china-saucers with some pomade in them, one or two thin old shoes, a piece of flannel carefully pinned up enclosing some small white onions, several damask table-napkins, some coarse crash towels, some twine and darning-needles, and several broken papers, from which sundry sweet herbs were sifting into the drawer.

HARRIET BEECHER STOWE, *Uncle Tom's Cabin*

"Do you think," said Candide, "that mankind always massacred one another as they do now? Were they always guilty of lies, fraud, treachery, ingratitude, inconstancy, envy, ambition, and cruelty? Were they always thieves, fools, cowards, gluttons, drunkards, misers, calumniators, debauchees, fanatics, and hypocrites?"

VOLTAIRE, *Candide*

Closing the door upon himself, Israel advanced to the middle of the chamber, and looked curiously round him.

A dark tessellated floor, but without a rug; two mahogany

chairs, with embroidered seats, rather the worse for wear; one mahogany bed, with a gay but tarnished counterpane; a marble washstand, cracked, with a china vessel of water, minus the handle. The apartment was very large; this part of the house, which was a very extensive one, embracing the four sides of a quadrangle, having, in a former age, been the hotel of a nobleman. The magnitude of the chamber made its stinted furniture look meagre enough.

But in Israel's eyes, the marble mantel (a comparatively recent addition) and its appurtenances, not only redeemed the rest, but looked quite magnificent and hospitable in the extreme. Because, in the first place, the mantel was graced with an enormous old-fashioned square mirror, of heavy plate glass, set fast, like a tablet, into the wall. And in this mirror was genially reflected the following delicate articles:—first, two bouquets of flowers inserted in pretty vases of porcelain; second, one cake of white soap; third, one cake of rose-colored soap (both cakes very fragrant); fourth, one wax candle; fifth, one china tinder-box; sixth, one bottle of Eau de Cologne; seventh, one paper of loaf sugar, nicely broken into sugar-bowl size; eighth, one silver teaspoon; ninth, one glass tumbler; tenth, one glass decanter of cool pure water; eleventh, one sealed bottle containing a richly hued liquid, and marked "Otard."

HERMAN MELVILLE, *Israel Potter*

"Odd fish!"
"Poor fellow!"
"Who can he be?"
"Casper Hauser."
"Bless my soul!"
"Uncommon countenance."
"Green prophet from Utah."
"Humbug!"

"Singular innocence."

"Means something."

"Spirit-rapper."

"Moon-calf."

"Piteous."

"Trying to enlist interest."

"Beware of him."

"Fast asleep here, and, doubtless, pick-pockets on board."

"Kind of daylight Endymion."

"Escaped convict, worn out with dodging."

"Jacob dreaming at Luz."

Such the epitaphic comments, conflictingly spoken or thought, of a miscellaneous company, who, assembled on the overlooking, cross-wise balcony at the forward end of the upper deck near by, had not witnessed preceding occurrences.

Meantime, like some enchanted man in his grave, happily oblivious of all gossip, whether chiseled or chatted, the deaf and dumb stranger still tranquilly slept, while now the boat started on her voyage.

HERMAN MELVILLE, *The Confidence Man*

Among the odd volumes in my father's library, was a collection of old European and English guide-books, which he had bought on his travels, a great many years ago. In my childhood, I went through many courses of studying them, and never tired of gazing at the numerous quaint embellishments and plates, and staring at the strange title-pages, some of which I thought resembled the mustached faces of foreigners.

Among others was a Parisian-looking, faded, pink-covered pamphlet, the rouge here and there effaced upon its now thin and attenuated cheeks, entitled, *"Voyage Descriptif et Philosophique de L'Ancien et du Nouveau Paris: Miroir Fidèle"*; also a time-darkened, mossy old book, in marbleized binding, much resembling verd-antique, entitled, *"Itinéraire Instructif de Rome, ou Description Géné-rale des Monumens Antiques et Modernes et des Ouvrages les plus Remarquables de Peinteur, de Sculpture, et de Architecture de cette Célébre Ville"*; on the russet title-page is a vignette representing a barren rock, partly shaded by a scrub-oak (a forlorn bit of land-scape), and under the lee of the rock and the shade of the tree, ma-ternally reclines the houseless foster-mother of Romulus and Remus, giving suck to the illustrious twins; a pair of naked little cherubs sprawling on the ground, with locked arms, eagerly engaged at their absorbing occupation; a large cactus-leaf or diaper hangs from a bough, and the wolf looks a good deal like one of the no-horn breed of barn-yard cows; the work is published *"Avec privilege du Sou-verain Pontife."* There was also a velvet-bound old volume, in brass clasps, entitled, *"The Conductor through Holland"* with a plate of the Stadt House; also a venerable *"Picture of London"* abounding in rep-resentations of St. Paul's, the Monument, Temple-Bar, Hyde-Park-Corner, the Horse Guards, the Admiralty, Charing-Cross, and Vaux-hall Bridge. Also, a bulky book, in a dusty-looking yellow cover, reminding one of the paneled doors of a mail-coach, and bearing an elaborate title-page, full of printer's flourishes, in emulation of the cracks of a four-in-hand whip, entitled, in part, *"The Great Roads, both direct and cross, throughout England and Wales, from an actual Admeasurement by order of His Majesty's Postmaster-General: This work describes the Cities, Market and Borough and Corporate Towns, and those at which the Assizes are held, and gives the time of the Mails' arrival and departure from each: Describes the Inns in the Metropolis from which the stages go, and the Inns in the country which supply post-horses and carriages: Describes the Noblemen and Gentlemen's Seats situated near the Road, with Maps of the Environs of London, Bath, Brighton, and Margate."* It is dedicated *"To the Right Honorable the Earls of Chesterfield and Leicester, by their Lordships' Most Obliged, Obedient, and Obsequious Servant, John Cary, 1798."* Also a green pamphlet, with a motto from Virgil, and an intricate coat of arms on the cover, looking like a diagram of the Labyrinth of Crete, entitled, *"A Description of York, its Antiquities and Public Buildings, particularly the Cathedral; compiled with great pains from the most authentic records."* Also a small scholastic-looking volume, in a classic vellum binding, and with a frontispiece bringing together at one view the towers and turrets of King's College and the magnificent Cathedral of Ely, though geographically sixteen miles apart, entitled, *"The Cambridge Guide: its Colleges, Halls, Libraries, and Museums, with the Ceremonies of the Town and University, and some account of Ely Cathedral."* Also a pamphlet, with a japanned sort of cover, stamped with a disorderly higgledy-piggledy group of pagoda-looking structures, claiming to be an accurate representation of the *"North or Grand Front of Blenheim,"* and entitled, *"A Description of Blenheim, the Seat of His Grace the Duke of Marlborough; containing a full account of the Paintings, Tapestry, and Furniture: a Picturesque Tour of the Gardens and Parks, and a General Description of the famous China Gallery, &c.; with an Essay on Landscape Gardening: and embellished with a View of the Palace, and a New and Elegant Plan of the Great Park."* And lastly, and to the purpose, there was a volume called "THE PICTURE OF LIVERPOOL."

HERMAN MELVILLE, *Redburn*

This royal throne of kings, this scepter'd isle,
This earth of majesty, this seat of Mars,
This other Eden, demi-paradise,
This fortress built by Nature for herself
Against infection and the hand of war,
This happy breed of men, this little world,
This precious stone set in the silver sea,
Which serves it in the office of a wall,
Or as a moat defensive to a house,

Against the envy of less happier lands,
This blessed plot, this earth, this realm, this England,
This nurse, this teeming womb of royal kings,
Fear'd by their breed and famous by their birth,
Renowned for their deeds as far from home,
For Christian service and true chivalry,
As is the sepulchre in stubborn Jewry,
Of the world's ransom, blessed Mary's Son,
This land of such dear souls, this dear dear land,
Dear for her reputation through the world,
Is now leased out, I die pronouncing it,
Like to a tenement or pelting farm:
England, bound in with the triumphant sea
Whose rocky shore beats back the envious siege
Of watery Neptune, is now bound in with shame,
With inky blots and rotten parchment bonds:
That England, that was wont to conquer others,
Hath made a shameful conquest of itself.
Ah, would the scandal vanish with my life,
How happy then were my ensuing death!

WILLIAM SHAKESPEARE, *Richard II*

Comming to kisse her lyps, (such grace I found)
Me seemd I smelt a gardin of sweet flowres:
that dainty odours from them threw around
for damzels fit to decke their louers bowres.
Her lips did smell lyke vnto Gillyflowers,
her ruddy cheekes lyke vnto Roses red:
her snowy browes lyke budded Bellamoures,
her louely eyes lyke Pincks but newly spred,
Her goodly bosome lyke a Strawberry bed,

her neck lyke to a bounch of Cullambynes:
her brest lyke lillyes, ere theyr leaues be shed,
her nipples lyke yong blossomd Iessemynes,
Such fragrant flowres doe giue most odorous smell,
but her sweet odour did them all excell.

EDMUND SPENSER, *Amoretti* 64

Where are Elmer, Herman, Bert, Tom and Charley,
The weak of will, the strong of arm, the clown, the boozer,
    the fighter?
All, all, are sleeping on the hill.

One passed in a fever,
One was burned in a mine,
One was killed in a brawl,
One died in a jail,
One fell from a bridge toiling for children and wife—
All, all are sleeping, sleeping, sleeping on the hill.

Where are Ella, Kate, Mag, Lizzie and Edith,
The tender heart, the simple soul, the loud, the proud, the
    happy one?—
All, all, are sleeping on the hill.

One died in shameful child-birth,
One of a thwarted love,
One at the hands of a brute in a brothel,
One of a broken pride, in the search for heart's desire,
One after life in far-away London and Paris
Was brought to her little space by Ella and Kate and Mag—
All, all are sleeping, sleeping, sleeping on the hill.

Where are Uncle Isaac and Aunt Emily,
And old Towny Kincaid and Sevigne Houghton,
And Major Walker who had talked
With venerable men of the revolution?—
All, all, are sleeping on the hill.

They brought them dead sons from the war,
And daughters whom life had crushed,
And their children fatherless, crying—
All, all are sleeping, sleeping, sleeping on the hill.

Where is Old Fiddler Jones
Who played with life all his ninety years,
Braving the sleet with bared breast,
Drinking, rioting, thinking neither of wife nor kin,
Nor gold, nor love, nor heaven?
Lo! he babbles of the fish-frys of long ago,
Of the horse-races of long ago at Clary's Grove,
Of what Abe Lincoln said
One time at Springfield.

EDGAR LEE MASTERS, "The Hill"

The box of pawn tickets at his elbow had just been rifled and he
took up idly one after another in his greasy fingers the blue and
white dockets, scrawled and sanded and creased and bearing the
name of the pledger as Daly or MacEvoy.

1 Pair Buskins.

1 D. Coat.

3 Articles and White.

1 Man's Pants.

Then he put them aside and gazed thoughtfully at the lid of the

box, speckled with louse marks, and asked vaguely:
—How much is the clock fast now?

JAMES JOYCE, *A Portrait of the Artist as a Young Man*

I could not forbear shaking my head, and smiling a little at his ignorance. And being no stranger to the art of war, I gave him a description of cannons, culverins, muskets, carabines, pistols, bullets, pow-
der, swords, bayonets, battles, sieges, retreats, attacks, undermines,
countermines, bombardments, sea fights, ships sunk with a thousand men, twenty thousand killed on each side, dying groans, limbs
flying in the air, smoke, noise, confusion, trampling to death under
horses' feet, flight, pursuit, victory; fields strewed with carcases, left
for food to dogs and wolves and birds of prey; plundering, stripping, ravishing, burning, and destroying. And to set forth the val-
our of my own dear countrymen, I assured him, "that I had seen
them blow up a hundred enemies at once in a siege, and as many in
a ship, and beheld the dead bodies drop down in pieces from the
clouds, to the great diversion of the spectators."

JONATHAN SWIFT, *Gulliver's Travels*

MORNING and evening
Maids heard the goblins cry:
"Come buy our orchard fruits,
Come buy, come buy:
Apples and quinces,
Lemons and oranges,
Plump unpeck'd cherries,
Melons and raspberries,
Bloom-down-cheek'd peaches,

Swart-headed mulberries,
Wild free-born cranberries,
Crab-apples, dewberries,
Pine-apples, blackberries,
Apricots, strawberries;—
All ripe together
In summer weather,—
Morns that pass by,
Fair eves that fly;
Come buy, come buy:
Our grapes fresh from the vine,
Pomegranates full and fine,
Dates and sharp bullaces,
Rare pears and greengages,
Damsons and bilberries,
Taste them and try:
Currants and gooseberries,
Bright-fire-like barberries,
Figs to fill your mouth,
Citrons from the South,
Sweet to tongue and sound to eye;
Come buy, come buy."

CHRISTINA ROSSETTI, "Goblin Market"

When in bygone days I gazed from these rocks upon yonder mountains across the river, and upon the green, flowery valley before me,
and saw all nature budding and bursting around; the hills clothed
from foot to peak with tall, thick forest trees; the valleys in all their
varied windings, shaded with the loveliest woods; and the soft river
gliding along amongst the lisping reeds, mirroring the beautiful
clouds which the soft evening breeze wafted across the sky,—when
I heard the groves about me melodious with the music of birds, and

saw the million swarms of insects dancing in the last golden beams of the sun, whose setting rays awoke the humming beetles from their grassy beds, whilst the subdued tumult around directed my attention to the ground, and I there observed the arid rock compelled to yield nutriment to the dry moss, whilst the heath flourished upon the barren sands below me,—all this displayed to me the inner warmth which animates all nature, and filled and glowed within my heart. I felt myself exalted by this overflowing fullness to the perception of the Godhead, and the glorious forms of an infinite universe became visible to my soul!

JOHANN WOLFGANG VON GOETHE,
The Sorrows of Young Werther

"Speed up the film, Montag, quick. *Click, Pic, Look, Eye, Now, Flick, Here, There, Swift, Pace, Up, Down, In, Out, Why, How, Who, What, Where, Eh? Uh! Bang! Smack! Wallop, Bing, Bong, Boom!*"

RAY BRADBURY, *Fahrenheit 451*

"What more easily explained and natural? With school turning out more runners, jumpers, racers, tinkerers, grabbers, snatchers, fliers, and swimmers instead of examiners, critics, knowers, and imaginative creators, the word 'intellectual,' of course, became the swear word it deserved to be."

RAY BRADBURY, *Fahrenheit 451*

Sunday, George Gudger:
Freshly laundered cotton gauze underwear.

Mercerized blue green socks, held up over his fist-like calves by scraps of pink and green gingham rag.

Long bulb-toed black shoes: still shining with the glaze of their first newness, streaked with clay.

Trousers of a hard and cheap cotton-wool, dark blue with narrow stripes; a twenty-five-cent belt stays in them always.

A freshly laundered and brilliantly starched white shirt with narrow black stripes.

A brown, green, and gold tie in broad stripes, of stiff and hard imitation watered silk.

A very cheap felt hat of a color between that of a pear; and that of the faintest gold, with a black band. . . .

Saturday, Mrs. Gudger:
Face, hands, feet and legs are washed.
The hair is done up more tightly even than usual.
Black or white cotton stockings.
Black lowheeled slippers with strapped insteps and single buttons.
A freshly laundered cotton print dress held together high at the throat with a ten-cent brooch.
A short necklace of black glass beads.
A hat.

JAMES AGEE, *Let Us Now Praise Famous Men*

There were too many dangers for Yossarian to keep track of. There was Hitler, Mussolini and Tojo, for example, and they were all out to kill him. There was Lieutenant Scheisskopf with his fanaticism for parades and there was the bloated colonel with his big fat mustache and his fanaticism for retribution, and they wanted to kill him, too. There was Appleby, Havermayer, Black and Korn. There was Nurse Cramer and Nurse Duckett, who he was almost certain

wanted him dead, and there was the Texan and the C.I.D. man, about whom he had no doubt. There were the bartenders, brick-layers and bus contractors all over the world who wanted him dead, landlords and tenants, traitors and patriots, lynchers, leeches and lackeys, and they were all out to bump him off. That was the secret Snowden had spilled to him on the mission to Avignon— they were out to get him; and Snowden had spilled it all over the back of the plane.

There were lymph glands that might do him in. There were kid-neys, nerve sheaths and corpuscles. There were tumors of the brain. There was Hodgkin's disease, leukemia, amyotrophic lateral sclero-sis. There were fertile red meadows of epithelial tissue to catch and coddle a cancer cell. There were diseases of the skin, diseases of the bone, diseases of the lung, diseases of the stomach, diseases of the heart, blood, and arteries. There were diseases of the head, diseases of the neck, diseases of the chest, diseases of the intestines, diseases of the crotch. There were even diseases of the feet. There were bil-lions of conscientious body cells oxidating away day and night like dumb animals at their complicated job of keeping him alive and healthy, and every one was a potential traitor or foe. There were so many diseases that it took a truly diseased mind to even think about them as often as he and Hungry Joe did.

JOSEPH HELLER, *Catch-22*

A book which tells why colonies have nearly as many uses as the yare to have now.
A book which makes no difference between one jeweler and an-other.
A book which mentions all the people who have had individual chances to come again.
A book in translation about eggs and butter.

A book which has great pleasure in describing whether any
    further attention is to be given to homes where homes have
    to be homes.
A book has been carefully prepared altogether.
A book and deposited well.
A book describing fishing exactly.
A book describing six and six and six.
A book describing six and six and six seventy-two.
A book describing Edith and Mary and flavouring fire.
A book describing as a man all of the same ages all of the same
    ages and nearly the same.

GERTRUDE STEIN, "Descriptions of Literature"

Over and over again Dorian used to read this fantastic chapter, and
the two chapters immediately following, in which, as in some curious tapestries or cunningly-wrought enamels, were pictured the
awful and beautiful forms of those whom Vice and Blood and
Weariness had made monstrous or mad; Filippo, Duke of Milan,
who slew his wife, and painted her lips with a scarlet poison that her
lover might suck death from the dead thing he fondled; Pietro
Barbi, the Venetian, known as Paul the Second, who sought in his
vanity to assume the title of Formosus, and whose tiara, valued at
two hundred thousand florins, was bought at the price of a terrible
sin; Gian Maria Visconti, who used hounds to chase living men, and
whose murdered body was covered with roses by a harlot who had
loved him; the Borgia on his white horse, with Fratricide riding be-
side him, and his mantle stained with the blood of Perotto; Pietro
Riario, the young Cardinal Archbishop of Florence, child and minion of Sixtus IV., whose beauty was equaled only by his debauchery,
and who received Leonora of Aragon in a pavilion of white and
crimson silk, filled with nymphs and centaurs, and gilded a boy that

he might serve at the feast as Ganymede or Hylas; Ezzelin, whose melancholy could be cured only by the spectacle of death, and who had a passion for red blood, as other men have for red wine—the son of the Fiend, as was reported, and one who had cheated his father at dice when gambling with him for his own soul; Giambattista Cibo, who in mockery of the name of Innocent, and into whose torpid veins the blood of three lads was infused by a Jewish doctor; Sigismondo Malatesta, the lover of Isotta, and the lord of Rimini, whose effigy was burned at Rome as the enemy of God and man, who strangled Polyssena with a napkin, and gave poison to Ginevra d'Este in a cup of emerald, and in honour of a shameful passion built a pagan church for Christian worship; Charles VI., who had so wildly adored his brother's wife that a leper had warned him of the insanity that was coming on him, and who, when his brain had sickened and grown strange, could only be soothed by Saracen cards painted with the images of Love and Death and Madness; and, in his trimmed jerkin and jeweled cap and acanthus-like curls, Grifonetto Baglioni, who slew Astorre with his bride, and Simonetto with his page, and whose comeliness was such that, as he lay dying in the yellow piazza of Perugia, those who had hated him could not but choose to weep, and Atalanta, who had cursed him, blessed him.

OSCAR WILDE, The Picture of Dorian Gray

Dorian murmured a graceful compliment, and looked round the room. Yes; it was certainly a tedious party. Two of the people he had never seen before, and the others consisted of Ernest Harrowden, one of those middle-aged mediocrities so common in London clubs who have no enemies, but are thoroughly disliked by their friends; Lady Ruxton, an over-dressed woman of forty-seven, with a hooked nose, who was always trying to get herself compromised, but was so peculiarly plain that to her great disappointment no one

would ever believe anything against her; Mrs. Erlynne, a pushing nobody, with a delightful lisp, and Venetian-red hair; Lady Alice Chapman, his hostess's daughter, a dowdy dull girl, with one of those characteristic British faces, that, once seen, are never remembered; and her husband, a red-cheeked, white-whiskered creature who, like so many of his class, was under the impression that inordinate joviality can atone for an entire lack of ideas.

OSCAR WILDE, *The Picture of Dorian Gray*

What past consecutive causes, before rising preapprehended, of accumulated fatigue did Bloom, before rising, silently recapitulate?

The preparation of breakfast (burnt offering): intestinal congestion and premeditative defecation (holy of holies): the bath (rite of John): the funeral (rite of Samuel): the advertisement of Alexander Keyes (Urim and Thummim): the unsubstantial lunch (rite of Melchisedek): the visit to museum and national library (holy place): the bookhunt along Bedford row, Merchants' Arch, Wellington Quay (Simchath Torah): the music in the Ormond Hotel (Shira Shirim): the altercation with a truculent troglodyte in Bernard Kiernan's premises (holocaust): a blank period of time including a cardrive, a visit to a house of mourning, a leavetaking (wilderness): the eroticism produced by feminine exhibitionism (rite of Onan): the prolonged delivery of Mrs. Mina Purefoy (heave offering): the visit to the disorderly house of Mrs. Bella Cohen, 82 Tyrone street, lower and subsequent brawl and chance medley in Beaver street (Armageddon): nocturnal perambulation to and from the cabman's shelter, Butt Bridge (atonement).

JAMES JOYCE, *Ulysses*

Notes

✳ ❄ ✳

CHAPTER 1: *The Literary List*

1. Jarrell, *Poetry and the Age,* 114.

2. In his *Observations on "The Fairy Queen" of Spenser,* Thomas Warton notes how fitting it is that the Knight and his companions are drawn deeper and deeper into the wood, lured by the beauty of the grove, until at length they arrive at the Cave of Error.

3. Hamilton, introduction to Spenser, *Faerie Queene,* 8.

4. Ferry, *Art of Naming,* 151. Note that in the original "occasion" of Ovid's tree catalogue in *Metamorphoses* the trees, like the types Spenser presents, are put to use, moved—in two senses—by Orpheus to provide shade "most grateful to the hill" (translation by Brookes More). In the Ovidian model, the trees demonstrate their utility without being consumed in the process.

5. Hofstadter, *Gödel, Escher, Bach,* 215, quoted in White, *Gatsby's Party,* 94.

6. Johnson, "Lives of the Poets," *Johnson: Selected Poetry and Prose,* 481–482.

7. Spufford, *Cabbages and Kings,* 7.

8. Gass, "And," 117.

9. Barney, "Chaucer's Lists," 192.

10. Summarized from Gaur, *History of Writing,* 13–17. Gaur also discusses other nonwritten forms of communication in which objects in specific series are important for idea transmission. These include knotted cords, used from China to South America for statistical records, and the sequences of cowrie shells used by the Yoruba to communicate such concepts as defiance, relationship, and hostility. Furthermore, Gaur relates, in the Yoruba language some words are homonyms with numbers: concepts such as attraction or agreement can be communicated by sending a message of a fixed number of shells, the word for *six* being the same as the word for *attracted,* and for *eight* the same as for *agreed.*

11. Schmandt-Besserat, "Two Precursors of Writing," 27–41.

12. Green, "Early Cuneiform," *Origins of Writing,* 43.

13. Fowler, *Kinds of Literature,* 153.

14. C. Whitman, *Homer and the Heroic Tradition,* 84.

15. Ibid. The practice of enumerative prayer or supplication is not peculiar to pre-Christian religions. Litany, a form of petition consisting of a series of invocations and tropes of different praises, has been a central vehicle for prayer in the Roman Catholic Church. This form has undergone its own evolution and speciation, and the number and types of titles have changed over the centuries. Lengthy, involved litanies lost favor to shorter, simpler versions. The Marian litany known as the Litany of Loredo is an example of a version that displaced others as a form of public devotion. The titles used in the praise of the Blessed Virgin include those derived from Scripture and popular medieval Latin poetry. New titles with official sanction have been added over time. As described in the *New Catholic Encyclopedia,* the Litany of Loredo has its own precise internal configuration which divides the invocations into sequential categories: titles which indicate the dignity of the Virgin's relationship to God, titles drawn from Old Testament prophecy and symbolism, titles attesting to her power and office, and titles attesting to her queenship.

16. Howe, *Old English Catalogue Poem,* 19. Cedric Whitman notes factual errors such as the inclusion in the list of a Sparta that was unfounded at the date of the drama, and a Larisa settlement similarly founded later (*Homer and the Heroic Tradition,* 42). G. S. Kirk observes that the Boetians command a privileged first position in the list even though they had a relatively minor role in the siege (Kirk, "*Iliad,*" 36).

17. Hunter, "Milton's Laundry Lists."

18. Edgar Dryden observes that "for Ishmael, knowledge does not result from bringing man face to face with a collection of pure facts. It involves, paradoxically, turning away from the factual world" (*Melville's Thematics of Form,* 84).

19. Villon, "The Legacy," *Poems of François Villon,* ll. 125–128. Or, further, consider Nathaniel Hawthorne's masonry in "The Celestial Rail-road": "You observe this convenient bridge. We obtained a sufficient foundation for it by throwing into the slough some editions of books of morality, volumes of French philosophy and German rationalism, tracts, sermons, and essays of modern clergymen, extracts from Plato, Confucius, and various Hindoo sages, together with a few ingenious commentaries upon texts of Scripture—all of which, by some scientific process, have been converted into a mass like granite" (*Nathaniel Hawthorne's Tales,* 132).

20. Howe, *Old English Catalogue Poem,* 27.

21. Gass's article "And" explores the myriad of subtly differentiated usages of the conjunction.

22. Burke, "Policy Made Personal," 78.

23. Rosenmeyer, *Green Cabinet,* 258. Rosenmeyer also notes that the list creates a space where "the herdsman's sensory experience" can be parceled out into discrete impressions and where the variety can be savored. E. R. Curtius provides a further example of this distributiveness in a *locus amoenus* lyric by Tiberianus, though he considers "impressionism" an incorrect categorization of the poem because of the precise formal structure that he finds in its scenic description. "The finest fruit ripens on espaliers," he notes, a statement one might apply to the best of literary listings (Curtius, *European Literature and the Latin Middle Ages,* 197).

24. Barney, "Chaucer's Lists," 190.

25. Spufford, *Cabbages and Kings,* 11.

26. White, *Gatsby's Party,* 104.

27. Lévi-Strauss, *Savage Mind,* 19.

28. Whitman, *American Primer,* 14.

29. Gass, "And," 106.

30. Cohen, "The Augustan Mode in English Poetry," 174.

31. Booth, *Shakespeare's Sonnets,* 340–341.

32. Villon, "The Testament," *Poems of François Villon,* ll. 370–371.

33. Howe, *Old English Catalogue Poem,* 27.

34. Milic, *Stylists on Style*, 416.

35. Gass, "And," 111.

36. Milic, *Stylists on Style*, 416.

37. Dupriez, *Dictionary of Literary Devices*, 108–109.

38. William Faulkner, "A Note on Sherwood Anderson," *Essays, Speeches and Public Letters* (New York: Random House, 1965), 4.

39. Milic, *Stylists on Style*, 15; Curtius, *European Literature and the Latin Middle Ages*, 285.

40. Barney, "Chaucer's Lists," 209; Puttenham, *Arte of English Poesie*, 232.

41. Stein, *George Herbert's Lyrics*, 108.

42. Greenwood, "George Herbert's Sonnet 'Prayer,'" 29.

43. As with lists in general, for any absolute statement an example can be found or made that counters it. Thus in *Through the Looking Glass* the White Queen's question "What's one and one and one and one and one and one and one and one and one and one?" is not boring in the least but serves to add to the delightful absurdity of the work.

44. Barney, "Chaucer's Lists," 193–194.

CHAPTER 2: *Emerson*

1. Thomas Carlyle, letter of 3 November 1844, in Slater, *Correspondence of Emerson and Carlyle*, 371. On Emerson's cataloguing sources see, e.g., Hodder, *Emerson's Rhetoric of Revelation*, and Buell, *Literary Transcendentalism*.

2. Buell, "Transcendentalist Catalogue Rhetoric," 331, 335.

3. Ellison, *Emerson's Romantic Style*, 188; Wilbur, *Responses*, 120.

4. Emerson, *Journals*, vol. V, p. 39.

5. Emerson, "Lord Bacon," *Early Lectures*, vol. I, p. 335; Ellison, *Emerson's Romantic Style*, 188.

6. Packer, *Emerson's Fall*, 40.

7. Ellison, *Emerson's Romantic Style*, 168.

8. Hodder, *Emerson's Rhetoric of Revelation*, 78.

9. Ellison, *Emerson's Romantic Style*, 173.

10. This is nicely shown in "Compensation": "Polarity, or action and reaction, we meet in every part of nature; in darkness and light; in heat and cold; in

the ebb and flow of waters; in male and female; in the inspiration and expiration of plants and animals; in the equation of quantity and quality in the fluids of the animal body; in the systole and diastole of the heart; in the undulations of fluids, and of sounds, in the centripedal and centrifugal gravity; in electricity, galvanism, and chemical affinity. Superinduce magnetism at one end of a needle; the opposite magnetism takes place at the other end. If the south attracts, the north repels. To empty here, you must condense there. An inevitable dualism bisects nature, so that each thing is a half, and suggests another thing to make it whole; as, spirit, matter; man, woman; odd, even; subjective, objective; in, out; upper, under; motion, rest; yea, nay" (*E*, 28).

11. Ellison, *Emerson's Romantic Style*, 170, 180.

12. Buell, "Transcendentalist Catalogue Rhetoric," 335; Maurice Gonnaud, "Introduction to the Second Edition," in Whicher, *Freedom and Fate*, xviii; Whicher, in Emerson, *Selections*, 407.

13. Whicher, in Emerson, *Selections*, 411.

14. Hyatt Waggoner notes that though blank verse predominates the opening stanza, "there is poetry enough in these bare lists of names and farm products." He goes on to speculate on "what principle led Emerson to select just *these* names from the much longer list of founding fathers given in the address ["Historical Discourse, at Concord, on the Second Centennial Anniversary of the Incorporation of the Town, September 12, 1835"]. It seems to me very possible that it was Emerson's much maligned poetic 'ear' that guided him in selecting names for the sound of them. There is assonance in B*u*lkeley and H*u*nt and in W*i*llard and Fl*i*nt; alliteration in *H*unt and *H*osmer; and a kind of internal 'rhyming' for which there is no name in Flin*t* and Hun*t*" (*Emerson as Poet*, 153, 149).

15. Bromwich, *Choice of Inheritance*, 139.

16. Emerson, "The Naturalist," *Early Lectures*, vol. I, p. 73, discussed in Matthiessen, *American Renaissance*.

17. Matthiessen, *American Renaissance*, 45–46.

18. Bishop, *Emerson on the Soul*, 118.

19. Bloom, *Figures of Capable Imagination*, 62.

20. Bishop, *Emerson on the Soul*, 5.

CHAPTER 3: *Whitman*

1. Emerson, cited in Daiches, "Walt Whitman," 112.

2. Bailey, *Walt Whitman*, 57.

3. Santayana, "The Poetry of Barbarism," *Interpretations of Poetry and Religion,* 180.

4. Swayne, "Whitman's Catalogue Rhetoric," 178.

5. Edward Dowden, review of 1871, cited in Price, *Walt Whitman,* 194.

6. Burke, "Policy Made Personal," 83.

7. Daiches, "Walt Whitman," 116.

8. Jakobson, "Two Aspects of Language and Two Types of Aphasic Disturbances," *Fundamentals of Language,* 69–96.

9. Buell, "Transcendentalist Catalogue Rhetoric," 330.

10. Dowden, review of 1871, 194.

11. Coffman, "'Crossing Brooklyn Ferry,'" 226. Although Emerson found the "endless passing of one element into new forms" exciting, he too approached the list with some degree of discernment, noting that "a too rapid unity or unification and a too exclusive devotion to parts are the Scylla and Charybdis" (*Journals,* vol. IX, p. 304).

12. Buell, "Transcendentalist Catalogue Rhetoric," 330.

13. Waskow, *Whitman: Explorations in Form,* 107.

14. I borrow this terminology from Richard Marotta, who employs it in "Milton and the Art of the Catalogue."

15. Buell, *Literary Transcendentalism,* 170, 172.

16. White, "Culture of Criticism," 67.

17. Howells, "Drum-Taps," *The Round Table,* 11 November 1865, 147–148.

18. Borges, "The Analytical Language of John Wilkins," *Other Inquisitions,* 103.

19. Buell, *Literary Transcendentalism,* 167.

20. Grossman, "Poetics of Union in Whitman and Lincoln," 188. My discussion of phrasal and clausal alternation derives from the observations of James Perrin Warren in his article "'The Free Growth of Metrical Laws.'"

21. Rukeyser, *Life of Poetry,* 85; Pearce, *Continuity of American Poetry,* 73.

22. Emerson considers the question of whether Nature actually outwardly exists irrelevant. His oration in *Nature* is confidently untroubled: "In my utter impotence to test the authenticity of the report of my senses, to know whether the impressions they make on me correspond with the outlying objects, what difference does it make, whether Orion is up there in heaven, or some god

paints the image in the firmament of the soul? The relation of parts and the end of the whole remaining the same, what is the difference, whether land and sea interact, and worlds revolve and intermingle without number or end,— deep yawning under deep and galaxy balancing galaxy, throughout absolute space,—or whether, without relations of time and space, the same appearances are inscribed in the constant faith of man? Whether nature enjoy a substantial existence without or is only in the apocalypse of the mind, it is alike useful and alike venerable to me" (*E*, 32).

23. Pearce, *Continuity of American Poetry*, 73; Grossman, "Poetics of Union in Whitman and Lincoln," 195.

24. Santayana, "Poetry of Barbarism," 178.

25. In *Moby-Dick,* Melville comments on the idiosyncracies of seeing: "So long as a man's eyes are open in the light, the act of seeing is involuntary; that is, he cannot then help mechanically seeing whatever objects are before him. Nevertheless, any one's experience will teach him, that though he can take an understanding sweep of things at one glance, it is quite impossible for him, attentively, and completely, to examine any two things—however large or however small—at one and the same instant of time, never mind if they lie side by side and touch each other" (*MD*, 376).

26. A slightly different way of interpreting these catalogues can be adapted from Charles Feidelson: "Instead of referring to a completed act of perception, [the catalogues constitute] the act itself, both in the author and in the reader" (*Symbolism and American Literature*, 18). For Coffman, however, "Crossing Brooklyn Ferry" embodies a movement between the opposing poles of sympathy and pride through its two catalogues, as the ferry moves between the two shores. At one shore, the sense of self is lost in receptive sympathy with the environing world; at the other, the sense of self is so fortified that it leads to the belief that the external world is an extension of the individual. It is the transit between the two shores that the poem strives to illustrate.

27. Foucault, *Order of Things*, 18.

28. Ibid., 19.

29. Price, *Whitman and Tradition*, 22.

30. Thurin, *Whitman Between Impressionism and Expressionism*, 86.

31. Jakobson, in *Fundamentals of Language;* De Selincourt, "The Form"; Spitzer, "Explication de Texte," 236.

32. Whitman, *Notes and Unpublished Manuscripts*, vol. IV, p. 1349.

33. De Selincourt, "The Form," 142.

34. Buell, "Transcendentalist Catalogue Rhetoric," 334.

35. Grossman, "Poetics of Union in Whitman and Lincoln," 200.

36. Pearce, *Continuity of American Poetry,* 77.

37. Hollander, "Introduction," to Whitman's *Leaves of Grass,* xviii.

CHAPTER 4: *Melville*

1. Bezanson, "*Moby-Dick:* Document, Drama, Dream," 192.

2. Review of *Moby-Dick* from the *London Atlas,* 1 November 1851, cited in Higgins and Parker, *Melville,* 362.

3. Frank Swinnerton, "Not Everybody's Book," *New York Bookman* 53 (May 1921), cited in Higgins and Parker, *Melville,* 149.

4. Brown, "Getting in the Kitchen with Dinah."

5. Bezanson, "*Moby-Dick:* Work of Art," 436–437.

6. Hollander, *Gazer's Spirit,* 4.

7. Brodhead, "Trying All Things," 6.

8. Foucault, *Order of Things,* 152.

9. Spitzer, *Linguistics and Literary History,* 6.

10. Colie and Lewalski, *Resources of Kind,* 22–23, and Lewalski, *"Paradise Lost" and the Rhetoric of Literary Forms,* 18–19.

11. Almost prophetically the sign reads *"Grand Contested Election for the Presidency of the United States"* and "BLOODY BATTLE IN AFGANISTAN" (*MD,* 29).

12. Dimock, *Empire for Liberty,* 114.

13. Greenberg, "Cetology."

14. In "Herman Melville and the Example of Sir Thomas Browne," Brian Foley investigates Melville's thematic and stylistic indebtedness to Browne. As Foley notes, one of Browne's characteristic tactics was to dismantle the "vulgar errors" of the best scientific and historical authorities, and the ill-founded popular opinions based on them, and to celebrate their failure to penetrate the world's great mysteries. In addition, Foley also notes Browne's habit of "doubleting," or using a conjunction to link two words, frequently an Anglo-Saxon word and its Latinate synonym. Foley suggests that this phraseology, which Melville adopts, highlights fitting constraints of language: "This reaching for two words where one would do presumably calls attention to the limitations of

language, [and] suggests that in a world in which the physical and the spiritual coexist, man can only approximate or approach Truth" (269).

15. It is this twofold character that probably leads Northrop Frye to identify *Moby-Dick* as a "romance-anatomy" in *Anatomy of Criticism*. Frye also notes the consequence of this mixed classification: "It is the anatomy in particular that has baffled critics, and there is hardly any fiction writer deeply influenced by it who has not been accused of disorderly conduct" (313).

16. Foucault, *Order of Things*, 129–130.

17. Compte Buffon, *Discours sur la manière de traiter l'histoire naturelle,* cited in Foucault, *Order of Things,* 147.

18. Murray's letter to Melville, 3 December 1847, and Melville's reply, 25 March 1848, are both published in Melville, *Correspondence*. Future citations from this volume will be given parenthetically by date in text.

19. Davis, *Melville's "Mardi,"* 66. Davis's work has consistently revealed Melville's prodigious reading and his meticulous study of the styles of numerous writers. To make the assertion that Melville in some way repudiated the authors he so clearly revered, and devoured, as Valerie Babb does in *Whiteness Visible,* is to overlook the facts and to misread gravely. Babb's argument—for example that the "higgledy-piggledy whale-statements" collected in "Extracts" imply that Melville sought to undermine "an ideology asserting the superiority of whiteness" by showing that the works cited were faulty in their incomplete grasp of the whale—is specious. Although her comments regarding Melville's skeptical treatment of phrenology are insightful, her appraisal that the "Extracts" merit debunking because they are "all products that in one way or another have disseminated values and notions deriving from Western European thought and have been employed at various points in the course of Western European history to lionize that civilization over others" (101) is misdirected.

20. Stephen, *Hours in a Library,* 34.

21. Parker, *Herman Melville,* vol. 1, p. 843.

22. Arvin, *Herman Melville,* 149.

23. Pommer, *Milton and Melville,* 324. In addition, Howard P. Vincent writes in *The Trying-Out of Moby-Dick* that "in any book of adventure built on such a special area of life, as philately, campanology, or baseball, there are always certain necessary details of the method and manner peculiar to them, which require expository treatment before the narrative may efficiently proceed" (123).

24. Arvin, *Herman Melville*, 169. Lewis Mumford's comments are worth quoting at length. Regarding the respect for fact, Mumford notes, "In the nineteenth century it was for the first time completely wedded to the imagination. It no longer means a restriction, a dried-up quality, an incompleteness. . . . For Ahab's hate and the pursuit of the whale is only one part of the total symbol: the physiological character of the whale, its feeding, its mating, its whole life, from whatever sources Melville drew the data, is equally part of it. Indeed, the symbol of Moby Dick is complete and rounded, expressive of our present relations to the universe, only through the passages that orthodox criticism, expressed on lesser works and more meagre traditions, regards as extraneous or unimportant!" (*Herman Melville*, 192).

25. The cheerfulness and geniality of the *Samuel Enderby*, and the tolerant attitude of her commanders toward Moby Dick, stand in marked contrast to the doggedness on Ahab's *Pequod*. Despite the fact that the captains of both ships share common insults from Moby Dick, the *Enderby* sails on in prosperity, as Ishmael's narrative implies, while the *Pequod* goes down.

26. Dimock, *Empire for Liberty*, 121.

27. Mumford, "Aesthetics: A Dialogue," *Findings and Keepings*, 89.

28. Mumford, *Herman Melville*, 191–192. Mumford states that the entire "physiological character of the whale," which includes "its feeding, its mating, its whole life," is now available as source material for the artist or poet (193). Of another mind, Walter Harding declares that such facts "occasionally irritate the modern reader" (*Variorum "Walden,"* 300). For more sympathetic assessments, see Walls, *Seeing New Worlds*, and Brown, *Emerson Museum*.

29. Etymologically, *fiction* comes from the Latin *fingere*, "to form, mold, shape." For my purposes here, I do not wish to misrepresent poetry and fiction writing by suggesting that they are deceptive or dissembling. I rather intend to consider them as modes of expression that attempt to "pass off" one thing for something else, such as occurs in the fashioning that poetry accomplishes by figuration or, as Michael Riffaterre pithily describes the "basic law" of poetry, that "says one thing and signifies something else" ("On the Prose Poem's Formal Features," in *The Prose Poem in France: Theory and Practice*, ed. Mary Ann Caws and Hermine Riffaterre, 117–132 [New York: Columbia University Press, 1983]). In a slightly different modality, the art of good fiction and drama is intended to effect the willing suspension of disbelief, in which what is "imaginatively invented" moves the audience as if it were fact.

30. Levine, "One Culture," 3.

31. Sewall, *Orphic Voice*, 9.

32. Consider Melville's letter to Evert A. Duyckink concerning the sinking of a ship by a whale, written only a week before the publication of the U.S. edition of *Moby-Dick* (7 November 1851): "Your letter received last night had a sort of stunning effect on me. For some days past being engaged in the woods with axe, wedge & beetle, the Whale had almost slipped me for the time (& I was the merrier for it) when Crash! comes Moby Dick himself (as you justly say) & reminds me of what I have been about for part of the last year or two. It is really & truly a surprising coincidence—to say the least. I make no doubt it is Moby Dick himself, for there is no account of his capture after the sad fate of the *Pequod* about fourteen years ago. . . . I wonder if my evil art has raised this monster." Note here also the interpenetration of fact and fiction as Melville claims the true existence of the *Pequod*, and fears to have conjured the leviathan by his writing.

33. Mumford, *Herman Melville*, 246.

34. Brodtkorb, *Ishmael's White World*, 119.

35. Guetti, *Limits of Metaphor*, 29.

36. This is no doubt why one early review, from the *London Leader*, dared readers to read the chapter "at midnight, alone, with nothing but the sounds of the wind moaning without, and the embers falling into the grate within" (8 November 1851).

37. Levin, *Power of Blackness*, 221–222.

38. Buell, "Transcendentalist Catalogue Rhetoric," 334.

39. Dryden, *Melville's Thematics of Form*, 100–101.

40. Irwin, *American Hieroglyphics*, 213. Irwin also brilliantly considers the relation implicit in the "black/white opposition of writing" (if somewhat differently from the way I have): "The letter is dead because it is dark, the lithic shadow of an inanimate literality, like the engraving on a tombstone; while the meaning that must be interpreted or translated from the dark script, the quickening sense that hovers about the writing like the white page about the black outline of the characters or the nimbus about the body, is the radiant spirit" (216).

41. Husni, "The Whiteness of the Whale," 211.

42. Chase, *Herman Melville*, 62; Mason, *Spirit Above the Dust*, 133; Feidelson, *Symbolism and American Literature*, 33.

CHAPTER 5: *Thoreau*

1. Peck discusses Thoreau's "Kalendar" in *Thoreau's Morning Work*.

2. Paul, *Emerson's Angle of Vision*, 74.

3. Buell, "Thoreau and the Natural Environment," 182–183.

4. Thoreau, "The Natural History of Massachusetts," *Collected Essays and Poems*, 32.

5. Emerson, "Thoreau," *Selections from Emerson*, 393.

6. Thoreau, "Natural History of Massachusetts," 41.

7. Ibid., 40–41.

8. Ibid., 24–25.

9. Monte, "Invisible Fences," 20.

10. John Simon, *Princeton Handbook*, cited in Michel Beaujour, "Short Epiphanies: Two Contextual Approaches to the French Prose Poem," in *The Prose Poem in France: Theory and Practice*, ed. Mary Ann Caws and Hermine Riffaterre, 35–59 (New York: Columbia University Press, 1983), 40; Buell, "Transcendentalist Catalogue Rhetoric," 336; Harding, *Variorum "Walden,"* 15.

11. A colleague reminds me that he did and he was. The reception of *Moby-Dick* was disappointing: Ishmael's prolixity evidently fatigued his readers and was neglected for many years in consequence.

12. Whitman, *Specimen Days*, 112. As an additional point of comparison *Specimen Days* contains a few simple columnar lists introduced as "perennial blossoms and friendly weeds I have made acquaintance with" (81) and "trees I am familiar with here," much in the manner of Thoreau's journals. Thoreau seems to take such delight in measuring and recording that his part-time employment as a surveyor brings to mind Frost's lines on gratifying labor in "Two Tramps in Mud Time": "My object in living is to unite / My avocation with my vocation."

13. Hildebidle, *Thoreau: A Naturalist's Liberty*, 94.

14. Paul, *Emerson's Angle of Vision*, 15–17.

15. Cavell, *Senses of "Walden,"* 33–34, and 30.

16. Ibid., 65.

17. Ibid., 33, 74.

18. Emerson, "Thoreau," 391.

19. Matthiessen, *American Renaissance*, 100.

20. Hildebidle, *Thoreau: A Naturalist's Liberty,* 34.

21. Mumford, *Golden Day,* 111; Hildebidle, *Thoreau: A Naturalist's Liberty,* 97.

22. Emerson's obituary for Thoreau tellingly interprets Thoreau's aversion to such scientific societies, emphasizing his extreme adherence to truth and individualism. Emerson quotes Thoreau's response in declining to share a memoir of his observations with such a group: "Why should I? To detach the description from its connection in my mind would make it no longer true or valuable to me" ("Thoreau," 388).

23. Strauss, "Persecution and the Art of Writing," *Persecution and the Art of Writing,* 24–25.

24. Fink, "Language of Prophecy," 160.

25. Simmel, *On Individuality and Social Forms,* 54.

26. Cavell, *Senses of "Walden,"* 43.

27. Sewall, *Orphic Voice,* 14.

28. Ovid, *Metamorphoses,* 463–464.

29. Neufeldt, "Thoreau in His Journal," 120.

30. James McIntosh judges Thoreau's post-1854 journal entries "collections of named but unpoeticized facts" (*Thoreau as Romantic Naturalist,* 53–54).

31. Goethe, quoted in Sewall, *Orphic Voice,* 261.

32. Hildebidle, *Thoreau: A Naturalist's Liberty,* 119.

Bibliography

※ ⬡ ※

Arvin, Newton. *Herman Melville*. Westport, Conn.: Greenwood, 1950.

Babb, Valerie. *Whiteness Visible*. New York: New York University Press, 1998.

Bailey, John. *Walt Whitman*. New York: Macmillan, 1926.

Barney, Stephen. "Chaucer's Lists." In *The Wisdom of Poetry: Essays in Early English Literature in Honor of Morton W. Bloomfield*, ed. Larry Dean Benson and Siegfried Wenzel, 189–223. Kalamazoo: Western Michigan University Press, Medieval Institute, 1982.

Bezanson, Walter. "*Moby-Dick:* Document, Drama, Dream." In *A Companion to Melville Studies*, ed. John Bryant, 169–210. New York: Greenwood, 1986.

———. "*Moby-Dick:* Work of Art." In *Critical Essays on Herman Melville's "Moby-Dick,"* ed. Brian Higgins and Hershel Parker, 421–440. New York: Hall, 1992.

Bishop, Jonathan. *Emerson on the Soul*. Cambridge: Harvard University Press, 1964.

Bloom, Harold. *Figures of Capable Imagination*. New York: Seabury, 1976.

Booth, Stephen. *Shakespeare's Sonnets*. New Haven: Yale University Press, 1977.

Borges, Jorge Luis. *Other Inquisitions, 1937–1952*. Austin: University of Texas Press, 1964.

Brodhead, Richard. "Trying All Things: An Introduction to *Moby-Dick.*" In *New Essays on "Moby-Dick,"* ed. Richard Brodhead, 1–21. Cambridge: Cambridge University Press, 1966.

Brodtkorb, Paul. *Ishmael's White World.* New Haven: Yale University Press, 1965.

Bromwich, David. *A Choice of Inheritance.* Cambridge: Harvard University Press, 1989.

Brown, Gillian. "Getting in the Kitchen with Dinah: Domestic Politics in *Uncle Tom's Cabin.*" *American Quarterly* 36:4 (1984): 503–523.

Brown, Lee Rust. *The Emerson Museum.* Cambridge: Harvard University Press, 1997.

Buell, Lawrence. *Literary Transcendentalism: Style and Vision in the American Renaissance.* Ithaca: Cornell University Press, 1973.

————. "Thoreau and the Natural Environment." In *The Cambridge Companion to Henry David Thoreau,* ed. Joel Myerson, 171–193. New York: Cambridge University Press, 1995.

————. "Transcendentalist Catalogue Rhetoric: Vision Versus Form." *American Literature* 40:3 (1968): 325–339.

Burke, Kenneth. "Policy Made Personal: Whitman's Verse and Prose—Salient Traits." In *"Leaves of Grass": One Hundred Years After,* ed. Milton Hindus, 74–108. Stanford: Stanford University Press, 1955.

Cavell, Stanley. *The Senses of "Walden."* New York: Viking, 1972.

Chase, Richard. *Herman Melville: A Critical Study.* New York: Macmillan, 1949.

Coffman, Stanley K., Jr. "'Crossing Brooklyn Ferry': A Note on the Catalogue Technique in Whitman's Poetry." *Modern Philology* 51 (1954): 225–232.

Cohen, Ralph. "The Augustan Mode in English Poetry." In *Studies in the Eighteenth Century: Papers Presented at the David Nichol Smith Memorial Seminar,* ed. R. F. Brissenden, 171–192. Canberra: Australian National University Press, 1968.

Colie, Rosalie, and Barbara K. Lewalski. *The Resources of Kind: Genre-Theory in the Renaissance.* Berkeley: University of California Press, 1973.

Curtius, E. R. *European Literature and the Latin Middle Ages.* Princeton: Princeton University Press, 1990.

Daiches, David. "Walt Whitman—Impressionist Poet." In *"Leaves of Grass": One Hundred Years After,* ed. Milton Hindus, 109–122. Stanford: Stanford University Press, 1955.

Davis, Merrell R. *Melville's "Mardi": A Chartless Voyage.* New Haven: Yale University Press, 1952.

Defoe, Daniel. *Robinson Crusoe.* New York: Norton, 1975.

De Selincourt, Basil. "The Form." In *A Century of Whitman Criticism,* ed. Edwin Haviland Miller, 135–145. Bloomington: Indiana University Press, 1969.

Dimock, Wai-Chee. *Empire for Liberty: Melville and the Politics of Individualism.* Princeton: Princeton University Press, 1989.

Dryden, Edgar A. *Melville's Thematics of Form.* Baltimore: Johns Hopkins University Press, 1968.

Dupriez, Bernard Marie. *Dictionary of Literary Devices, Gradus A–Z.* Toronto: University of Toronto Press, 1991.

Ellison, Julie. *Emerson's Romantic Style.* Princeton: Princeton University Press, 1984.

Emerson, Ralph Waldo, *Early Lectures,* ed. Stephen Whicher and Robert Spiller. Cambridge: Harvard University Press, 1959.

———. *Essays and Lectures.* New York: Vintage, 1983.

———. *Journals and Miscellaneous Notebooks of Ralph Waldo Emerson,* ed. Merton M. Sealts, Jr. Cambridge, Mass.: Belknap, 1965.

———. *Selections from Ralph Waldo Emerson,* ed. Stephen Whicher. Boston: Houghton Mifflin, 1960.

Feidelson, Charles. *Symbolism and American Literature.* Chicago: University of Chicago Press, 1953.

Ferry, Anne. *The Art of Naming.* Chicago: University of Chicago Press, 1988.

Fink, Steven. "The Language of Prophecy: Thoreau's 'Wild Apples.'" *New England Quarterly* 59 (1986): 212–230.

Foley, Brian. "Herman Melville and the Example of Sir Thomas Browne." *Modern Philology* 81:3 (1984): 265–277.

Foucault, Michel. *The Order of Things.* New York: Pantheon, 1971.

Fowler, Alastair. *Kinds of Literature.* Cambridge: Harvard University Press, 1982.

Frye, Northrop. *Anatomy of Criticism.* Princeton: Princeton University Press, 1957.

Gass, William. "And." In *Voicelust: Eight Contemporary Fiction Writers on Style,* ed. Allen Wier, 101–125. Lincoln: University of Nebraska Press, 1985.

Gaur, Albertine. *A History of Writing.* London: British Library, 1987.

Green, M. W. "Early Cuneiform." In *The Origins of Writing,* ed. Wayne M. Senner, 43–57. Lincoln: University of Nebraska Press, 1989.

Greenberg, Robert M. "Cetology: Center of Multiplicity and Discord in *Moby-Dick.*" *ESQ* 27:1 (1981): 1–13.

Greenwood, E. B. "George Herbert's Sonnet 'Prayer': A Stylistic Study." *Essays in Criticism* 15 (1965): 27–45.

Grossman, Allen. "The Poetics of Union in Whitman and Lincoln: An Inquiry Toward the Relationship of Art and Policy." In *The American Renaissance Reconsidered,* ed. Walter Benn Michaels and Donald Pease, 183–208. Baltimore: Johns Hopkins University Press, 1985.

Guetti, James. *The Limits of Metaphor.* Ithaca: Cornell University Press, 1967.

Harding, Walter. *The Variorum "Walden."* New York: Twayne, 1962.

Hawthorne, Nathaniel. *Nathaniel Hawthorne's Tales.* New York: Norton, 1987.

Higgins, Brian, and Herschel Parker, eds. *Herman Melville: The Contemporary Reviews.* Cambridge: Cambridge University Press, 1995.

Hildebidle, John. *Thoreau: A Naturalist's Liberty.* Cambridge: Harvard University Press, 1983.

Hodder, Alan. *Emerson's Rhetoric of Revelation: Nature, the Reader, and the Apocalypse Within.* University Park: Pennsylvania State University Press, 1989.

Hofstadter, Douglas. *Gödel, Escher, Bach: An Eternal Golden Braid.* New York: Basic, 1979.

Hollander, John. *The Gazer's Spirit.* Chicago: University of Chicago Press, 1995.

Howe, Nicholas. *The Old English Catalogue Poem.* Copenhagen: Rosenkilde and Bagger, 1985.

Hunter, William B., Jr. "Milton's Laundry Lists." *Milton Quarterly* 18:2 (1984): 58–61.

Husni, Khalil. "The Whiteness of the Whale: A Survey of Interpretations, 1851–1970." *College Language Association Journal* 20:2 (1976): 210–221.

Irwin, John. *American Hieroglyphics: The Symbol of the Egyptian Hieroglyphics in the American Renaissance.* New Haven: Yale University Press, 1980.

Jakobson, Roman, and Morris Halle. *Fundamentals of Language.* The Hague: Mouton, 1971.

Jarrell, Randall. *Poetry and the Age.* New York: Vintage, 1959.

Johnson, Samuel. *Samuel Johnson: Selected Poetry and Prose,* ed. Frank Brady and W. K. Wimsatt. Berkeley: University of California Press, 1977.

Kirk, G. S. *The "Iliad": A Commentary.* Cambridge: Cambridge University Press, 1985.

Levin, Harry. *The Power of Blackness.* New York: Knopf, 1958.

Levine, George. "One Culture: Science and Literature." In *One Culture: Essays in Science and Literature,* ed. George Levine and Alan Rauch, 3–32. Madison: University of Wisconsin Press, 1987.

Lévi-Strauss, Claude. *The Savage Mind.* Chicago: University of Chicago Press, 1966.

Lewalski, Barbara K. *"Paradise Lost" and the Rhetoric of Literary Forms.* Princeton: Princeton University Press, 1985.

Marotta, Richard. "Milton and the Art of the Catalogue." Ph.D. diss. City University of New York, 1977.

Mason, Ronald. *The Spirit Above the Dust: A Study of Herman Melville.* London: Lehmann, 1951.

Matthiessen, F. O. *American Renaissance.* New York: Oxford University Press, 1971.

McIntosh, James. *Thoreau as Romantic Naturalist.* Ithaca: Cornell University Press, 1974.

Melville, Herman. *Correspondence.* Evanston: Northwestern University Press, 1993.

————. *Mardi*. Evanston: Northwestern University Press, 1998.

————. *Moby-Dick*. New York: Vintage, 1991.

Milic, Louis. *Stylists on Style*. New York: Scribner's, 1969.

Miller, F. DeWolfe. *Christopher Pearse Cranch and His Caricatures of New England Transcendentalism*. Cambridge: Harvard University Press, 1951.

Monte, Steven. "Invisible Fences: Prose Poetry as a Genre in French and American Literature." Ph.D. diss. Yale University, 1996.

Mumford, Lewis. *Findings and Keepings: Analects for an Autobiography*. New York: Harcourt, 1975.

————. *The Golden Day: A Study in American Literature and Culture*. New York: Norton, 1934.

————. *Herman Melville*. New York: Harcourt, 1929.

————. *Herman Melville: A Study of His Life and Vision*. London: Secker and Warburg, 1963.

Neufeldt, Leonard. "Thoreau in His Journal." In *The Cambridge Companion to Henry David Thoreau*, ed. Joel Myerson, 107–124. Cambridge: Cambridge University Press, 1995.

Norris, Frank. *Mcteague: A Story of San Francisco*. New York: Vintage, 1990.

Ovid. *Metamorphoses*. Trans. Brookes More. Boston: Marshall Jones, 1978.

Packer, Barbara. *Emerson's Fall*. New York: Continuum, 1982.

Parker, Hershel. *Herman Melville: A Biography*. Vol. 1. Baltimore: Johns Hopkins University Press, 1996.

Paul, Sherman. *Emerson's Angle of Vision*. Cambridge: Harvard University Press, 1952.

Pearce, Roy Harvey. *The Continuity of American Poetry*. Princeton: Princeton University Press, 1987.

Peck, Daniel. *Thoreau's Morning Work*. New Haven: Yale University Press, 1990.

Pommer, Henry. *Milton and Melville*. Pittsburgh: University of Pittsburgh Press, 1950.

Price, Kenneth. *Whitman and Tradition*. New Haven: Yale University Press, 1990.

Price, Kenneth, ed. *Walt Whitman: The Contemporary Reviews*. Cambridge: Cambridge University Press, 1996.

Puttenham, George. *The Arte of English Poesie*. Kent, Ohio: Kent State University Press, 1970.

Rosenmeyer, Thomas G. *The Green Cabinet*. Berkeley: University of California Press, 1969.

Rukeyser, Muriel. *The Life of Poetry*. New York: Current, 1949.

Santayana, George. *Interpretations of Poetry and Religion*. New York: Scribner's, 1916.

Schmandt-Besserat, Denise. "Two Precursors of Writing: Plain and Complex

Tokens." In *The Origins of Writing*, ed. Wayne M. Senner, 27–41. Lincoln: University of Nebraska Press, 1989.

Sewall, Elizabeth. *The Orphic Voice: Poetry and Natural History*. New Haven: Yale University Press, 1960.

Simmel, Georg. *On Individuality and Social Forms*. Chicago: University of Chicago Press, 1971.

Slater, Joseph, ed. *The Correspondence of Emerson and Carlyle*. New York: Columbia University Press, 1964.

Southey, Robert. *The Doctor*. London: G. Bell, 1930.

Spenser, Edmund. *The Faerie Queene*, ed. A. C. Hamilton. New York: Longman, 1992.

Spitzer, Leo. "Explication de Texte as Applied to 'Out of the Cradle Endlessly Rocking.'" *Journal of English Literary History* 16 (1949): 229–249.

———. *Linguistics and Literary History: Essays in Stylistics*. Princeton: Princeton University Press, 1948.

Spufford, Francis. *Cabbages and Kings: The Chatto and Windus Book of Literary Lists*. London: Chatto and Windus, 1989.

Stein, Arnold. *George Herbert's Lyrics*. Baltimore: Johns Hopkins University Press, 1968.

Stephen, Leslie. *Hours in a Library*. London: Smith, Elder, 1909.

Strauss, Leo. *Persecution and the Art of Writing*. Westport, Conn.: Greenwood, 1952.

Swayne, Mattie. "Whitman's Catalogue Rhetoric." *University of Texas Studies in English* 21 (1941): 162–178.

Thoreau, Henry David. *Collected Essays and Poems*. New York: Vintage, 1989.

———. *Journals*, ed. John Broderick. Princeton: Princeton University Press, 1981.

———. *"A Week on the Concord and Merrimack Rivers," "Walden," "The Maine Woods,"* and *"Cape Cod,"* ed. Robert F. Sayre. New York: Vintage, 1985.

Thurin, Erik Ingvar. *Whitman Between Impressionism and Expressionism*. Lewisburg, Pa.: Bucknell University Press, 1995.

Twain, Mark. *The Adventures of Tom Sawyer*. New York: Viking, 1990.

Villon, François. *The Poems of François Villon*. Trans. Galway Kinnell. Hanover, N.H.: University Press of New England, 1982.

Vincent, Howard P. *The Trying-Out of Moby-Dick*. Boston: Houghton Mifflin, 1949.

Waggoner, Hyatt. *Emerson as Poet*. Princeton: Princeton University Press, 1974.

Walls, Laura Dassow. *Seeing New Worlds: Henry David Thoreau and Nineteenth-Century Natural Science*. Madison: University of Wisconsin Press, 1995.

Warren, James Perrin. "'The Free Growth of Metrical Laws': Syntactic Parallelism in 'Song of Myself.'" *Style* 18:1 (1984): 27–42.

Warton, Thomas. *Observations on "The Fairy Queen" of Spenser.* London, 1807.

Waskow, Harold J. *Whitman: Explorations in Form.* Chicago: University of Chicago Press, 1966.

Whicher, Stephen. *Freedom and Fate: An Inner Life of Ralph Waldo Emerson.* Philadelphia: University of Pennsylvania Press, 1971.

White, Hayden. "The Culture of Criticism." In *Liberations: New Essays on the Humanities in Revolution,* ed. Ihab Hassan, 55–69. Middletown, Conn.: Wesleyan University Press, 1971.

White, Patti. *Gatsby's Party: The System and the List in Contemporary Narrative.* Purdue, Ind.: Purdue University Press, 1992.

Whitman, Cedric H. *Homer and the Heroic Tradition.* Cambridge: Harvard University Press, 1958.

Whitman, Walt. *An American Primer.* Boston: Small, Maynard, 1904.

———. *Leaves of Grass.* New York: Vintage, 1992.

———. *Notes and Unpublished Manuscripts,* ed. Edward Grier. New York: New York University Press, 1984.

———. *Specimen Days.* Boston: Godine, 1971.

Wilbur, Richard. *Responses: Prose Pieces.* Ashland, Ore.: Story Line, 2000.

Index

✳ ✺ ✳

DATE DUE

GAYLORD | No. 2333 | | PRINTED IN U.S.A.